How to Complete
and *Survive*
a Doctoral Dissertation

How to Complete *and* *Survive* a Doctoral Dissertation

by DAVID STERNBERG

ST. MARTIN'S PRESS · *New York*

For information, write: St. Martin's Press,
175 Fifth Avenue, New York, N.Y. 10010
Manufactured in the United States of America

Library of Congress Catalogue Number: 80-28938
ISBN: 0-312-39605-8
ISBN: 0-312-39606-6 (pbk.)

DESIGN BY DENNIS J. GRASTORF

10 9 8 7 6 5 4 3 2 1

FIRST EDITION

This book is for the tens of thousands of courageous ABDs confronting the great task in the years to come.

Table of Contents

A Finnish proverb goes, strong *sisu* (guts) will help get a person even through a gray rock. Now I chant "Sis-u, sis-u," inside my head as I lug myself up those weary hills toward the end of a long run.

RICHARD ROGIN, in *The Runner Magazine*

CHAPTER 1

The Loneliness of the
Long-Distance Writer

THE DISSERTATION DOCTORATE: A LONG-STANDING AND POORLY UNDERSTOOD PROBLEM.

The status of ABD (All But the Dissertation) is the critical one in American graduate education. Since the 1960s its poignancy, sometimes permanency, has been growing. We all seem to know someone—a friend, relative, spouse, colleague—who is either filled with apprehension confronting the task fresh after completed course work or bogged down for years in stop-again, start-again efforts to finish.

Although dissertation woes are generally familiar in the context of the private lives of obscure graduate students, they have been know to obstruct revolutions and revolutionaries! Rosa Luxemburg's longterm lover and fellow political activist, Leo Jogiches, couldn't finish his dissertation, the cause of much wrangling between the two: "When she moved to Berlin, Leo stayed behind in Zurich, working at an interminable doctoral thesis which he never completed. Years went by . . . before she could persuade him to leave Switzerland and join her." [1]

No such prolonged crisis confronts the doctoral candidate in hard/ life sciences or "professional degree" programs, where a full dissertation (see below for a delineation of the elements defining a full dissertation) is not required. It is in the social sciences, education, humanities and letters disciplines that people have their lives disrupted and even sometimes permanently scarred by a dissertation-writing experience.

1

American society is not aware, excepting personal acquaintance of particular ABDs, of the almost larger-than-life trials, fortitude, despair, courage and even heroics experienced in writing a doctoral dissertation. One never sees a TV program or movie, for example, about a handicapped, disadvantaged, full-time-employed, or alcoholic-addicted person who, against all odds, completes a dissertation in political science or educational psychology. Skating championships, law and medical degrees, attainment of political office, yes; doctoral dissertations, no. Nor is there any modern fiction about people writing dissertations, depicting them as central heroic or tragic characters caught up in a great struggle, or any "how-to-do-it" books.[2] Again, books abound about fiction writers as heroes, about studies of fiction "writers at work" and about how to write poetry, short stories and novels, even, recently, general nonfiction.[3]

The first, and only, nonfiction book about dissertation writing I was able to find was John Almack's *Research and Thesis Writing: A Textbook on Principles and Techniques of Thesis Construction for the Use of Graduate Students in Universities and Colleges,* published half a century ago! [4] This book is not without merit on the "mechanical" side of thesis construction, but, reflecting its times, it says absolutely nothing about the structural/bureaucratic and emotional dimensions ringing dissertation writing. It seems long overdue for a book on writing a dissertation in tune with its time, when such a project has to be understood to be as much of an emotional and human relations enterprise as an exercise in library research, hypothetheses construction, and gathering and analysis of data. Although not slighting the "mechanical" aspects of the dissertation, the greater weight of the present volume is toward sociological and personal issues that the dissertation writer must confront and master.

The frequency of the ABD status has become so large that it has been legitimated in its own right: Professional journals, like the *Employment Bulletin* of the American Sociological Association, frequently contain openings for an "instructor or assistant professor to teach introductory and family courses: ABD," or, "will consider M.A.; prefer ABD." A recent perusal of the Sunday *New York Times Careers in Education* section indicated the ABD status as an acceptable credential for teaching positions in history, psychology, human relations, bilingual-teacher education and English-language studies.

Implicit in these offerings is the understanding that one will soon get his doctorate or not be retained beyond a limited number of reappointment years in the teaching position, but understood as well is the hard fact that many will never complete the dissertation.* A social science trade joke, recognizing the limited mileage of the ABD, goes, "An ABD and fifty cents will get you a cup of coffee."

In the last years of the 1970s colloquia/workshops on "How to Write a Doctoral Dissertation" were held at major metropolitan New York graduate centers, including New York University and City University of New York (CUNY). All sessions played to standing-room-only crowds of graduate students. In March of 1980 Kingsborough Community College of CUNY advertised in *The New York Times* for a major doctoral-candidate workshop dealing with problems like writers' blocks, oral examinations, statistical analysis and publishing professional articles. In May 1980 the following advertisement appeared in *The New York Times:* "Doctoral Candidates. Can't get that dissertation off the ground? Enroll in intensive workshop, June 5–7 . . . Leave workshop with a detailed draft of your proposal. Limited to 7." This last workshop appears much closer to a business venture than the other more academic, nonprofit, sponsored ones. Profit-oriented dissertation "counseling," probably involving no small measure of actual thesis *writing*, appears to be growing in response to the desperation of many ABDs.

Most social science and some humanities doctoral programs themselves schedule (often require) anticipatory socialization for students near the end of their course work in the form of routine thesis prospectus or dissertation seminars, but veterans of these efforts are nearly unanimous in evaluating them as very little help for the great task. (Read on for reasons why in-department forums are ineffective.)

This book is intentionally entitled: "How to Complete *and Survive* a Doctoral Dissertation." Two potential emotional/career nightmares

---

* Throughout this volume the male pronoun and possessive pronoun—"he" and "his"—are used generically to refer to both male and female dissertation candidates. Since, as we shall soon see, nearly half the candidates are women, the writer wishes to disavow any sexist intention in using male nomenclature. Constantly substituting "he/she," or "one" or "the candidate" is awkward and tedious. Using "they" is just plain grammatically wrong, which wouldn't do in a "how-to" book concerned with writing. So I am more or less stuck with "he" and "his," and hope all men and women reading the book construe them as intending to embrace both human genders equally.

face the ABD: *Not* to finish is practically to guarantee a years-long, if not lifelong, mood of a flawed or somehow incompleted life, where the ABD is constantly explaining/rationalizing to others (e.g., university employers, colleagues, friends, spouses, lovers, family) and to himself just why he didn't finish. The emotional energy expended in often decades-long apologizing and soul-searching is incalculably debilitating and humiliating.

On the other hand, I have often heard ABDs remark (indeed, sometimes said it myself), "If only I could finish my thesis, my troubles would be over." Although such a statement has some validity, *finishing* often scars the successful laureate as well: All along the dissertation course, from initial topic selection and proposal to defense, are strewn potential dangers to self-preservation (dignity), *inter alia,* a sadistic (or lecherous) professor on one's committee; "selling your soul" to a committee which won't pass your thesis unless you excise what you consider to be its (and thus your) guts or add what you judge to be anathema; situations where the fieldwork data contradicts one's hypotheses and causes one to feel (wrongly, as the book will show) that the alternatives are either giving up the project or "fudging" the data; lying to or manipulating (thus depersonalizing) your sample in order to get data deemed "absolutely essential" for the thesis.

A last-stage emotional correlate of finishing is often postpartum dissertation depression, where the writer is so emotionally exhausted, that years of unproductive drifting can follow. One function of this book is to anticipate the surfacing of many of these emotionally crippling conditions and train the candidate in self-compassion and self-healing along the dissertation course.

Statistics of the Problem.

When I researched this book I discovered something akin to a "cover-up" regarding information about doctoral candidates in dissertation-required programs. Not only are there no national statistics on ABDs; there are no national statistics on how many students are enrolled in doctoral programs separate from master's degree enrollments. At the local level of particular universities, graduate registrars were either vague and defensive about hard statistics on this group or, even when eager to help, hard put to give satisfactory answers since

4

their coding categories did not include attention to this specific status. My review of much statistical data on universities (an enormous body of facts and figures on nearly every conceivable aspect of university programs, faculty and student characteristics), together with my interviews with registrars and educators, convince me that the dissertation doctorate is certainly the least understood institution in American higher education. (Some tentative answers to why this should be so come later in the chapter.) The statistical picture of the ABD problem in the United States that follows, then, was necessarily constructed by me through indirect measures, formula suggestions from prominent registrars, educators, statisticians at the National Center for Education and educated guesses from my own experience as a sociologist and dissertation adviser.

What we are trying to ascertain here is an estimate of the number of people currently in the same boat in the early 1980s. Table I gives the national statistics for graduate students, full and part-time, enrolled beyond the first year of graduate school in the twelve fields of study requiring a dissertation for the doctorate, as of 1976 (the last year for which figures were available when this book was written). Although a small portion of this population are master's candidates, the great majority are doctoral:

Table 1.1: Enrollments in Dissertation-Required Doctoral Programs, 1976

Field of Study	Beyond First Year Full-time Enrollment	Beyond First Year Part-time Enrollment Divided by Three
1. Area Studies	1,206	250
2. Communications	1,262	555
3. Education	29,942	26,936
4. Foreign Languages	4,015	907
5. Home Economics	1,108	520
6. Letters	10,524	3,280
7. Library Sciences	1,400	744
8. Psychology	10,789	2,336
9. Public Affairs and Services	10,057	2,419
10. Social Sciences	18,115	4,697

Field of Study	*Beyond First Year Full-time Enrollment*	*Beyond First Year Part-time Enrollment Divided by Three*
11. Theology	5,510	1,259
12. Interdisciplinary Studies	2,942	1,492
Subtotal	96,870	45,395

Total: 142,265 full-time *or* full-time-equivalent doctoral students in dissertation-required fields

Source: *Digest of Education Statistics,* National Center for Education Statistics, HEW, 1979, p. 95

Note that the part-time total was divided by *three* to get a full-time equivalent of that portion of the doctoral population which roughly controls for students who pursue doctoral courses well beyond the conventional two full-time years that most catalogs and authorities indicate as normative.[5] The total of 142,265 must be corrected additionally for growth in graduate student populations since 1976 (dissertation-required doctoral enrollments *are* growing, although not at a striking rate, despite general decline in college enrollments). A "medium growth" projection would be 1.5 percent per year.[6] To come up to 1981, then, the total would be 152,935 doctoral students.

The reader will have noted a large variance in enrollments by field. Education doctorate enrollments (about 60,000) account for nearly three times the next largest category, social sciences (23,000), followed by psychology, letters, and public affairs and services (each with about 13,000). The smallest fields are area studies, communications, home economics and library science, each with 2,000 or fewer candidates.

Do doctoral program enrollments differ substantially by sex? Despite considerable rhetoric from feminist quarters, the data do not support a general claim that women are discriminated against in current dissertation-required doctoral *enrollments.* Data is not available for assessing their proportionate representation as ABDs. We do know, however, that they still represent a minority of doctorates received: In 1973, 30 percent of doctorates granted in sociology went to women; in 1978, 37 percent.[7] Table 1.2 gives the percentage distribution of men and women enrolled in the twelve fields:

6

Table 1.2: Enrollments in Dissertation-Required Doctoral Programs by Sex, 1976

Field of Study	Male %	Female %
1. Area Studies	55	45
2. Communications	58	42
3. Education	42	58
4. Foreign Languages	39	61
5. Home Economics	15	85
6. Letters	51	49
7. Library Sciences	25	75
8. Psychology	55	45
9. Public Affairs and Services	54	46
10. Social Sciences	68	32
11. Theology	83	17
12. Interdisciplinary Studies	54	46

Source: *Digest of Education Statistics,* National Center for Education Statistics, HEW, 1979, p. 95

A totaling of male and female *full and part-time* students in 1976 comes to 116,806 men and 116,251 women, virtually a 50–50 split between the sexes. Of the twelve areas, only two were significantly male-dominated (defined as showing a skewed distribution of at least 60–40)—theology and social science—and three significantly female-dominated—foreign languages, home economics and library science. Increasing pressures from affirmative-action groups make it likely that the 1980s will see even further reductions in the enrollment inequalities by sex that do exist, as well as moves toward near-parity in degrees conferred.[8] In any event, the drastic biases against women candidates in "professional studies," such as medicine and law, have no real analogue in the dissertation-required fields. This may well be because sexism is always most evident in those institutional and educational sectors where the most money and power are implicated, and, by and large, regardless of the relatively high prestige attached to winning, say, an humanities or social science doctorate, these twelve fields rank relatively low on both financial and power scales. In my judgment, sexism practiced by faculty members against her ranks relatively low on the list of hurdles facing the female dissertation writer. Certainly, she may have to combat debilitating sexist attitudes on the part of an unsympathetic or often outright hostile husband who wants dinner on the table at six, no matter what the dissertation time schedule demands. But such problems can be dealt with in a way that historic institutionalized resistance to female membership in fields like medicine cannot. The major hurdles to completing and surviving a dissertation, discussed at great length in this volume, are not sex-linked.

Approximating the number of ABDs within the larger doctoral population is even chancier than estimating the number of doctoral students. I divided the population by *three*, reasoning that this would give the number of candidates who had most likely finished all (two full years) of their course work, and were either squarely up against the dissertation, or soon to be so after their last qualifying written and/or oral preliminary (to the thesis) examinations. This calculation yielded a figure of 50,978 ABDs. This is a very considerable figure in its own right, but an even more important point to stress is its perennial nature: Each academic year throughout the 1980s more than 50,000 *new* ABDs will be generated by the American graduate school system. We will have over half a million ABDs during the decade.

In this sense the ABD is in a very large boat with lots of company. It is one of the key paradoxes of the ABD that it is a "lonely crowd" status. Statistically large in numbers as ABDs may be, the context and contours of graduate education institutions, and perhaps the very structure of the dissertation doctorate itself (see discussion below), make almost all successful doctorates products of an individual, and usually lonely, agency.

If 51,000 ABDs per year is a reasonably close estimate, what is the completion, or success, figure? Again, as of this writing no research, certainly on a national scale, has ever been conducted. Certain individual departments in particular disciplines may have carried through studies of their own shops, but that information is available on a "need-to-know" basis only. The best, although far from entirely satisfactory, model one can use is an "in-out" scheme. Simply put, one asks how many finished-product doctorates come out as compared to

ABDs going in. Let's look first at the number of doctorates awarded yearly in the twelve areas:

Table 1.3: Doctorates Awarded in Dissertation-Required Doctoral Programs, 1976–1977

Field of Study	Number of Doctorates Awarded
1. Area Studies	153
2. Communications	171
3. Education	7,955
4. Foreign Languages	752
5. Home Economics	160
6. Letters	2,199
7. Library Sciences	61
8. Psychology	2,761
9. Public Affairs and Services	335
10. Social Sciences	3,784
11. Theology	1,125
12. Interdisciplinary Studies	304
Total	19,760

Source: *Digest of Education Statistics,* National Center for Education Statistics, HEW, 1979, pp. 112–116

Perusal of all the (albeit admittedly incomplete) available statistics leads to the conclusion that no matter how one cuts the pie, each year in the 1980s will see upward of 50,000 ABDs go in and about 20,000 earned doctorates come out of the graduate education machine. Obviously, one cannot simply compare brand-new ABDs of a given year with awarded doctorates for the *same* year to get a success figure, since normally it takes one to two years to write the dissertation. But, for example, we generated about 47,400 new ABDs in 1976; 19,760 doctorates were awarded the next year. Assuming the 1976 ABDs had now worked on their dissertations for at least a year, their finishing rate was about 42 percent. Obviously, there is some statistical distortion here, since all the 1977 awards were not conferred upon 1976 starters; some could have begun five years earlier. So one cannot talk about cut-and-dried success and failure rates, given the often idio-syncratic time phasing of particular dissertation writers in particular fields and the far from satisfactory statistics. Still, a "catch-up" process that significantly alters the numbers does not appear to be operating; for every one hundred ABDs that go in, only forty-some doctorates come out, year after year.

The "in-out" figures vary drastically from field to field. Here are the percentages of finishers (based on 1976–1977 data) for the twelve fields:

Table 1.4: Ratio of Awarded Doctorates to Entering ABDs

Field of Study	Awarded Doctorates (in %) Entering ABDs
1. Area Studies	32
2. Communications	28
3. Education	42
4. Foreign Languages	46
5. Home Economics	29
6. Letters	48
7. Library Sciences	9
8. Psychology	63
9. Public Affairs and Services	8
10. Social Sciences	50
11. Theology	50
12. Interdisciplinary Studies	21

Source: *Digest of Education Statistics,* National Center for Education Statistics, HEW, 1979, p. 95; pp. 112–116

To get some understanding of what is behind the enormous fluctua-tions among finishers in different fields would require a book in its own right. Among the larger enrolled fields, psychology has the best track record, and public affairs and services egregiously the worst. Even operating with a relaxed and optimistic model of "catch-up," it seems likely that, at best, no more than about half of 1980s American ABDs will be getting their degrees.

It is my sense that university chairpersons, deans and even highest officials intuit these substantial nonfinishing rates (unparalleled in other kinds of graduate, undergraduate, indeed any type of American educational program) but do not undertake or commission a "body count" for fear that public access to such data would (1) reduce enrollments in graduate programs; (2) lead to student demands for far-reaching changes in graduate program guidelines and requirements; (3) threaten lucrative "maintaining matriculation" fees now paid by many ABDs for periods sometimes up to a decade; (4) entail faculty and administrative shakeups and housecleanings.

Even keeping in mind the caveat of not translating the in-out figures into success-failure rates per se, the probabilities of not converting the ABD into a Ph.D. in the candidate's foreseeably near future are alarmingly high. Certainly, if you are a five-year-old ABD pounding the pavement at your regional or national convention and avoiding old classmates with the embarrassment that "everybody finished but me" (one of a list of counterproductive dissertation myths discussed in this book), you are flailing yourself with a statistical unreality.

FOR WHOM IS THIS BOOK?

This volume is intended primarily for doctoral candidates in fields of study—ordinarily one of the twelve discussed above—where a dissertation is required. By a full dissertation is meant a thesis which requires (1) exhaustive library review/survey of related literature; (2) construction of a researchable problem, and related hypotheses, which makes some original contribution to the field; (3) experimental work and/or fieldwork with subjects and/or groups; (4) an elaborate methodology for analyzing the data collected; (5) a lengthy, literary write-up, analysis and discussion of the results of such experimental work or fieldwork; (6) a formal, oral defense of the dissertation before a committee. Non- or quasidissertation doctorates are those which require from none to some, but less than all of the above elements of a full dissertation.

Nondissertation fields include those such as medicine, dentistry and engineering. Law doctorates (the J.D.) often require a major senior paper for graduation, but this paper is not comparable in terms of the six elements to the scope and arduousness of a dissertation. Hard and life science doctorates require a "dissertation," but the form and strict faculty supervision (see below) of these projects are not like a full dissertation. With disciplines such as letters, history, languages and philosophy we have a midground, where elements three and four are usually not salient, but the other requirements are in full force. Full dissertations must be written by candidates in the social sciences (here including psychology as a social science), public administration and in the majority of education doctorates.[9]

This book, then, will be relevant and useful for all kinds of doctoral candidates, except those in the so-called "professional" and hard/life science areas.[10] It will be instructive even for *them* in correcting any smugness or patronizing attitudes that many hold about the inability of so many dissertation candidates to finish. The book should also be helpful to those who have to "live with" a dissertation writer through his trials in understanding some of the enormities of the project and the accompanying strains to which a candidate is exposed.

Although a candidate writing a thesis in, say, French or comparative literature will not have to complete an "experiment," issues addressed in this volume—such as deciding to write a dissertation, building a dissertation file, how to get out of a dissertation depression and how to deal with one's proposal/dissertation committee—are as pressing for him as for a student writing a sociology, psychology or public administration thesis.

As already noted, there are over 150,000 full-time or full-time-equivalent students in relevant dissertation-required doctoral programs in any given year. In the broadest sense, the book speaks to all of these people. For purposes of answering just what a specific student might look for in the volume, we might break this population down into four groups: (1) students in their first or second year of course work who are still deciding about whether to write the dissertation, or, having already decided that fundamental question, are looking for a viable topic, or want some sense of what is in store for them; (2) students still doing course and/or qualifying examinations who have already concurrently started a dissertation; [11] (3) the 50,000-plus new ABDs generated each year by the American university system, faced with the immediate task of climbing the Matterhorn looming above them; (4) the "veteran" ABDs, still in a holding pattern of "maintaining matriculation," often five or more years after completion of their other requirements. No one knows the size of this last group; indeed, when I interviewd graduate registrars, the cover-up element seemed most prominent, perhaps, in the long-term ABD area.

THE DISSERTATION WRITER ADRIFT.

In the introduction to their generally valuable *Guide to American Graduate Schools,* Livesey and Doughty, both graduate registrars at one time or another at a major university, state that the dissertation is the most rewarding phase of a doctoral program. This is a most astonishing statement. I have never encountered a dissertation writer, most certainly while writing his thesis, who would acquiesce in such a judgment. When I ask my students or clients to word-associate to their dissertations, some combination of the following responses is typical: fear, agony, torture, guilt, no end in sight, indefinitely postponed gratification, "ruining my life, "I'm drowning in it," anxiety, boredom, hate, despair, depression, humiliation, powerlessness. Should the reader object that I may see a "deviant" part of the candidate spectrum, I would answer that discussions with successful colleagues in various fields over more than ten years have yielded the same kind of negative emotional response when recalling the days of our dissertations.

The truth of the matter is that, although the American educational system is characterized at almost all levels by "support systems"— remedial programs, tutors, counselors, pass/fail options—for students unparalleled in the world, virtually the entire support structure vanishes for doctoral candidates undertaking a dissertation in education, social science, humanities or letters. Abrupt withdrawal of the support system leads to the candidate's feeling some or most of the unhappy emotions listed above.

Interestingly, the support system continues intact for "hard" science and "professional" candidates. In physics or zoology, for example, Ph.D. candidates are assigned by their graduate mentors/advisers to pursue some relatively narrow and well-defined experiment for their dissertation project; in law or medicine, a senior-year long paper or comparable project may be required, but its proportionate weight in obtaining the doctorate is tiny compared to a dissertation in political science or educational psychology. Hard science and professional-degree candidates know that if they attend two to four years of classes

13

along with their mates and carry out the last-year project, closely supervised by their advising professor, they will—excepting contingencies like banana-peel slippage—almost always receive their doctorates. As we have already demonstrated, and as the ABD knows all too well, no such certainty is available to doctoral candidates in fields with which this book is concerned.

The degree of uncertainty and magnitude of eventual nonfinishers in "soft" science doctorates is astounding and puzzling, not only because of the contrast with "hard" science and professional doctorate prognoses, but because of the length and arduousness of predissertation course and examination work that dissertation-degree candidates must log. Certainly, a sociology or history candidate has put in as much, if not considerably more, work (often including acquisition of an M.A. en route) by the time he reaches the ABD status as the law student at the end of three years of law courses, but the law student is by then a Juris Doctor and the ABD has yet to *begin* the major project required for his doctorate! [12]

Professional students might counter with the fact that they must additionally pass state licensing boards, but, again, the reality is that the vast majority of medical and law college graduates pass the boards/bars, even though some of them must try a number of times. There is no analogue to this "second (or even third and fourth) chance" in dissertation doctorate "licensing." It is a rare event—of dissertation lore—for a candidate to be (fully) failed on his dissertation and then go out and try another one, partly because doctoral committees/programs do not generally allow it, but, more importantly, because the dissertation course is so long and debilitating that a second effort is almost unthinkable to the candidate.

People do not understand how matters stand for the dissertation candidate: his family has trouble grasping the magnitude of the task; friends may be sympathetic, but in a general way which gets to none of the nuances of the loneliness and uncertainty involved. Most often, relatives and friends cannot understand why your high school and college classmates got their law, medical, engineering or dentistry degrees right on schedule, and you seem to be floundering and having so much *angst*. Holders of professional and hard-science doctorates are generally patronizing toward the struggling ABD: the doctors and lawyers see it in terms of somebody snared by impractical or unprag-

14

matic projects; the scientists see the delays as inevitable results of fooling around with "fuzzy," "soft-headed" and nonrigorous ideas and methods. All too often, the candidate himself internalizes some of this derogation and impatience toward his own project.

From all the evidence I have been able to gather, ABDs seem to have been caught unawares by the problematic nature of finishing their degrees. That is, the typical ABD entered graduate school three to four years previously with high hopes and the feeling that the main victory had already been won: getting over the GREs and acceptance into a program. Up to this point, his situation is very similar to someone accepted by a law or medical school. Next follows involvement with course work and preparation for predissertation comprehensives. The concern is with doing well in both phases so that he will be allowed to write the dissertation, not that the dissertation will perhaps turn out to be near-impossible to write. Very often, even graduate students at the top of their classes and feeling confident and quite highly motivated right through completion of course work (even though interest seems generally to decline in graduate programs after the first year, including some professional programs) [13] describe their realization that the dissertation does not necessarily follow smoothly as "a hell of a shock," or "the sky falling in," or "a whole new ball game." The following section examines some of the most prominent features of the dissertation writer's adriftness and essays some account both of its timing in the doctoral course and its causes.

Specific Features of the ABD Problem.
Dissertation anomie. Only the statistically rare (e.g., a favored graduate or teaching assistant, often bitterly resented by the rest of the students because of his connections) among ABDs, or those approaching that status, doesn't get the message that nobody down at the department is seriously concerned with helping him work through a multiyear project on a continuous, serious basis. Dissertation anomie is the occupational disease of the ABD. Structurally, it is a dislocation between stated official goals of a doctoral program, on the one hand, and the unavailability of means—particularly faculty personnel, tutelage and support—for the candidate's successful pursuit of his goals. Psychologically, the dislocation is experienced by individual candidates in feelings of drifting, powerlessness and despair. Dissertation

15

anomie as internalized by ABDs cannot fairly be described as "pathological," "neurotic" or "deviant." It is the cluster of predictable feelings, given the structural dislocations in the programs.

Each kind of anomie has a "chronic" and "acute" phase. Departments appear to go through cycles of anomie: some years, under some chairpersons, the policing of and standards for writing dissertations might be tightened up, after a preceding period of slackness; when this occurs, a candidate writing during that latter administration will probably have a somewhat less anomic experience. But one can never count on continuities within the administration, either at the field of study/departmental level or the cross-discipline dean's level; both are subject to change of personnel and policy at any time. The only reliable constant is the possession of a set of dissertation-writing savvys, skills and attitudes which this book tries to teach.

Faculty unreliability. Why should the faculty and administration be dilatory or delinquent in helping future junior colleagues get over the last great hurdle to full membership in a discipline? One might understand the indifference of people (including relatives and friends) in terms of lack of interest in long-term intellectual projects that have less than dramatic practical "payoff," but this cannot account for faculty (near) indifference and reluctance to help.[14] Or can it? Wilensky demonstrated that American university professors were nearly as unread and "practical" oriented as nonacademics.[15] But giving faculty some benefit of the doubt, regardless of their general attitude toward matters of the mind, surely they must be interested at least in work in their *own* disciplines. Although this is usually more or less true (not without exceptions that every doctoral candidate can identify within his own department), it is not the same as saying that graduate professors are interested in students' doctoral dissertations.[16]

One can scale faculty from one to ten on dissertation interest and helpfulness. Excepting infrequent "round-robin" systems (as rare as round-robin chairmanships), where each graduate faculty member is assigned an equal number of dissertation candidates, a very large majority of faculty members constitutionally empowered by the university to be dissertation advisers, readers or committee members will score three or below on the scale. In every department there are one or two nines or tens, known to all candidates by the student grapevine, besieged by numbers they cannot adequately handle. Such men and women have a way of moving on, either through exhaustion, lack of recognition for their efforts by administrations or bitterness with colleagues who won't help with the load; so that even they cannot really be relied upon to see one through a lengthy endeavor, no matter how close one feels to them. The message bears repeating and will be driven home throughout the book: When it comes to doing a dissertation, the buck stops with the candidate and the resources he can bring to the project. Outside help will be appreciated and utilized when available, but the bottom line must be, "I am going to do this thing myself," so that if—usually when—allies withdraw their divisions, the dissertation front doesn't collapse.

Why isn't the faculty (consistently) helpful? From a sociological perspective, dissertation advising rates low as a career-promoting activity. People are promoted, given tenure, receive more attractive offers from other universities, principally in terms of what they *publish themselves,* certainly not for editing and advising the writings and publications of graduate students. Graduate professors will often baldly tell one as much.

Sometimes they offer a somewhat less self-interested and not totally specious reason for reluctance to get heavily involved with dissertation candidates. Advising a doctoral dissertation is a most time-consuming affair. Most of the ABDs who come to graduate professors about dissertations have only the fuzziest notions of what they would like to pursue as topics. Very often, after "fooling around" with half a dozen "pipedreams," the student vanishes, either quite literally into the limbo of "maintaining matriculation" from where many never return, or goes on to the next "sympathetic" professor, where the process starts all over again. Very quickly, say the professors, one gets cynical, or at least very cautious about commitment to an ABD.

For many professors, the ABD is viewed like the bookmen and women who come by their offices with regularity: one gives them a few quick minutes of partial attention and then gets rid of them, either by making a promise to "consider" a new book for course adoption or sending them down the hall to an unsuspecting colleague who is "really the person you should be talking to about this."

This faculty definition of the ABD as Fuller Brush salesman, interloper and time waster, combined with techniques for brushing him off, exacerbates dissertation anomie and often sets tragedies in motion. ABDs are run around from professor to professor in a downward spiral of powerlessness, increasing discouragement and embarrassment. ABDs who felt fairly comfortable with faculty during course work begin to feel like strangers in their own departments, cooling their heels in waiting rooms and becoming increasingly apologetic for taking up (more of) a professor's time.

Not infrequently, a professor will sign his approval to a dissertation proposal or prospectus (which he may or may not have read with care) of a persistent student to get him off his back, when the prospectus is not viable as a dissertation; somewhere along the way—usually longer than shorter given faculty's relaxed attitudes toward dissertation beginnings—a dissertation committee is going to veto the whole project, after the candidate has invested considerable work and hope. Most of the time, that candidate will walk away from the doctorate and become another forgotten casualty of American graduate education.

Lack of graduate student community. Four principal factors determine how much or how little student community, solidarity and support a given doctoral program will exhibit:

1. whether the program is located in a rural or urban university setting.
2. the size of the enrollment.
3. the percentage of doctoral candidates enrolled full- versus part-time.
4. the percentage of candidates with full-time or substantial part-time employment outside the program/university.

A megapolis-based, subway campus program with hundreds of matriculated students, many of whom are matriculated part-time and hold full-time jobs, will be the atomized/alienated/anonymous pole along a continuum of graduate student community/lack of community. A small (under fifty) rural program where the students all are sequestered in the same university town, enrolled full-time and usually working part-time in some capacity connected with the university, very often the program itself, will approach the *gemeinschaft* pole, where students will band together to study for courses, research projects and qualifying exams.

Fewer and fewer programs contain any longer all four of the opti-

18

mal elements for graduate student community; e.g., the *size* of rural-based enrollments is exceeding the limits necessary for most of the students to get to know each other well. Many programs in many disciplines, including the largest ones, contain all four of the negatively synergistic elements. The Midwest seems to be the major region of the nation where schools containing some measure of most of the optimal conditions can still be found, although there are many exceptions to this rule in the giant state universities.

Even with the presence of optimal conditions for graduate student community, surprisingly little seems to materialize. For reasons more closely scrutinized in Chapter Four, doctoral candidates have been reluctant to band together either during course or (especially) the later dissertation-writing stage. Attempts to organize graduate students to take a stand against specific faculty or university policies have met with conspicuously less success than with undergraduate students. There is an abiding fear of graduate program faculty and a cultural norm of "doing your own time"; joining together can be labeled as "trouble-making," thus jeopardizing one's doctorate.

Added to fear of faculty retaliation has been an abiding sense of *competition* among doctoral candidates who have read into low finishing rates a kind of quota system which pits them against their fellow students. I argue in this book that no such quota system exists, and that others writing dissertations should be sought out to form support groups (see Chapter Seven). There indeed seems to be such a slowly developing trend in many universities and disciplines, both large and small, urban and rural. But for every presently developing enclave of doctoral student solidarity, there still exist countless undifferentiated masses of enrolled graduate students and ABDs who are going it almost completely alone. There is certainly a lonely, solitary component to writing a doctoral dissertation, but the size of this element may have been exaggerated by the dissertation subculture. In some instances, this loner view of the thesis has led to study groups, formed for various predissertation purposes, being terminated when ABD status has been reached—a most serious error.

Candidates' unpreparedness.[17] Faculty constantly complain that even graduate students at the ABD level are "unprepared" to write a dissertation. This statement is puzzling since it appears to discount the worth of the numerous theoretical, substantive and methodological

19

courses that the student has negotiated in, say, sixty credits of his field of study. But I do not believe they mean unprepared in the narrower sense of having no grasp of the literature in the discipline, or unequipped to carry through statistical analyses of data, or unable to write with minimum clarity (although any or all of these failings may, in fact, characterize a minority of ABDs). Unprepared here means more in the way of *unsocialized* to the scope and meaning of a doctoral dissertation.

The idea and institution of a doctoral dissertation which foreran the current American model developed in Western Europe, principally in Germany and France (Johns Hopkins was its transplanter from the Old to the New university world). The European doctorate was an enormous project, often the capstone of a career, generally achieved later in life than in the American case, demanding a thesis of originality, great length (and thus years to write) and very often controversy. Doctoral dissertation defenses were, like hangings, public affairs (this public quality continues to a limited extent, even today), where any interested person could attend and even pose contentious questions from the audience to the candidate. It was not unknown for these defenses to break up in melées.

Nothing in the contemporary American student's prior twenty-year educational experience could possibly "prepare" him for a dissertation akin to the traditional model. Indeed, very few of the current supervising professors were any more prepared when they wrote *their* dissertations (never mind their bemoaning of decline of standards since their day). Credentialed faculty look back upon the dissertation like veteran marines see boot-camp days at Paris Island: a hell-and-brimstone initiation into the corps. And since the veterans went through hell (and it made better men of them), why shouldn't today's ABDs have to take it? Indeed, such attitudes about the initiation-like quality and function of the dissertation, usually unstated, may play a major role in faculty indifference to the ABD's plight. For all we know, distinguished docents like Weber in Germany, Freud in Austria and Durkheim in France may have held the same notions about their students struggling with their dissertations.

Transcending the revenge or "get-even" function that the thesis may—or may have—played for present and past faculty, there exists a widespread faculty conviction that the dissertation is the instrument that forges a full-fledged colleague out of a graduate student, in that it forces him to combine the disparate skills and ideas he has picked up in graduate courses into a coherent piece of professional work. The correlative attitude here is that one really has to go this route alone, forge the product oneself. This is the position that, with certain qualifications, I myself hold. In any event, the basic point to be underscored is that even those professors who have a positive and sympathetic attitude toward ABDs cannot be relied upon to work closely with the candidate, since they are apt to feel, partly through their own dissertation experience and partly because of professional convictions, that the dissertation is necessarily a lonely affair of the mind and heart. It may even be that, operating under this paradigm of the dissertation, they are not alarmed at the high "dropout" rate among ABDs, seeing in that process a kind of doctoral Darwinian natural selection and survival of the fittest.

Again, simply consider the American graduate student's reaction when facing such a "switch" in expectations right at the end of his academic career. From grade school through high school through college and graduate school (course work), students are officially and/or informally encouraged to pursue learning styles and goals almost diametrically opposed to those required for a dissertation (certainly in the European understanding of the doctorate, but even within the later American tradition, I believe). The American educational system encourages working together with peers.[18] Student peer groups devalue serious and sustained intellectual pursuit in favor of social and athletic skills. American teachers positively sanction memorization and rote learning of conventional wisdom, discourage or even punish creative and nonmidstream thought. Even colleges and universities have always weighted their curricula in favor of "practical" matters, with "free-floating" intellectual courses and enterprises much more often eulogized than practiced or funded.[19]

Nor is it generally true that the term papers of college or even graduate school prepare the student to some extent for the dissertation. Remembering the six elements of the dissertation (above), one need only reflect on numerous term papers (if indeed one can even recall them) distinctly lacking in these features. Graduate students themselves consistently report that their term papers are synthetic reports, where one takes an idea from X, a quote from Y, a prayer from Z. Rarely are the papers *analytical* or *critical* in a sense approaching the demands of a dissertation. The professors are, of course, im-

21

plicated in this corruption; still hoping for the occasional well-researched and finely honed analytic performance, they have come to settle for some reasonable regurgitation of their lectures or assigned texts whose prose transcends word-salad. To insist on first-rate, carefully prepared papers would be (1) to fail many more people than the administration would allow; (2) to bring a double or treble load of end-of-term (just when one wants to start vacation) work upon the professor's shoulders in the form of rereadings of revised papers; and (3) to insure widespread unpopularity among even graduate students who simply are not "prepared" for such stringent demands and see them as "unreasonable," "sadistic" or as some kind of specific "personal" animosity toward particular students.

Then, too, term papers so often seem to be done in a rush, on the fly, started as the term is ending, competing with the demands of two or three other papers. Students sometimes appear to spend more time considering the color of the cover page or the style of plastic folder in which to encase the paper than in the contents itself. Such fast-food writing habits and schedules, so endemic to and reflective of our contemporary life-style in general, practically guarantee failure to write an acceptable dissertation, unless a candidate is prepared to make changes along the lines indicated in this book.

It is probably true that the *master's thesis* used to serve as a kind of anticipatory socialization halfway house between term papers of one kind or another and the dissertation.[20] However, in an attempt to streamline graduate programs and cut down on required years of matriculation (studies at the turn of the 1970s indicated that the average successful candidate in most disciplines was taking from seven–nine years after completion of his undergraduate degree to finish) in a time of tight money, inflation and aversion to "idleness" and "time wasting," the master's degree, and related thesis, is becoming extinct, at least as part of doctoral programs.[21] Although nowhere near as demanding as the dissertation, the master's thesis did require some attention to many, if not most, of the six elements of the full dissertation.

Most ironically, it is now being used primarily as a "terminal" degree to "cool out" students not considered by departments as "Ph.D. material." With an M.A. in hand one could—very often can, even today—get a research and even long-term (albeit usually not tenurable) teaching post. Today's "elite" ABD often doesn't have a master's degree to fall back upon should he fail or seriously delay in negotiating the dissertation. This all-or-nothing condition (where on paper and in employment reality all he has is his bachelor's degree) further increases the anxieties of the ABD status.

THE SCHEME OF THE BOOK.

This first chapter's intention is to give the ABD candidate, or any other person considering writing a dissertation, a general picture of the situation he faces along statistical, emotional, general interpersonal and faculty-relations dimensions. One theme that emerges very clearly is the statistical "togetherness" but personal "aloneness" of the dissertation-writing status. Another is the less than heartening rate of finishing the degree. A third is the generally lukewarm, at best, cooperation of the faculty in this large endeavor. The last is the "unpreparedness" of the typical candidate to mount the dissertation without some turnabout in his accustomed manner of approaching intellectual problems, studying, researching and writing. The remainder of the book is designed to help the candidate understand, face up to and surmount the hurdles that have been outlined.

The chapters constitute a dual-track, psychological-emotional *and* practical "guidebook," with the writer traveling shoulder-to-shoulder with the candidate along all the sequential stations of the dissertation course. Issues discussed at length include:

1. Deciding whether you really want to write the dissertation, involved herein a "cost accounting" of the career and emotional credits and debits.
2. Picking a dissertation topic that will "go."
3. Making the dissertation the top priority in your life: building a dissertation-writing frame of mind and place.
4. Building a dissertation file: the philosophy and construction code.
5. Writing a successful dissertation proposal, or prospectus, including picking a committee you can work with.
6. The dissertation itself: researching it, writing it and presenting it to the faculty.
7. Down in the dissertation dumps: how to get out.
8. The dissertation defense: how to pass it.
9. Beyond the dissertation: getting professional mileage out of it.

23

10. Beyond the dissertation: surviving it.
11. Myths versus realities about the dissertation: dangerous traps, bugaboos and myths about the thesis which have ensnared, weakened and defeated candidates.

The contents of this guidebook stem directly from the personal successful theses (four of them) experiences of the author, acquaintance with numerous dissertations of his colleagues in various fields, his extensive supervision of dissertations and M.A. theses over a period of twelve years, five years of a dissertation-therapy practice during which the writer has helped (but never *written:* the main input must always come from the candidate) a significant number of clients complete, or make significant progress on, dissertations in which they were previously bogged down for years.* Along the way, at relevant points and junctures, anecdotes and parts of "case studies" will be related (including the author's own dissertation), with which many a reader will surely identify, or at least empathize.

HOW TO USE THIS BOOK.
I assume that a person who has reached, or is nearing, ABD status is minimally literate, conversant with the basic theories and methodologies of his field, thoroughly experienced in library research, knows an *op. cit.* from an *ibid.* If one needs serious remedial work in any of these areas, one is ready for neither the dissertation nor this volume. So the book is in no way a "style manual" or "writer's tool" in the sense of a work like Crosby and Estey's *College Writing.*[22] *How to Complete and Survive a Doctoral Dissertation* does contain "nuts and bolts" on organizing a dissertation file, writing a proposal and the dissertation itself, but they are of a very different order from style, grammatical or citation guidelines. In this book usually even "mechanical" problems (e.g., constructing a file) are infused with equally important emotional themes (e.g., getting into an attitudinal frame of mind to keep your file humming along).

---

* In the following chapters I make liberal use of my own doctoral dissertation whenever I feel it is highly relevant to illustrating an important point. I also want the reader to bear in mind constantly that I have personally experienced most of the dissertation's travails.

24

How to use the book will depend, of course, at what station on the dissertation path the reader finds himself. Ideally, it should be read prior to, or just at the time of, reaching ABD status, so that all the chapters will be relevant to the candidate's unfolding experience. As the project moves along, specific sections, corresponding to the candidate's stage of development, should be consulted again. The book is designed to be a constant companion to the writer from start to finish, and beyond.

The book is equally relevant for long-term ABDs, since most of the time they are going to have to turn around their attitudes, working/writing habits and sometimes even a "no-go" topic, if they seriously hope to finish and survive.

It must be remembered from the start that the writer is, perforce, discussing the basic issues of a general dissertation's life history in American graduate schools; there are, of course, hundreds of particular programs which are bound to vary in detail and even sometimes in basic requirements. Still, I believe that the basic "variance" has been covered; naturally, a particular candidate in a particular program will have to make adjustments in the book's guidelines to tailor it to his department, its peculiar faculty composition, his particular dissertation and his own personality. Nonetheless, it is clear to me how similar "under the skin" are most programs' demands about dissertations. Certainly, the requirements of qualities and habits the *writer* must possess or cultivate to complete the dissertation are virtually identical throughout the nation.

So, I would have the reader turn to the book for information, strategies and reshaping of attitudes toward the great project. More generally, and perhaps most importantly, the book is intended to convey support and hope, without being Pollyanna-like; all too often, I have found, the doctoral dissertation candidate is his own worst enemy (as if he needed any more!), torpedoing himself with doomsday myths about the dissertation. Hopefully, this book will demythologize and remove some of the terror from the thesis experience. At the same time, it intends to train the candidate in anticipation and self-compassion, so that dissertation crises along the way don't take him unawares, throw him completely off, stall his progress or ruin the next five or ten years of his life.

Now, let's get on the dissertation course.

SUMMARY.

1. ABDs (All But the Dissertation) have become a substantial "minority group" in American society but have achieved very little public understanding, sympathy or support. Currently, each year some 51,000 new ABDs are produced, facing the task of carrying through a huge project for which they have been ill prepared, either in college or graduate school itself. The 1980s will see more than half a million ABDs generated, a substantial percentage of whom will never finish the thesis. If one adds to the new ABDs the large, if precisely undetermined, number of "veteran" ABDs who hang on year after year without progress, we see a large "social problem," perhaps even a crisis, in the midst of American graduate education.

2. The writer had to construct his own statistical picture of and projections for ABDs when he discovered that no national data on that specific status existed. Such a situation seems to be the combined result of "cover-up" and indifference factors. The author's statistical workup shows that more than half of all ABDs writing full-fledged dissertations never finish, although the percentages vary considerably from discipline to discipline. Such a high failure rate is startling in contrast with ABDs' prior successful completion of two to four arduous years of all other degree requirements, and with the infinitely lower failure rates for "professional," non-dissertation-required doctorates, such as law, medicine and dentistry. It is difficult to see how any other factor but the differential thesis requirement can account for the very different success rates. Men and women are about equally represented in the ABD population, although men are over-represented in doctorates conferred. But projections from 1970s data indicate that women will make substantial strides toward parity with men by 1990.

3. After completion of predissertation requirements, the candidate finds himself adrift, with accustomed educational support systems withdrawn to a degree unprecedented in American education at any level. Particular conditions implicated in this situation are dissertation anomie, faculty "unreliability," lack of a graduate student community and candidates' "unpreparedness" for the great task.

4. The book is addressed to (a) graduate students still doing course work, who want anticipatory socialization to the demands of the upcoming dissertation course; (b) the 51,000 new ABDs squarely up

26

against the thesis task; (c) the undetermined but large number of "veteran" ABDs; (d) families, spouses, lovers and friends of ABDs, to aid them in living with their candidate through this difficult time in his life by providing some in-depth background on the project with which he is wrestling; (e) graduate educators, administrators and faculty, in the hope that this exposition will prompt structural reforms of the callousness and even disrespect with which programs currently treat ABDs.

5. The volume is designed to be a constant companion or "guidebook" for the writer along all the major stations of the dissertation course: the initial deliberate decision to write the thesis; proposal; data collection; data analysis; actual writing of chapters; thesis defense; postdegree aftermath. Throughout, four essential dimensions of the project are consistenly treated and interwoven: "nuts-and-bolts" issues; emotional difficulties of the candidate caused by the thesis experience; possible changes and disruptions in interpersonal relations; strategies and tactics for dealing with dissertation-supervising faculty.

NOTES

1. Neal Ascherson's review of E. Ettinger's ed., *Comrade and Lover: Rosa Luxemburg's Letters to Leo Jogiches*, in *New York Review of Books*, March 6, 1980, p. 4.
2. In the early 1930s, George Stewart, an English professor at Berkeley, wrote a novel called *Doctor's Oral*, describing the disruptions in intimate relations, and anxieties generated by writing a dissertation. I am indebted to my former professor, Robert Bierstedt, for calling this book to my attention.
3. W. Zinsser, *On Writing Well: An Informal Guide to Writing Nonfiction*, 2nd ed. (New York: Harper and Row, 1980).
4. John Almack, *Research and Thesis Writing: A Textbook in Principles and Techniques of Thesis Construction for the Use of Graduate Students in Universities and Colleges* (Boston: Houghton-Mifflin, 1930).
5. H. Livesey and H. Doughty, *Guide to American Graduate Schools*, 3rd ed. (New York: Viking, Compass Books, 1975), page xx.
6. *Projections of Education Statistics* to 1986–87 (Washington, D.C.: National Center for Education Statistics, HEW, 1978), Table 9, pp. 28–29.
7. Wilkinson, "A Profile: Minorities in Sociology and Other Behavioral Sciences," American Sociological Association *Footnotes*, November

1978, pp. 6–8; "Women in the Profession: Data Sources for the Eighties,[11] Sociologists for Women Society, SWS *Newsletter,* January 1980.

8. If the Wilkinson statistical trend continues in social science, 1990 should see equal numbers of candidates and conferred degrees for both sexes. For a more doubtful view of rapidly approaching parity, especially in doctoral *degrees,* see Dearman and Plisko, *The Condition of Education* (Washington, D.C.: National Center for Education Statistics, HEW, 1979), p. 231, and their "Projections of Degrees, by Level and Sex to 1987–1988," forthcoming management bulletin.

9. Usually, education doctoral dissertations have to do with some basic institutional element, such as faculty or student personnel, administration of some level of education system, instructing a particular type of student and the like. The substantive and methodological perspectives are ordinarily psychology, sociology, political science or public administration. See *Digest of Education Statistics,* Table 108 (on degrees conferred by field and subfield of study, 1976–1977), (Washington, D.C.: National Center for Education Statistics, HEW, 1979), pp. 113–114.

10. Even in the more rigorous sciences, a concern with writing lucid English for popular and lay audiences, as well as for colleagues, is growing, although it probably has not yet substantially affected dissertation style. See R. Barass, *Scientists Must Write: A Guide to Better Writing for Scientists, Engineers and Students* (New York: Wiley, 1978).

11. Although precise numbers are not known, pre-ABD dissertation starts are apparently not infrequent. See Livesey and Doughty, op. cit., pp. xxii–xxiii.

12. In the 1970s, in a little-known debate and decision, the Board of Higher Education of the City University of New York (CUNY) ruled that a J.D. qualified as a "doctor's degree" required to hold a tenured professorial line. I have always disagreed with this decision, since the J.D., in my judgment and experience, amounts to little more than an M.A., especially since no dissertation is required. The decision was made on lobbying and "political" grounds, rather than on academic ones.

13. Derek C. Bok, "A Challenge to Legal Education" *Harvard Law School Bulletin,* Fall 1979, pp. 12–15.

14. Cf., R. Hofstadter, ed., *Anti-Intellectualism in American Life* (New York: Knopf, 1963).

15. H. Wilensky, "Mass Society and Mass Culture," *American Sociological Review,* April 1964; see also Anderson and Murray, eds., *The Professors: Work and Life Styles Among Academicians* (Cambridge, Mass.: Schenkman, 1971).

16. When the term "graduate faculty" is used, a distinction has to be made

between the minority situation, usually in elite schools, where graduate professors teach and work only in the graduate program; and the much more usual case, where professors have assignments in both undergraduate and graduate, say, education or sociology programs. In the former cases, of course, faculty are much more apt to be forthcoming with supervision and guidance of theses.

17. Those candidates in the minority elite programs may be *partially* exempted from some of the remarks in this section on unpreparedness; but even there I would contend that the issues of the dissertation task are never squarely met in course work, term papers or class projects.

18. Educators never seem to discuss the inconsistencies between emphasis on peer group learning and phobias against "cheating." Particularly with young students, when "moral judgment" is not fully developed, a distinction between cooperation and cheating must be very difficult to see. Many students, I believe, carry a genuine lack of distinction right through college.

19. With the near-depression economics of the late 1970s and early 1980s, even the most traditionally liberal arts-oriented of universities, notably Harvard, have retrenched to a more "practical" focus on the Three Rs, giving way to the demands of many (corporate) employers (often endowers) and even many students that marketable skills be emphasized.

20. I wrote a 191-page master's thesis in sociology and found it helpful, up to a point, for doing my dissertation three years later.

21. The late 1970s saw a burgeoning of "uncolleges," where one spent all his time in the shop learning a skilled trade (machine, computer programming, TV or air-conditioning repairs) and was promised by television commercials there would be no "hassles" with useless drivel like foreign languages, history or sociology. The growth of "uncolleges" is certain for the 1980s as well. One wonders how their advertisements might strike, or tempt, a floundering ABD.

22. H. Crosby and G. Estey, *College Writing*, 2nd ed. (New York: Harper and Row, 1975).

CHAPTER 2

The Great Decision: Reordering Priorities and Choosing a (Viable) Topic

THE DISSERTATION: STARTING ALL OVER AGAIN

In medical or law school, the decision to *enter* these graduate programs is the last great decision, since faithful course attendance and examination passing virtually ensure acquisition of an M.D. or J.D. in four or three years' time. It is the crux of the ABD problem that dissertation-required doctorates demand an extra great decision—to write or not to write—and that the average candidate is unaware, until far down the program's line, of its importance and necessity. It is the failure to confront this decision peculiar to dissertation doctorates that accounts for more nonfinishes or long delays than any other single factor.

It is probably not exaggerating matters very much to assert that course work and even preliminary examinations, on the one hand, and writing the dissertation, on the other, have no relationship. Certainly, as we have seen, successful (even outstanding) performance up to the dissertation is no guarantee of completion of the degree. What the catalogs, deans and faculty don't tell the candidate is that graduate school success really involves the negotiation of *two* separate programs, one ending with passing course work and preliminaries (and sometimes obtaining a master's degree as well), and the other beginning with "applying" for admission to write a dissertation through submission of an acceptable proposal. In a very real sense, dissertation writers are starting over again, and very little in their past two or three years of performance counts for much. That matters shouldn't stand this way (and many program spokespersons will indignantly howl that what I am claiming is false or exaggerated), that there should be continuity between the two parts of a doctorate, that it is unfair, even a disgrace and should be rectified forthwith—with all this the writer concurs. But the "two-program" model is here to stay for the foreseeable future, certainly going to span the reader's dissertation-writing experience. If the candidate wants to work to alter this system, fine. But do it after you finish your doctorate.

It is just this failure to understand that the dissertation and the preceding parts of the program are independent that makes questions such as "Do you really want to write your dissertation?" or "Have you thought through some changes in your life you are going to have to make while doing the project?" sound puzzling or even silly. "Of course I want to do my dissertation; I'm in graduate school, aren't I? I'm here to get my doctorate," the candidate will answer. But he or she has usually "bought" the "professional school" model of the doctorate, the one minus the zinger: the dissertation. Omission of the dissertation as its "own ball game" makes these questions and answers unreflexive to each other.

Cost Accounting the Dissertation.

The dissertation is definitely not for everybody, not even for all ABDs, particularly since most have failed to consider the independent demands and related skills and attitudes of that project. All ABDs, or near-ABDs, should undertake a serious "cost analysis" prior to undertaking the dissertation.[1] Involved in the equation are considerations such as one's goals/priorities in life, a sober appreciation of the specific demands of writing a dissertation, an honest inventory of one's *intellectual/literary strengths and weaknesses* vis-à-vis these demands, an inventory of one's *emotional strengths and weaknesses* vis-à-vis the dissertation demands, a projection of the "rewards" and "punishments" awaiting one along the dissertation way, and beyond. As the candidate reads through this book, he will get a fuller understanding of just what changes in life-style the dissertation is going to demand and be able to make a more reliable and convincing decision as to

31

whether he possesses what Tom Wolfe has called, in another context, the "right stuff" for the task.[2]

Some Wrong Reasons for Writing the Dissertation.

I am terming those reasons which generally won't sustain a candidate through the project as "wrong." If you are contemplating a dissertation chiefly for one or more reasons akin to the following (selected) types, you are, my "actuarial" experience dictates, in for a great deal of trouble:

1. "I've got an exciting topic." More specific discussion about choosing a dissertation subject will ensue later in the chapter, but here let me state that, although an "exciting" topic (sometimes connected with a "chance-in-a-lifetime" research access) can serve as a first-stage motivator, all dissertation topics become predictably frayed, frustrating, often boring, infuriating for the writer at points down the course. When students tell me that their problem is that they picked the "wrong"—say, sociology—topic, I relate to them the agonies and ennui that fellow candidates who chose "in" topics on sex roles or more bizarre types of deviant behavior are experiencing. One picks a dissertation topic—a relatively secondary concern—after serious commitment to the primary goal of writing a doctoral dissertation; to reverse the sequence of these two decisions is to misunderstand the nature of the dissertation and invite nonfinishing.

2. "If I don't write the dissertation, I'll have wasted years of study and money." It is true in large part that you will have wasted both. I am not going to patronize you with talk about how learning is valuable in its own right, regardless of material reward (even though that is undoubtedly universally true up to a point), living as we are in the financially tight 1980s. But the dissertation is not like a business venture, or even like a professional school (business school included) where just "hanging in there" or "toughing it out" more often than not will pay off or bring you even. If an ABD's cost accounting yields debits in lack of skills and/or motivations for the long-distance dissertation, he should quit, or at the very least take some time off, do something else for a while, to rethink priorities and willingness to work on deficiencies. Better to waste two or three years than five or six.

3. "Everybody's expecting me to write it and get my doctorate." The problem here is that "everybody," including the candidate, until very

recently was operating on the doctorate *qua* law, medicine or dentistry model. These good folks, including one's nearest and dearest, don't understand about the extra requirement (any more than you really did). In any situation where one allows others in possession of less crucial intelligence than oneself to dictate a decision, a self-destructive delegation and abdication of agency and authority is being committed. In my experience, one can still—after very serious and thorough conclusions about the costs of a dissertation being too high, or one's "set" toward the task just not being up to it—walk away from two or three years of course work, certainly hurt for a while, but survive quite whole. Such is not the case after putting in an additional year or two on a dissertation with no end in sight. Those years are more than waste: each succeeding one bores into one's strength, making it harder and harder to walk away whole and get on to another task or profession where the prognosis is better and interest higher.

4. "I'm not quitting this one too." Oftentimes, candidates in dissertation-requiring programs have a biography of leaving other disciplines or careers. Such earlier abdications, changes of mind, reversals of field may weigh heavily on the state of mind of a candidate who is contemplating not pursuing the dissertation: "Here I go again. Another time of not seeing it through." I believe American society puts entirely too much pressure on its young adult persons to "find themselves," usually equating that discovery with hitting upon a lifetime job or career. The equation is quite false: many people who successfully pursue one line of employment never really "find themselves" in the sense of internally experienced feelings of gratification; on the other hand, many occupational "drifters" move from field to field, feel reasonably good about themselves and experience shame (not internal guilt) only when denigrated by others for their spotty employment records.

In any event, the dissertation doctorate is the worst place for a career-uncertain person to make his last stand, if that mood is his chief one for continuing in a program, since the dissertation prerequires the very kind of commitment which is most problematic in the case of this type of candidate.

The Right Reason for Undertaking the Dissertation.

Although one can catalog a list of wrong (insufficiently motivating) reasons for undertaking the dissertation, only one general "right" reason exists: The candidate is deeply interested in his specific discipline and has every intention of pursuing a career within the field immediately upon (or at least soon after) completion of the thesis. This reason must not be confused with that of finding a "sexy" or "in" dissertation topic, which is a fleeting and often effervescent motivator.

One of the most troublesome aspects of the dissertation is the relative absence of short-term, even middle-term rewards. Dissertation writers constantly complain about not being able to see the end of the road as the months and seasons of proposals, research, analysis and writing go on. (There are certain ways, which the book will discuss, in which along-the-way rewards can be built in by the writer, but they only partially break up the built-in burden and dreariness of the thesis course.) The dissertation-writing situation parallels long-distance running in this respect. How do runners keep going, mile upon mile, in, say, a twenty-six-mile marathon? Experienced harriers, such as James Fixx, note that when their feet and souls begin to drag along the way, they constantly remind themselves that there were well-thought-out reasons for wanting to finish the race before they began; some even repeat these reasons to themselves right through the entire course of the run.[3]

It is my conviction that only the candidate's firm intention to become a full (the doctorate bestowing full membership) professional in his dissertation field, combined with his constant self-reminders of that intention and eventual gratification through the ups and downs of the long dissertation "run," is an adequate long-range reward for the task confronting him. Since the time I was in college, there was talk, and lore, about the so-called "gentleman scholar" (who in undergraduate school received the "gentleman's C" grades), who pursued graduate school and even the dissertation at his leisure, with no serious thought about finishing in a relatively limited time, or especial concern with taking up a career in the field. I have come to doubt that (a) such people exist, or (b) if they do, that they ever finish their theses. Even in the serious academic and research employment recessions of the 1970s and 1980s, almost all the earnest and committed dissertation writers I have known believed they would obtain (although very often not without a good deal of initial perseverance and disappointment at the start of employment search) a full-time "line" position.

This is to say that people who are in the dissertation game on "spec" are most often not going to make it. Those who believe they are going to "pick up" a dissertation doctorate and then "see what happens" are a particularly high-casualty group. I am not asserting that one cannot successfully negotiate a dissertation while working another job (including running a household with children)—there may sometimes even be advantages to such a dissertation-writing situation. But if one's *attitude* is leisurely and uncommitted to a definite switch in full-time employment to the doctorate field, the "moonlight" candidate has small hope of completing.

Let me point up again the distinction between interest in one's field and in one's dissertation subject. In the past few years I have had a number of clients in psychology Ph.D. programs who were interning as clinical psychologists/psychotherapists. Invariably, their dissertation topics and methodologies—whether they were matriculated in clinical psychology, educational psychology, counseling psychology or another specialty—were *experimental* projects. It is one of the dislocations of graduate psychology programs—parallel ones can no doubt be found in many of the disciplines with which we are concerned—that no matter what eventual subfield of psychology a Ph.D. pursues (a National Science Foundation report indicated that three-fourths of psychologists pursue "service" careers working with patients or clients, and only one-fourth "research" ones), he is almost always required to write an experimental-model dissertation.

My psychology dissertation clients always disliked, sometimes even hated, their dissertations because there was so little relationship (or the relationship was a *negative* one, as they saw it; the "objective" methods of the dissertation research and experiment were opposed to the "intuitive" approach in therapy) to their present and future work in psychotherapy. Thus, on top of the usual aversion to necessarily making the dissertation the center of one's life was the additional complication that the content, methodology and *ideology* of the topic conflicted with the substance, approach and ideology of their clinical work, even though the dissertation and their jobs were both in the general field of psychology. Yet, most of these persons finished their theses (most even came to "like" their dissertations, or at least feel terribly proud and gratified that they were able to complete them), because the doctorate was absolutely essential for them to become

35

licensed as clinical psychologists. Each of these candidates possessed a very strong *general commitment* to psychology and was able, with struggle, to transfer that drive to a topic to which he or she was certainly less than committed. My input consisted in large part in getting these candidates to remind themselves constantly that the lifelong gratification of being "Dr. Jones," practicing their professions in a fully credentialed and societally prestigious manner, was worth an all-out eighteen-to-twenty-four-month effort now.[4]

Getting into the Driver's Seat of Your Dissertation.

As we have taken pains to note, American graduate schools, let alone lower-level systems of education, do not enculturate their students for the task of the dissertation. Accordingly, ABDs come to the dissertation assuming—to the problematic extent they think much about it at all—that their lives are going to proceed pretty much along SOP lines during their project. The dissertation is hazily adumbrated as not much more than a long term paper. Many candidates never get past this erroneous picture of the thesis, never get a handle on its true scope, never finish. The dissertation experience, until they give up, is one long puzzle for them: "Every time I go down to the department they find something else wrong, or something else for me to add. I can't understand it." Or: "I go to one professor, and she tells me I better take her course in theory construction before I continue my proposal; I go to another, and he tells me I need work in statistics. What's going on here? I feel like I'm getting the runaround."

What's going on is that the candidate is continuing to play the *reactive role* in which he has been so heavily trained by our school system, rather than taking the *active role* the dissertation demands. To do a dissertation one has to see the big picture: if you fail to have the grand design blocked out, then you are constantly at the compartmentalizing mercies of faculty and various advice givers, since they can capriciously change the shakily charted direction of your thought and inquiries. The candidate has to get into the driver's seat of his dissertation, and this means jettisoning long-seated, dysfunctional intellectual—and even life-—styles. A main goal of this book is to plot out, in the following chapters, specific strategies and tactics for converting the typically shaky ABD from a reactive, passive, childlike taker of advice and instructions to an adult, autonomous forger of his own dissertation. Without such a "conversion," the thesis will rarely be completed,

36

or, even if completed, fail to bestow its chief potential benefit—aside from the doctorate—infusing the rest of one's life with a sense of achievement in completing an enormous project which so few men and women are able to negotiate.

Making the Dissertation a Top Priority in Your Life.

It is only when the dissertation is first or second on the ABD's priority list that he is able to devote to it the time, attention and motivation to grasp its big picture, or grand design. Only with the thesis constantly on one's mind can one "call the shots." Think of the candidate as a stagehand straining to push the "set" of his dissertation to the middle of his life stage. But a theater grip has to move props and set pieces around. Everything can't be center-stage; some must be moved upstage, downstage or even offstage for the duration of important scenes.

The successful candidate is going to have to rearrange his social and psychological priorities—and even relationships—during the dissertation course if he is to get on top of the thesis and drive it home to completion. Many, if not most, ABDs offer fierce resistance to setting a new scene onstage. And yet, nearly all the successful writers I have known had to make the dissertation close to an obsession (magnificent or otherwise). This is almost indescribably difficult to convey, especially to American students, who find the concept so alien. The idea of lovers, spouses, children, social life in general being relegated to a back burner, virtually put "on hold" for much of the dissertation course, is horrifying, often incomprehensible to people. Yet the rigors of the research and writing are such that a candidate has no strength, stomach or time for extensive quarrels, grand passions, backbiting. The "shutting down," or at least severe "cutback," of extradissertation concerns for the year or two of writing is poignantly if humorously underscored by a "personal" ad in the *New York Review of Books* (November 22, 1979): "33-YEAR-OLD ATTRACTIVE WOMAN, having just finished her doctorate, is ready to enjoy life again and would like to meet an adventurous man."

Friends and Lovers During the Dissertation: Differential Association.

But, you may protest indignantly, do I seriously expect you to give up your husband, your lover, your family, your job? Believe me, none

37

of these would be bad ideas, at least in certain cases. But I am not suggesting across-the-board cutting off of one's intimate and employment connections, even if this were possible. Rather, I am suggesting the need to create a "space" for oneself of relative tranquillity and freedom to think about and work on the dissertation. Management of one's particular extradissertation relationships has to be dictated by answering the question: "Is the content or tone of this relationship helpful, detrimental or neutral in getting my dissertation finished?" Depending on your biographical answers to these questions, you are going to have to nurture, withdraw from or accept various associations. Dissertation writing demands a kind of "differential association" with people determined by how they affect the progress of your thesis.[5]

Obviously, some detrimental dissertation associations can't be completely cut off: Your husband may be intractable about not supporting your need for dissertation space, but a good provider, father and lover. You'll need him, and want him, at a later date, after the doctorate is conferred. What you must do in the meantime is try to negotiate with *him* to give you some time off and with *yourself* to point mentally and emotionally in the dissertation direction without a new debilitating *guilt* burden of neglecting the family. Such alterations in associations or emotional investments in associations are possible only if you have genuinely put finishing the thesis virtually at the top of your list.

Dissertation time is no time for emotional crises in one's personal life; the crises of the dissertation are quite enough to bear and surmount. Candidates "swept away" by a new grand passion can get shipwrecked on the dissertation rocks. Actually, if one is totally committed to a dissertation, getting swept away is unlikely, but the early stages of writing (e.g., the proposal) are dangerous times; many candidates, frightened by the extent of the commitment, are seeking a way out.

Figure 2.1 delineates the salient status positions and corresponding role relationships a "typical" ABD is likely to possess and have to deal with. (Obviously, some candidates will not be incumbents of all of these statuses, although most will occupy some version of all or nearly all of them.) The doctoral candidate status is much further refined and analyzed in terms of specific role partners in Chapter Six, on presenting the unfolding dissertation to faculty (see Figures 6.1 and 6.2, below).

Figure 2.1: An ABD's Status-and-Role Sets

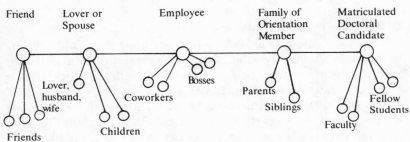

At the point of seriously undertaking the project, the candidate is urged to diagram his own differential association map/model, taking Figure 2.1 as a point of departure:

1. List your key statuses, and with whom you deal within them on a regular basis.
2. Evaluate each personal, family, student and work association (a) in terms of whether it helps, hurts or is neutral to dissertation progress, and (b) *in what specific ways.*
3. For each association map out a strategy for maximizing or minimizing your contacts (not merely on a numerical dimension, but in terms of emotional investment) during the dissertation writing.
4. Make the exercise an ongoing one; every couple of months re-evaluate both the nature of the associations and how well you have managed to deal with them in the interests of moving ahead with your dissertation.

Some of these alterations in your association model, first construed by the candidate as temporary, may turn out to be permanent. Sometimes the dissertation experience, by changing a person, permanently alters certain personal/social as well as occupational relationships. This is almost inevitable in a project demanding reaching way down inside oneself for resources perhaps never before realized. A dissertation has a way of making a *mensch* of a man or woman no longer satisfied with all of the old arrangements and associations in life.

There is, then, risk, but also promise in doing the dissertation. Any way one cuts it, the doctoral dissertation is not for the fainthearted (see Chapter Nine, "Beyond the Dissertation: Surviving It and Professionally Exploiting It").

Of Work and the Dissertation.

Can a candidate who is working full-time hope to make the dissertation a near top priority in his life, possibly rearrange his associations and life-style in line with the kind of program outlined above? This is a vital question for over 160,000 part-time ABDs facing the dissertation in the 1980s (part-time because the vast majority of them are working). No one *knows* what the differential finishing rates for full-time and part-time writers are. Almost everyone concerned with the issue *guesses* that full-timers have higher success rates, or, at the least, faster finishing rates. The reliability and validity of these hunches, observations and guesses are complicated by many "mixed" cases; an ABD may stop work, say, for a year to work on his thesis, then returns not having finished, or someone may continue to work and complete his dissertation.

I am cautious about overall negative correlations between working and effectively writing and finishing the dissertation. Some of that caution comes from my own dissertation experience: During at least half of my dissertation course (eighteen months from its start to finish), I held a part-time teaching job, which did not, upon reflection, impede my progress (although at the time I cursed it roundly and often for believing it to be doing so). Beyond my dissertation, I know that the most sustained, long-distance writing I did in the 1970s was during academic terms when I was teaching a four-course load.

Much depends upon the *nature* of one's employment. Going back to the differential dissertation association model, work can be classified as contributive, dysfunctional or neutral in reference to dissertation progress. Teaching or research jobs in the same or related field to one's thesis most often have a synergistic, positive effect on dissertation development. In my case, I used the classroom to get feedback from my students on problems I was having with my fieldwork. Having to delineate these issues in lecture form forced me to rethink and clarify them for myself. Then, too, sharing my work with my students was most stimulating and motivationally very crucial; students were awaiting the next episode in my dissertation research. The lectures I gave during my fieldwork were some of the most exciting, existential and "authentic" of my career. Students sense when you are talking about something you are actually carrying through, as opposed to giving a "secondary source" lecture.

One kind of dysfunctional job so physically and emotionally exhausts a candidate that the last thing on his mind is two hours of dissertation work after dinner. This kind of job creates the "weekend warrior" type of work style, where the candidate tries to give his project a few hours on the weekend (said hours being resented by the ABD himself who wants Saturday and Sunday to rest and recharge for Monday; his spouse and children, who want these hours shared with them). A *sine qua non* of progress is a regular, scheduled taking up of the dissertation cudgels. Weekend dissertation writing coupled with a physically demanding full-time job rarely yields a finished thesis.

Another kind of dissertation-disservice job involves soakage in forty hours of a chiefly antiintellectual or "practical" ambience. I would say that the majority of business and sales jobs fall into this category. The danger with such work locales is that they tend to instill in the candidate a cynicism, impatience and even deprecation toward the worth of his dissertation. Such debilitation is often as hindering to writing a dissertation as a physically demanding job. Although there is talk (there are even books) about the "academic marketplace," and although certain elements of dissertation negotiation (e.g., the proposal) have a definite contract element, the dissertation is not "doing business," in the sense of commercial affairs. The hustle, high-pressure sales techniques and ideology that "everybody and everything has its price" are most dysfunctional activity styles and attitudes for winning dissertation approval from a laid-back faculty accustomed to moving at a much more leisurely pace.[6]

There *is* one instance when a candidate can turn an aggressive business context to his advantage: when that site and its personnel are the subjects of his dissertation (see below in this chapter for choosing a dissertation topic). When this is the case, the "double agent" quality of the job can convert it into an exciting affair: one isn't really there as an employee, although that is one's "cover," but as a sociologist, political scientist, psychologist, recording the data for one's own purposes and project.

Sometimes a job has already conferred a relatively high status on

41

the incumbent, to the extent that he may seriously resist the role reversal and role abnegation built into the status of ABD in his dealings with supervising graduate faculty. High-placed business executives, ranking police officers, supervisors of public agencies and lawyers—to name a few groups—have all had authority conflicts and stresses when concomitantly pursuing a doctorate. Although a teaching position is usually a dissertation-promoting employment (see above), in the case of a long-term ABD who has taught for many years, holds tenure and perhaps a high rank (cases of tenured professors without a Ph.D. were more common ten or twenty years ago, but can still be found), it is not conducive to rematriculating and/or completing the dissertation. A fifty-year-old professor, mistakenly addressed by students, staff and faculty as Dr. Jones for fifteen years, comfortable with his teaching situation, has very little to gain (and perhaps a good deal to forfeit: his position might be jeopardized if the question of his incomplete credentials was raised anew) by reseeking the doctorate.

There is, of course, the other side to the picture where a "halo effect" mechanism transfers the ABD's "outside" prestige over to the graduate program setting and creates deferential or collegial treatment from faculty. A few years ago, for example, an MD entered the doctoral program in sociology at an Ivy League university. Within a year, a number of the faculty were asking him for prescriptions. Without necessarily postulating a causal relationship, it is instructive to note that he negotiated the doctoral/dissertation course with unusual smoothness. In my own case, I would hazard that my possession of a law degree when I entered the New York University sociology graduate program gave me some "points"; I recall being asked for, and giving, occasional legal advice to professors during my course years. But any leverage I might have gained during predissertation years vanished for a number of reasons, perhaps most saliently the fact that *I* vanished for a year or two upon completion of my course work and preliminary orals, and returned to confront new faculty whom I had never counseled and who were unfamiliar with my extrasociology credentials.

Neutral jobs are those which neither promote nor hinder progress on the dissertation. Although I couldn't possibly catalog them all, by a process of exclusion they would include work which didn't leave one bone-weary and jobs where at least some "life of the mind" element existed. Many nonprofit organization and/or public service jobs would qualify here; in the private sector, publishing and advertising probably won't hurt you, although they may not help. A number of my master's and doctoral advisees over the years have used "neutral" work sites, especially public service agencies (e.g., drug control divisions, court staffs, social welfare departments) as successful theoretical focuses and data bases.

An employed reader/candidate is going to have to construct his own personalized calculus in evaluating his job as functional, dysfunctional or neutral for getting his dissertation done. Certainly, my classification and assignment of particular jobs to one category or another does not presume to be "airtight." Some teaching jobs are permeated with cynicism and antiintellectualism; some business positions are rich in analytic thinking and long-range planning (both necessary features in a dissertation). But, if only to use my observations as a point of departure, the fully employed candidate has to evaluate his job with a view toward maximizing its dissertation-promoting aspects and containing or defusing its dissertation-discouraging elements. If such a calculus "prints out" as highly negative, the candidate is either going to have to change his job or face inevitable discouragement and delay in the progress of his thesis. It is at such a decision junction that being in touch with the reasons for writing one's dissertation becomes imperative.

Setting Up a Dissertation Office.

The need to rearrange social and psychological life priorities during the dissertation course is facilitated and reinforced by (indeed, requires) creating an objective base, or "office," designed exclusively for this project. Developmental psychologists have demonstrated that children with their own rooms perform better in school than matched children without one. The quality of the room's furnishings, luxurious or rather sparse, seems unimportant in affecting learning; the privacy is paramount. There is every reason to believe that such differentials stretch into adult performance of intellectual tasks.[7]

The office should (1) be in a separate room, or at least place, and (2) devoted as completely as possible, during the life of the dissertation, to thesis matters. Both of these requirements may present problems of

43

execution in a particular candidate's case. One's home or apartment may simply not have an extra room to convert into a dissertation office. A number of my clients lived with spouses in one-bedroom apartments. In each of these instances, they "carved out" a part of either the bedroom or living room, using some kind of room divider, such as bookcases or screens to isolate the office. Another ABD created an office under the loft bed she constructed in the bedroom. Particularly in the case of the bedroom office, it was agreed upon (eventually, but not without resistance) that the ABD's spouse would stay out of the bedroom during dissertation working hours. Until that ground rule was implemented, the office was so permeable and subject to interruption (from spouse) and even disruption (from children) that little sustained progress could be made.

It is also almost essential that the office not be the base for multiple enterprises, from paying bills, to letter writing, to collection and storage of mail, memorabilia and years of graduate school clutter in the form of notes, books and term papers. A desk and bookcase(s) in the "common area" of the home should do for these diverse activities and papers. The idea is to underscore both the "starting anew" and single-mindedness of the dissertation project. The clean desk signifies the clean slate of one's beginning. Every item that subsequently enters your office should be there only because of its necessity for and contribution to the dissertation. If this sounds like a rather "Spartan" organization plan, it is intended to; soon enough the office will begin to fill up.

So, the *privacy* of your office signifies to both you and those you live with the respect and importance you accord to your independent project. (It is most often the independent quality and implications of the dissertation course which cause a spouse or lover to resist the office rearrangement, not the specious reason that it is "inconvenient" or "unfair.") It also helps you get into the driver's seat of your dissertation by providing you with a dissertation space that is always waiting for you when you have scheduled time for work, or whenever you feel like (and you will) "just being" with your dissertation. Making the office *exclusive to the thesis* also underscores its uniqueness and importance, and gets one right down to a dissertation-writing frame of mind. No diversions await one in the office; one sits down and is squarely up against the task.

What should the office contain? You need a decent-size desk, one or more bookcases, writing materials and/or a typewriter, a filing cabinet (the building of a file is so crucial to mounting a dissertation that the next chapter is devoted to it), probably (à la Woody Allen in *Manhattan*) a tape recorder (the uses of which are discussed in Chapter Three) and perhaps a blackboard (particularly if you are a teacher and feel comfortable and familiar with getting down ideas in that fashion). Although, everything else being equal, the office should be as pleasant as possible, little time should be spent on interior decorating after the essential equipment has been set up. Establish privacy and exclusivity; further elaborations are usually "dissertation stall."

Dissertation Office Hours.

It is essential to set up a rather rigid schedule of hours to work each day (week) on the dissertation. You've set up an office; now you have to "punch in," with the important difference that *you* are the boss and have to police yourself in punctuality and attendance. The editors of the *Paris Review* have interviewed, since 1953, over fifty successful full-time novelists, essayists, poets and playwrights living in many countries to get a picture of how they worked at their craft.[8] Perhaps the most important common thread among such a diverse group of writers was that they maintained a virtually invariable daily writing time, five to seven days a week, for from two to four hours, and at the same time of the day (most often, mornings).[9] Another theme that emerged was how *systematic* and *businesslike* about their writing these people are (were), even in the case of those stereotyped as "unpredictable," "flamboyant," "wild" or "irresponsible" (e.g., William Faulkner, Ernest Hemingway, Henry Miller, Norman Mailer).

I have discovered that *some time each day* (or at least five days a week: even the most zealous candidate/writer has to reward himself with an occasional day of rest) at the office is the key effective variable. Optimally, the period should be a minimum of two hours, but this cannot always be arranged, particularly for full-time employed candidates. The point is that, say, ten hours a week spent in the dissertation office in two sittings (often at weekends) does not have the same punch as five two-hour sessions. What one needs on this job is to establish and maintain an ongoing rhythm and flow. Progress on the dissertation comes with day-to-day involvement: if you give it only

45

two "shots" a week, half of your allocated time session is apt to be spent just "catching up" or reminding yourself of where you left off the previous week. So, in terms of progress, a two-session ten-hour input is going to yield closer to five hours, because of deductions for "maintenance." Thus, it is probably more effective to spend only one hour each day in the office (five hours a week) than a whole afternoon on both weekend days.

The writer will discover that he will often want to exceed his daily minimum time, particularly when things are humming. Whenever feasible, one should try to leave an hour's breathing space after the scheduled time limit to allow one to continue when the blood is up. On the other hand, the writer should never "leave the office early" on a day when the project isn't speeding along. Very often, I know from my own experience, a person can sit stalled at his typewriter or day-dreaming for an hour and a half; suddenly a breakthrough can happen, and the next half hour is rapid, productive work. But you have to give yourself time, tough out some of the (seeming) doldrums if you are to be there to exploit the opportunity. Mark Twain once said, "The harder I work, the better my luck gets."

I rarely have a day anymore when nothing, or very little at all, comes out of two or three hours at my machine. But certainly, there are sessions when I am a good deal less than satisfied with what I have written. I make it a rule never to indulge in a past novice habit of angrily ripping up pages which I don't like and throwing them in the wastebasket. I find that the next day in the office I can almost always extract something from those imperfect pages which will, in fact, fit into my ongoing manuscript. Short of this, that output at least gives me a lead-in for the next day's hopefully more on-target production.

The discussion about time spent in the dissertation office has to be qualified with respect to library research and fieldwork that particular dissertations require. At certain stages of the dissertation, your work will undeniably require your being "out of the office" and "in the field" for days, or even weeks, at a stretch. Still, one always has to come back to the office to put together library and field research. During the fieldwork stage of my dissertation (lasting about nine months), I almost always spent an additional two or three hours (at the end of the day) in my office, reviewing my field notes, reminding myself what had to be followed up the next day, writing down impressions and hunches (see next chapter on "Building a Dissertation File" for a tabulation of these kinds of office activities). Despite the time demands of library attendance and fieldwork or conducting experiments, one must not relinquish a daily period at the dissertation office (although it may be necessary for limited periods to reduce the blocks of time); one must mind the store.

These guidelines about time apply to the employed ABD as well as the candidate who doesn't have to work during his dissertation course. The employed ABD is going to have to find ways to get in a daily hour or two at his office, even if this means confrontations with family and friends, and sacrifice of leisure, usually evening, hours for TV. If time is not found and a schedule not implemented, neither the working nor the nonemployed ABD is going to finish the dissertation. Additionally, there are going to be times with dissertations (particularly in social science and education fields) where the working candidate will have to take a few days off from employment, usually to gather data from subjects or groups who aren't available after 5 P.M. Again, during the writing of the dissertation, after all the data and statistical analyses are in, an employed ABD may want/need to take off some days or weeks to write "full-time" in the office. These contingencies must be anticipated and taken into account in evaluating the functional or dysfunctional effects of one's job on completing the dissertation.

Choosing a Dissertation Topic.

Contrary to a good deal of faculty and student mythology, the dissertation topic *per se* is at best a secondary factor both in determining whether a candidate finishes and the troubles he experiences at different stages of research and writing. Recall my argument about the topic as *dependent* variable, commitment to becoming a full-fledged member of the profession as the *independent, prior* one in the sequence of dissertation decisions. No matter how "exotic" the topic, e.g., "Swedish Prostitutes and Their Black American Pimps in Stockholm"; how "current" or "relevant," e.g., "Mary McCarthy and Susan Sontag: Contrasting Visions in Feminist Literature"; how obscure or arcane, e.g., "Effects of White Noise Occlusion of Voice Feedback on Superego Functioning"; all dissertations run into a predictable, common set of both "internal" problems, from hypothesis construction to sample issues, methodological difficulties, analytic contradictions and "external" difficulties connected with getting several faculty members

47

to agree upon not only the topic itself, but from what perspective and in what degree of emphasis and detail it should be pursued.

None of this is to say that one should not give careful consideration to the thesis topic. *Careful consideration* should be underscored here, because when a fresh ABD or near-ABD is buzzing with dozens of tentative topics, such consideration is going to render most of these inspirations unfeasible. One has to put four essential questions to every prospective topic:

Is it researchable? For a comparative-literature candidate, the issue might be whether relevant texts from other eras, countries or languages were available/accessible. For the psychology or sociology candidate, the key question is whether one has access to, or can gain admission to, topic-loaded samples or groups. For example, an undoubtedly worthwhile and "relevant" dissertation topic in social psychology would be "The National Security Council As a Small Group: A Test of Bales's Interaction Process Matrix." Bales and his associates, watching, recording and videotaping Harvard undergraduates for decades through one-way mirrors, have constructed a set of "laws" about how members will behave which they assert are generalizable to all small "task-oriented" groups. However, it is most unlikely that an ABD will get a chance to set up shop in a room adjacent to the NSC conference room, so that such a topic is going to have to be scratched and something a bit more pedestrian and a lot more accessible substituted, like *Tally's Corner: A Study of Negro Streetcorner Men.*[10] One must be virtually certain that the data for the dissertation will be available and accessible *when* the candidate comes around to the collection phase of his project. The timing of the operation is every bit as crucial as the topic per se in the calculation of its researchability. If the chances are higher than the .05 level that your target group or sample will disappear or disband six months or a year down the pike, or that its personnel will change, presenting you with members who may not "honor" their predecessors' generous offer of your entry (and such reversals transpire very often), then you must immediately drop that topic, no matter how attractive, and move on to the consideration of others.

Does it make a contribution to the field? Nearly all program catalogs makes some reference to the dissertation as required to "make a substantial contribution to the field (or to the literature)." Sometimes the qualifier "original" is added to the litany of the requirement. Although no one quite knows what these phrases mean—or, more accurately put, various faculty will differ as to their construction—they are not merely lip-service embroiderings. The *size* of the contribution bothers many dissertation donors: One of my clients, describing her education doctorate in nursing, told me, "I'm going to contribute my little mite here, and then somebody else her little mite there, and so on." This is what I would term "the dissertation-as-too-little" syndrome, where the ABD, steeped in the background of term papers and short-term projects, construes the dissertation as a kind of "quickie" to be knocked off in a few months. Other candidates initially (if they persevere in this attitude, they are in great trouble) see their dissertation as *the* contribution to the field. Here we have what I call the "dissertation-as-too-much," or "dissertation-as-*magnum opus*," syndrome. Although a dissertation must be a good deal more than a "mite" to be approved, it is, after all, in almost all cases the *first* large work in a candidate's career. The *tour de force* and the *magnum opus* come twenty or thirty years later. Although there can be no exact rules about how to find a middle ground between these two misconceived polar views of a dissertation, the ABD must reality-test this dimension of his dissertation. Generally, a resolution of this issue comes with day-to-day consideration of the issue in your "office," careful perusal of related literature, feedback from faculty and students.

Is it original? "Originality" gives many an ABD trouble as well, which is understandable, given the nonoriginal orientation of one's preceding educational exposure and experience. The problem is that rarely, if ever, has the student been asked to produce a sustained, serious input of his own. What the ABD has to be looking for in choosing an "original" thesis topic is "*daylight*," i.e., "after perusal and study of related literature, and appraisal of the scope and ambition of other recent theses in the field, do I find a hole, a gap, a missing link that my topic can contribute to plugging, bridging or forging?" For example, prior to my dissertation, there was a recent growing literature in socialization processes of health professionals; medical, dental, osteopathic and nursing students had been studied. In my Fuller brushman travels through the department, the chairman (interested in the sociology of occupations) mentioned that chiropractors' (a large group of some 23,000) education had never been studied. I did a calculus of researchability, contribution and originality and during the next twenty months researched and wrote my dissertation.[11]

The candidate must guard against panicking that the "originality" of his thesis has been extinguished or "scooped" by another ABD or professional sometime during the period of his research and writing. Suppose you are writing a dissertation on the sociology of the single life-style in Manhattan. One day you hear that another sociology student up at Columbia is doing his on "just the same thing," as your "commiserating" informer breathlessly puts it. Despair! Anguish! Everything lost! Nonsense, although many candidates go through a trauma like this, or are walking (and writing) around with a fear that the "bad news" is coming tomorrow. The truth, of course, is that *fifty* ABDs could write sociology dissertations on the enormous general topic of single or sex roles, or drugs, or homosexuality (and *have),* without the "daylight" or originality of any of them being trampled or usually even touched upon by the others. If you have chosen your "daylight" carefully, there is no chance that it will be occluded by another writer: to dwell on that kind of fear is "dissertation paranoia."

Will it blow up in your face? Will it come back to haunt you? A topic can qualify as researchable, contributory, and sufficiently original and still be rejected, or at least carefully reweighed, as potentially dangerous to your career, even, on occasion, to your personal safety. Dissertations which deal with unpopular ideologies or stigmatized or illegal groups are most apt to backfire in ways which are often unpredictable at the time of dissertation embarcation. I had little inkling of the threats from chiropractors about publishing my findings which were awaiting me at the end of the dissertation trail (see Chapter Nine for details). I was not to know that chiropractors would object, to the point of threatening me, to my publishing as a book my dissertation about chiropractic student culture. Journalist Anthony Thomas probably didn't expect the magnitude of attack from the Saudis and the NATO countries following the screening of his "dissertation" on contemporary sex roles in Saudi Arabia ("Death of A Princess," 1980); one of my sociology colleagues, worried himself half to death over supervising faculty's moralistic and sexist disapproval of his mid-1960s "insider" study of a militant homosexual organization.

Although I was not able to heed my own advice, I would counsel (perhaps precisely because of my own woes in this area) against doing a doctoral dissertation with even a slight smell of its topic putting off one's thesis committee or threatening one's career or safety. The dissertation, and doctorate it confers, is simply too pivotal and difficult a career step to make it any more problematic by introducing gratuitous elements of risk and anxiety. If one is thick-skinned, it is fine to pursue controversial research *after* obtaining at least some corona of protection and status which the doctorate confers.

Of Fate and the Dissertation Topic: José Moreno and the Dominican Revolution. Although superficially it appears that people hit upon an eventually viable dissertation topic through many routes—from "chance," to "out-of-the-blue," to methodical planning—ultimate topics almost always come out of extensive soaking in the literature and prior research of one's field, and are traceable consequences of that immersion. It may be arguable whether the final choice is determined by "fate" or "being in the right place at the right time," but prior to that right moment or right idea come months, even years, of selective reading and thinking about dozens of related issues.

An exception, which ultimately proves the rule about topics resulting from a long deliberative planning and screening process, was José Moreno's dissertation-turned-book, *Barrios in Arms: Revolution in Santo Domingo.*[12] In October of 1964 Moreno arrived in Santo Domingo with the intention of writing his dissertation for Cornell University's sociology department on structural anomie in formal Dominican organizations, such as labor, agricultural and "social welfare" groups. In the spring of 1965, when the revolution broke out, all the organizations he planned to study in his proposal were in disorder—so he studied, perforce, the revolution instead! Thus, once in a while your topic can be decided by a massive social upheaval, rather than a thesis committee or extensive library investigation.

But even though all his original proposal planning went down the drain, Moreno was able to use his general sociological skills to write an incisive and competent treatise on the role of various small (interest) groups in shaping the contours and coalitions of the rebellion. This highly unlikely turn of dissertation events only serves to underscore the point that particular topics are much less crucial to the thesis decision and writing process than a general competence grounded in the theory and methods of one's discipline.

51

Other avenues to picking a topic. Most often, a prospective candidate who is excessively worried about his specific dissertation topic, who feels bewildered about the vast array of choices confronting and confusing him, hasn't yet paid his dues in terms of soaking in the field.

If you feel that you have done this groundwork but are still shaky about nitty-gritty procedures for selecting a topic, let me finally suggest a few paths that have worked for some people:

1. Although, as noted in Chapter One, master's theses are being phased out of doctoral programs, you might just have had to write one (as I did). I have known of fine Ph.D. dissertations that have been "spun off" from master's thesis material. Not all M.A. theses have this potential for expansion and have to be scrutinized in terms of the substantial contribution and originality criteria. If there has been a few years' interval between the master's thesis and the dissertation, there may also have been a significant switch in faculty. Such a turnover might provide another kind of "daylight" for the M.A.-turned-doctorate, in providing it with new readers who would be less apt to see it as just a "rehash" of the master's. In any case, you should never consider the expansion as "an easier dissertation" because it won't turn out that way: the additional theoretical and methodological problems that you will have to confront and resolve in expansion will be very similar to those of a brand-new dissertation topic.

2. A candidate in search of a topic can read other recent successful proposals and dissertations in his department to determine acceptable standards of contribution, originality, competence and literary worth. Reading other proposals is often heartening, especially when a candidate is living with "the dissertation-as-too-much" myth. It is also advisable to correlate proposals whose topic and style seem related to what one might personally undertake with the particular faculty member(s) they were written for, in an attempt to find professors whose views and standards you can work comfortably with on a dissertation committee. Whether such faculty are still in your program (or whether they will continue to be in it two years hence when you are finishing up) or will be able to take you on are, of course, questions that have to be investigated. My own position is that although one may pick a thesis topic with a particular professor's counsel, encouragement and approval (indeed, such approval is often required), one should *never* pick it because that faculty member is going to see one through the two-odd years of the project. The topic must be

above "politics and personalities," stand alone on its own and the candidate's merits of researchablity, contribution and originality. Too many circumstances can intervene (and repeatedly have) in your relationship with a faculty member, from a falling-out you may have with him, to his losing or changing his position in the program or the department, to his leaving (for good, or taking a sabbatical) "just when you needed him most."

Although it is advisable to choose *tenured* full or associate professors as chief advisers, on grounds of more authority and less chance of departure, they certainly won't turn down a better job offer to stick around supervising your dissertation. Even in today's depressed academic market, there is still considerable lateral movement near the top.

Whenever possible, discuss program dissertations that appeal to you with their authors. This may often be difficult because such persons may have left for parts unknown, or you may feel reluctant to call them since you didn't really know them, or because you really *did* know them and are embarrassed because they've finished and you haven't. My clients have experienced very good luck in contacting earlier finishers in their programs. Almost invariably, such successful candidates have been very willing to share their time and dissertation experience with another candidate. Writing the thesis is such an enormous undertaking and triumph that it is apt to be on the finisher's mind for years hence. Convince him that you are seriously involved in the same great task, and he will most often embrace you. This eagerness to help is interestingly contrasted with the reluctance to help on the part of the faculty, primarily, I believe, because of the status differentials involved in the latter case, whereas the new Ph.D. can still recall in an instant his until-recent ABD status.

What you will get from the successful recent candidate in your program is an insider's story of everything from the mechanics of the thesis, to the operation of the stages of the dissertation course, to (depending on your relationship with the new finisher) personality profiles on various committee members. You will see quite quickly that the final "neat" version of his proposal, data gathering and analysis were, in fact, preceded by months of the "messy" issues with which this book is concerned. My position is that the candidate should write his dissertation with the bottom-line assumption that *nobody* is going to help him. Within that general guideline, recent successful candidates are better sources for advice and counsel than the graduate faculty, as outrageous as that assertion may appear to the uninitiated or naive.

3. A minority of candidates have previously worked with a particular professor, either as teaching or research assistants, the latter "RAs" sometimes connected with a grant won by the faculty member. Sometimes students take or are offered "spinoffs" from the mainline grant data pool to "work up" as their own dissertations. There is nothing inherently wrong with this approach to topic selection, although professors do have a way of leaving a program and taking their grants with them. I have personally seen too many cases of grant-spinoff nonfinishing to be overenthusiastic about such a selection process. Besides the "principal investigator's" outright departure, grants can and do get canceled, "fellows" upon whom the RAs are bestowed can fall out of favor with the investigator and not be reappointed. Again, the same basic rule is appropriate: If you are working on a grant and you are given a section of the data for your thesis, ask yourself, "Where would I and my thesis stand if the grant and its administrator were to disappear tomorrow?" If your answer in terms of research-ability, contribution and originality is, "My thesis stands just fine, and independent," go right ahead. Otherwise, if you are still at the initial topic-deciding stage, find a topic that can stand on its own feet.

SUMMARY.
1. Failure to examine thoroughly the reasons for which one wants to write the dissertation, and the changes its execution will force in life-style, is a major cause of nonfinishing. Starting candidates are usually unaware that writing the thesis is like beginning a new program—starting all over again—which has little connection with the "old" one of courses and preliminary examinations, and whose success or failure hardly correlates with performance in the predissertation program.
2. The dissertation is definitely not for all ABDs, and a particular person contemplating the project must candidly "cost account" his intellectual and emotional strengths and weaknesses in the face of what the dissertation will demand.
3. There is a range of "wrong" reasons for mounting a dissertation, all of which share the common flaw that they are not sufficiently motivating over the long run of the dissertation course. The only "right" reason for pursuing the dissertation is the candidate's deep interest

and commitment to his field, combined with his intention to pursue a full-time career in the discipline upon completion of the degree.

4. Getting into the driver's seat of one's dissertation involves making the thesis a top priority in life and correspondingly reducing for the length of the project, the scope of other spheres of relationships, such as intense love affairs or various emotional crises. The reader is presented with a model of differential dissertation association for maximizing or limiting those relationships with people which promote or reduce allocation of the dissertation to high priority.

5. Can one complete a dissertation while employed full-time? The answer depends on the kind of job which is held, since "work" is not of one piece. Various work conditions, sites, ideologies and ambiences which contribute to, work against or are neutral to dissertation progress are discussed.

6. It is essential for the ABD to set up a dissertation "office," devoted exclusively to the thesis and off limits to family and friends during working hours. Symbolically, the office testifies to and reinforces the candidate's single-minded, serious and ongoing commitment to his dissertation. Regular "office hours" and probably new writing habits, treated in the text, have to be instituted.

7. One's dissertation topic usually comes out of intimate familiarity with a discipline over a good deal of time, rather than from a "brainstorm." A well-trained candidate should be able to write a dissertation on any of a range of topics in his field, directing onto them his general theoretical grasp and methodological skills. A final topic is ordinarily culled from a list of potentiual ones according to how well it meets the standards of: 1. researchability; 2. contribution to the field; 3. originality; 4. stability (with no potential to blow up in one's face). For those having inordinate difficulties in selecting a topic, the chapter suggests a number of approaches.

NOTES

1. The long-term ABD must also, alas, undertake such an accounting. Although the writer is the last to advocate "quitting," there are most definitely a minority of cases where cutting one's losses is the only alternative to destroying one's life.

2. The "right stuff" was the combination of skills and emotional attitudes that determined, so the candidates believed, which test pilots would be chosen as the first astronauts. See Tom Wolfe, *The Right Stuff* (New York: Farrar, Straus and Giroux, 1979).

3. James Fixx, *The Complete Book of Running* (New York: Random House, 1977), p. 92.
4. It is undeniably one of the thrilling moments in life to receive one's doctorate. Although it is fashionable to play down the title and its use, almost all the Ph.Ds I know use their title with (deserved) pride. As a motivator and anticipatory socializer, I often address my graduate students and clients as "Doctor" and try to get them to see themselves with that status in the not-too-distant future.
5. In criminology, "differential association" is a model for predicting criminal behavior by frequency, priority, intensity and duration of contacts with other people disposed or opposed to law-breaking behavior. See Sutherland and Cressey, *Criminology* (New York: Lippincott, 1978).
6. This nonhurried pace, incidentally, seems to characterize the publishing world as well and exasperates many writers. But it has to be lived with.
7. Cf., Virginia Woolf, *A Room of One's Own* (New York: Harcourt, Brace and World, 1929). Although the volume is concerned with feminist independence, having a room/space of one's own is equally applicable and vital to dissertation independence and autonomy.
8. George Plimpton, ed., *Writers at Work, The Paris Interviews, Four Series* (New York: Penguin Books, 1977). The description of writing as "work" is most apt in the present dissertation-writing context.
9. A variation on the time standard is a fixed minimum word or page output per day, the writer generally stopping when, but not before, that quota is met. Hemingway, for example, kept a large chart of his daily word output, averaging around 500—"so as not to kid myself." When he missed a day to go fishing, he doubled up the next.
10. Elliot Liebow, *Tally's Corner* (Boston: Little, Brown, 1967). Anthropological and sociological literature is rich in "participant observation" studies of various groups. Oftentimes, such groups really don't want to be scrutinized, and researchers have to use great ingenuity to get access/entry. But difficulties have to be contrasted with near-impossibilities: the majority of studied groups are powerless people. For reasons that have to do with the political structure of modern societies, no systematic observational studies of high-level decision-making groups have been conducted.
11. David Sternberg, "Boys in Plight: A Case Study of Chiropractic Students Confronting a Medically Oriented Society," unpublished doctoral dissertation, New York University, 1969.
12. José Moreno, *Barrios in Arms: Revolution in Santo Domingo* (Pittsburgh: University of Pittsburgh Press, 1970).

CHAPTER 3
Building a Dissertation File: Philosophy and Construction Code

The key to completing a dissertation is not brilliance or even inspiration, but organization. Indeed, many a long-term ABD is overloaded with brilliant insights which keep him darting in various noncumulative directions; the definitive quality of brilliance is a short, blinding illumination that quickly burns out. This is precisely *not* what the ABD writer needs. What he does need is a master *plan* in the form of some kind of filing system which keeps him on the right track(s), helps him evaluate his progress on various dissertation fronts, keeps him on keel, "flash-freezes" occasional "brilliant" insights so that they can be reconsidered within the framework of the total plan.

I suspect all serious researchers and writers (at least nonfiction ones, and probably many novelists, as well) keep files at the nerve and communications centers of their "offices." [1] Yet, the concept is foreign or vague to most beginning ABDs, who continue to surprise me with blank responses to my questions about how they are coming along with their files. A dissertation candidate must have a file, and it has to be seriously constructed at the time a topic is decided upon, *prior* to undertaking both the proposal/prospectus and the dissertation itself. Because the file is so vital to success with the dissertation—and because its rationale and format are so poorly grasped by most beginning writers—it requires its own chapter.

Various metaphors can be used to describe the function of the file in negotiating a dissertation project. One can see it as the "scaffold" which supports the writer and his dissertation during the erection of the thesis. I like to conceive of it as a "vehicle" which the candidate builds and then "rides along" to the end of the dissertation. In my own theses and book-writing experiences, I have discovered that the vehicle metaphor is much more than that; as my file grows, it eventually *becomes* the particular project.

There is no doubt that one way in which we humans are moved and motivated is by seeing *tangible growth* as a consequence of our efforts. For the gardener, growth is measured by increase in flower size; for the weight lifter, inches on the triceps; for the dissertation writer, thickness of one's file. If the reader sets up his file properly from the start, he will discover many times down the dissertation course the "lift" pulling out his filing drawers can give him.

HOW TO BUILD A DISSERTATION FILE: HEADINGS, PROCEDURES, DISCUSSION.

What follows is a kind of "starter set" of essential file headings upon which any given candidate can build, elaborate, revise to suit the needs of his own particular discipline, program, topic, thesis style, relations with faculty and students, and personality. Note immediately that the file is much more than a straightforward nuts-and-bolts blueprint or recording system (although it is, of course, both of these, as well): it is a "life history" of the dissertation, taking into full account the human and emotional sides of the project. Note, too, that some of the file headings will have (or already have had) their own chapters—or at least chapter sections—in the book, e.g., choosing a topic, severe problems during the dissertation course, strained relationships with proposal and/or thesis committee. I certainly do not claim that my particular system is the only way to set up a file, only that it has worked for many candidates (including myself). I do believe that wherever one begins, he or she is going to end up with a file and headings quite akin to those outlined here, since ultimately it is the common nature of the dissertation demands that tell.

Dissertation Log.

A running time sheet of hours spent in the office, library and field should be assiduously kept. Such a log is important in its own right as a motivator and will play a part when the candidate periodically reviews his progress (or lack of it), or has to rebudget his time in light of job demands or new phases of his dissertation (e.g., spending more time in the field than in the office, or *vice versa).*

Choosing a Dissertation Topic.

Ordinarily, this won't be a very thick file, since the candidate will have settled on a topic at about the time the filing system is set up. But there should be an account of how—through a sifting process and calculus of researchability, contribution and originality—you finally decided to go with your topic. This will be important in the days of "dissertation doubt" you will confront from time to time over the next year and a half: "Why did I have to pick this damn topic?" or, "If only I'd chosen a topic like X did." If you have the record available, you can go back and read and review exactly *why* you carefully and patiently selected "Sartre's Contribution to Existentialism" (which is currently torturing you), instead of "Camus' Views on Nihilism" (which is currently attracting you).

Timetable for Proposal, Experiment, Fieldwork, Statistical Workup of Data, Write-up, Defense.

Although one rarely meets the originally blocked-out deadlines in an exact fashion and must revise them in the face of unforeseen circumstances and delays, a master time plan—and a quite delimited one, at that—is essential to avoid the no-end-in-sight syndrome so common to the dissertation course.

Relations with Proposal-and-Dissertation Committee Members.

Although "personalities" are not as important as the candidate's own steady and thorough input into his dissertation (and also because specific members often change through the dissertation course), one must certainly deal with them on a more or less regular basis throughout the phases of doing a dissertation. Even though less than sanguine relationships with faculty can rarely defeat a highly competent thesis, strained situations with one or more members can definitely delay completion and make the project period very unpleasant, just as good relationships with advisers and members can expedite and lessen the emotional burden of writing (at the very least, not *add* to it). Accordingly, a *dissertation differential association calculus* should be worked

59

out (and constantly *updated)* with each relevant faculty member evaluated in terms of whether he is promoting, obstructing or neutral to the dissertation's progress. Then strategies should be worked out to maximize or minimize contacts with faculty according to how they were scored.

Comparative Proposals and Dissertations from Other Successful (Recent) Candidates in the Program.

The guideline uses to which these sources can be put for constructing one's own proposal and thesis were discussed in Chapter Two. Prior successes should be scrutinized with the aim of answering questions such as, What content and ordering of sections does the department approve and prefer? How thorough a review of the literature is required? What kinds of methodological designs and variables, what kinds of statistics keep coming up? How long is the average proposal or dissertation? How extensive, and at what level of literary quality, are the "critical" reviews of the literature, analysis and discussion sections?

The Dissertation Proposal.

Herein, a heading for each important, discrete section of the proposal. Chapter Four is devoted to the various dimensions of constructing a viable proposal.

Contacts and Arrangements for Subjects and/or Groups in Your Experiment or Fieldwork.

ABDs are generally not prepared for the unreliability of data-source contacts. A vague promise from a colleague, for example, to give you half an hour of his introductory psychology class to administer your instrument "anytime you want" often never comes through, or the half hour isn't half enough, or you need to go back for a second session (which he can't give you), or the cross section of the sample is not representative. People have to be very seriously pinned down; commitments (sometimes on a *quid pro quo* basis) have to be obtained from colleagues, fellow researchers, friends, contacts in school systems, for the provision of a specific number of subjects on specific dates for specific/sufficient amount of (often classroom) time. Whenever possible, "backup" data sources should be arranged, so that fall-throughs don't catch the researcher in an "all-or-nothing" trap which may seriously delay the dissertation.

Troubleshooter File.
At what junctures in the project do intellectual problems or contra-dictions keep recurring? For example, no matter how often she reworked the proposal, one of my clients couldn't convincingly relate her two latter hypotheses to the first two. Another dissertation writer continued to have trouble in constructing a valid measure for "will to live" in connection with her dissertation on "Locus of Control Among the Terminally Ill." How can such difficulties be resolved? By altering the hypotheses, changing the methodology? Perhaps they cannot be solved, but at least "lived with"? Candidates should beware of the myth of the "perfect dissertation" (discussed later in this volume).

Serendipity/Inspiration File.
As work moves ahead, unexpected and/or contradictory ideas and data are going to arise. The experienced (read successful) researcher uses even contradictory and superficial-appearing "doomsday" data to advantage—rather than despairing (which is what the inexperienced ABD has a pronounced tendency to do)—banking it for an "alterna-tive" explanation of results. Most "finished" behavioral science work is, contrary to methodology textbook righteousness, revisionist. (See Chapter Five for elaboration of serendipity in thesis writing.)

Devil's Advocate File.
Here one raises himself the hardest, most unjust, off-the-wall ques-tions which proposal and defense committee members are likely to raise, and prepares answers. Since the candidate generally comes to know more about his particular topic than anyone else on earth be-fore he is through (often a dubious distinction among one's friends: I found, for example, during my dissertation that people at parties had a way of excusing themselves when I turned to an in-depth discussion of the world of chiropractors), eventual faculty questions can be fielded if the devil's advocate brief has been kept up and current, with both questions and answers.

61

"Ventilation" File.

Regularly, the candidate should get down (and to some extent *out* of his system) the *passions* of the dissertation, be they love, hate, boredom, frustration, anxiety, fear. Anthropologists and sociologists have long encouraged and practiced such ventilation about different phases of research, from relations with one's sample, to one's colleagues, to one's own writing.[2] During my research with chiropractic students, I kept a "journal" where I recorded prominent and recurrent *feelings* that kept surfacing; about once a month I summed these up in a memorandum for my ventilation file. During much of my fieldwork, I was in real danger of being expelled from the chiropractic college due to—what I termed in the dissertation—"chiropractic paranoia." This created enormous anxiety and occupied much of my journal. Then, too, in my role of "house sociologist" and general confidant to both students and faculty, I became "wise" to several cases of miscarriage of justice (in terms of grades, allotted transfer credits, suspensions from school) that reflected specific faculty-student animosities or vendettas. To retain my credibility as an objective observer and keeper of confidences, there was nothing I could do about these ethically troubling situations without jeopardizing further access to my sample, and thus completion of my dissertation. During some of these episodes, the ethical/human side of me was at war with the careerist side: the battle was fought in the journal. Researchers are constantly running into these kinds of ethical/emotional dilemmas.[3] Of course, a particular candidate's ventilative issues will be determined by the nature of his project and what steps are required, but even if fieldwork or an experiment isn't involved, plenty of emotional issues will surface. Whatever the structural demands of a given dissertation, the personality of a particular writer is the key intervening variable; another researcher in my place at the chiropractic college might not have been bothered by what I perceived as major conscience questions and have focused on different emotional qualms, e.g., personality conflicts with certain abrasive faculty or students.

"How'm I Doing?" [4]

About once a month an evaluative memorandum should be written by the researcher to himself, taking stock of the general progress of the various thrusts of the project. This memorandum should be written "cold," *before* work on the master review/progress file (see below), for a sense of how much the candidate is carrying in his head about his dissertation. Acquisition of a "gestalt" view of one's thesis is a major step toward completion, since henceforth whatever data one confronts in the office, library or field can be efficiently discarded or incorporated in line with whether they fit the big picture. Carrying the dissertation in one's head is also vital for the dissertation defense (see Chapter Eight, below).

Dissertation Group File.
The issues of formation, format, maintenance and uses of a dissertation support group are discussed in depth in Chapter Seven. If a candidate joins such a group, he must keep two subfiles on it. One must be a record (preferably taped) of the group's comments during sessions specifically devoted to his thesis. The other should be summaries, supplied by other members in the form of abstracts, outlines, statements of particular problems, of fellow group members' projects.

Successive Drafts of Dissertation Chapters.
In almost all cases, the candidate is going to have to write at least two versions of each dissertation chapter. All drafts, earlier and later, should be kept together for comparative purposes. At the point when a chapter has been more or less finalized, a copy should be made and placed for safekeeping in some location other than one's office. Dissertation horror lore abounds with stories about the careless or unfortunate ABD who loses the only copy of his completed dissertation to a fire, theft, flood, the destructive rage of a vengeful spouse, drunken movers, eviction.[5] In an actual case with which I am acquainted, a psychology candidate lost his only copy in a robbery of his briefcase. Totally shattered, he retired to a Mediterranean island for the better part of two years, returned to New York City, wrote a new thesis (undoubtedly making multiple copies this time of developing chapters) and is now a successful psychoanalyst (perhaps specializing in disaster victims). Where the second copy is placed is determined by the candidate's worst fear: a friend of mine, terrified of fire, kept a copy of his dissertation manuscript in the refrigerator, wrapped in plastic; another acquaintance, apprehensive of burglary, kept a copy in a heavy safe. Excepting some unusually developed paranoia like

63

the above cases, the best place to keep a legible copy is in a bank safety-deposit box.

Master Review/Progress File

1. Title a separate blank page for each of the salient headings in your file.
2. Provide a date slot for each page.
3. Xerox twelve–fifteen copies of each page.
4. Every month, without fail, the writer should date one set of the headings, and type or write in work progress and problems—carried out, confronted, resolved, unresolved—during that month for each file heading.

This is a most effective technique for overviewing which parts of the dissertation are forging ahead, standing still or lagging behind (more of this in Chapter Five on researching and writing the dissertation). These reviews lead to intensified or reduced efforts in one heading area or another in the forthcoming month. The writer must always precede a given monthly master review write-up with a review of at least the *prior* month's progress file. The key to cumulative progress is the sense of continuity that such a developmental comparison allows.

The master review/progress file is one where no time skimping should be tolerated. Of course, in a given month, one will normally have much more to say under some headings than others (sometimes because some files are right "on time," sometimes because no progress has been made). It is not at all inordinate that two or three entire office sessions should be spent on your review. Sometimes the exercise will flow beautifully; other months it will be a halting and painful business. Whatever the tone of a particular month's review writing, it must be pushed through.

Recently I attended a trial lawyers' review workshop in New York. The keynote speaker, a distinguished trial attorney, devoted his entire presentation to the development of an unexpected assertion that the bedrock of successful trial lawyering was *list keeping*! He detailed his own list-keeping styles, subjects and procedures, complete with an account of his continual checking and cross-listing. At first the relatively young audience of attorneys seemed skeptical about or bored by his insistence upon the centrality of a listing or filing scheme to presenting a winning case—anticipating probably that he would talk of the brilliant cross-examination, surprise witness or dramatic summing up. As the talk wore on they became, I believe, convinced, if not fascinated, that routine, day-to-day organization and collation of material was fundamental to a sound trial case. I, of course, could not help but be struck by the similarity between starting lawyers and beginning ABDs, the latter being as initially skeptical and unimpressed by repeated stress on a matter as routine or banal as the dissertation file, when the greener fields of boundless theories and inexhaustible inspirations lay before them.

Index File.

You must have an index file of your substantive files. Number the file folder as soon as you begin a new entry, and transcribe its number and title onto your master index sheets. A master index is indispensable when the files proliferate, and you want to find something quickly, or cross-file, in your cabinets. Always keep your files in *seriatim* order.

I can hear an early-stage dissertation writer saying, "All of this seems a pretty elaborate filing system for the three pages of a mini-proposal that I have at the moment!" But you will be astonished at how quickly your materials will grow as you work in earnest on your dissertation. The filing system reverses the ordinary dictum of "form follows function" with a sequence of "function follows form," based on my repeated observations that setting up an adequate and comprehensive operations base—or file—motivates, even forces, the ABD to go out into the world and gather the materials of his dissertation.

On cross-filing. As your files develop, it will strike you that some subjects, under whatever heading they started off, are equally weighted on, or appropriate under, two or more headings. Cross-filing may then be indicated. Now, one has to proceed with caution in cross-filing: in the largest sense, all sections of one's thesis are interrelated (or they better be), all cross-filable. Taken to an extreme, one could drown in an orgy and compulsion of filing, producing a brilliant ingrown file, but no dissertation. Never cross-file (i.e., place a duplicate copy of key ongoing materials under two or more headings), unless you feel a recurrent "tugging" with more or less equal force from two different headings. Cross-filing decisions are best made after the master/review progress file has been completed for a given month.

To give the reader some taste of a possible cross-file (obviously, the particular combinations for peculiar disciplines, topics and writers are vast) that cuts across many fields of study, consider a situation that might (often does) arise within the context and interfaces of file headings entitled "Relations with proposal and dissertation committee members" and "Ventilation." Dilatory ABDs often wake up to the fact that they have neglected their "fence mending" down at the department, that they are out of touch with faculty members with whom they worked and studied during predissertation days and perhaps do not even know faculty currently in charge of the doctoral program. It is most difficult for the candidate to reestablish connections with a department which he may not have visited for a year or two; every day he further delays, the resistance and embarrassment are enhanced. Here is an ideal problem for cross-filing and cross-solving. Use "Relations with committee members" to plot out strategies for effecting a rapprochement; use "ventilation" for getting out the humiliation and rage you may feel in taking up the Fuller Brush Man role. A strategy that has often proved effective in both reintroducing and reinstating oneself with the faculty and allaying some of one's most troubling "reentry" emotions is what I term "dissertation confession." Suppose you are a two-year-old ABD and have done very little toward a dissertation proposal, have not visited your department for about a year and the chairperson has changed. The very best approach is to schedule an appointment with the chairperson and "lay it on the line" with him. You acknowledge that you have delayed, give some reasons for such delay, recount for him the pain you have been undergoing in not making progress, reaffirm your intense commitment to finishing and promise to submit a proposal within some reasonable time limit.

The face-saving aspect of this approach is that it is truthful. Stopping short of begging for mercy, one asks for compassion. Most chairpersons see themselves as "shepherds" of their faculty and graduate student flocks. They like to play the "father/mother confessor" role. More often than not, they have heard such "confessions" or "repentances" frequently in the past; very likely, they personally experienced delays and doubts about their own dissertations. So, in this problem context, one can usually expect a sympathetic response—rather than indifferent or hostile—from faculty. You may well be off the hook, provided that you do, in fact, demonstrate some tangible written proof of progress before your memory begins to fade once again from the chairperson's mind.

The File and a Tape Recorder.[6]

A tape recorder is very valuable for certain aspects of the file and actual writing of the dissertation: In getting down an idea that can occur at any time of the day, office hours or not, but which you do not have time to develop at the moment. Sometimes such flashes relate directly to the file or chapter you are presently working on (say, a spied contradiction in your analysis or a required addendum); nearly as often they refer to work you "completed" weeks ago, or work coming up in the weeks ahead. In any event, try never to switch file horses in midstream: keep to the flow of your present work, and deal with the "intruder" later; it's there waiting on the cassette for subsequent calm and unobtrusive consideration.

Certain specific file headings lend themselves to the oral dimension, most particularly:

"How'm I doing?" Some candidates prefer to talk out, rather than write down, their monthly off-the-top-of-the-head summing up of their dissertation. Upon playback, they are able to ascertain how their presentation will sound to others, such as a thesis committee or dissertation adviser, and which parts of the thesis are still thin or less than convincing.

Devil's Advocate File. Every month after the dissertation is well underway, prepare a list of "The Ten Bitchiest Questions," read each onto the tape and proceed to answer them. Upon feedback, ask for each whether your response would satisfy a faculty interrogator. Did you sound confident? Shaky? Irritated? Proposal and dissertation defenses (about which more will be written in later chapters) are staged affairs, presentations of self with the aim of being accepted, "getting over." In the specific area of answering cantankerous, malicious or even stupid faculty questions, the candidate's best strategy is to take on all such comers as if they were serious and reasonable queries, worthy of in-depth and good-natured answers. The candidate should strive with his answers to create an atmosphere of collegial community with his examiners—all of you interestedly promoting the advancement of the discipline, at the moment through the vehicle of a dissertation. If your side of the presentation is convincing, it will be very hard for faculty not to "play along," to treat you as anybody less than a soon-to-be full colleague. Judge your audio performance in accord with such collegial-sounding criteria.

Ventilation. Most people find it more natural and satisfying to talk or laugh or cry or scream about their feelings than to write about them. Ventilation sessions cannot be scheduled like other file tapings; emotions don't know timetables. Whenever a strong dissertation emotion comes upon you—be it impatience with an adviser who is holding you up by reading your chapters at a maddeningly slow pace, anger with your husband who isn't keeping up his commitment to take over the children and household chores to give you your full time in your office, outrage over how one of your fieldwork sample was treated by a superordinate that day, frustration with inability to find a satisfactory analytic statistic for a key section of your data—get it down on tape.

Dissertation group discussions. Tape the sessions devoted to your thesis, since such a record is much more comprehensive than note taking. It will also allow you to gauge the effectiveness of your oral presentation in a context not too different from faculty appointments, hearings and defense regarding your dissertation.

Which tapes to save. My own habit is to label and save all cassettes I make in the office on a particular large project. Certainly, the candidate must keep, at the very least, taped material on the specific file headings discussed above. The exclusive goals of all the files and all the tapes are finishing and surviving the dissertation. Repeated reviews of all previous "How'm I doing?" devil's advocate and dissertation-group tapes give you a sense of developmental progress on your journey toward its end, and hone your speaking and debate skills for coping with defense hearings. Review of the ventilation tapes helps you to anticipate and better cope with dissertation traumas further down the line. ("Hey, I talked about that two months ago; let me go back and see how I felt about and dealt with it then.")

What to Tape and What to Write Out.

The tape recorder, as valuable as it is for the purposes noted above, has its limits as a dissertation tool. After all, the medium of the thesis is the written word, and even though there are crucial oral episodes, like discussions with dissertation committee members and the formal defense, the talk about the thesis is based on what the candidate has put down on paper in the form of working "position papers" on key issues of theory and methodology, and successive drafts of thesis chapters.

Written documents allow for scrutiny and overview nearly impossible with tapes. Inconsistencies and *non sequiturs* abound in even the best lectures. When the candidate sits down to write (about) his dissertation, he is clearly up against it, cannot "wing it" or "bullshit" his way through a talk-show version of his project. This *confrontational* quality of writing—where the words stare back at you, often with reproach on first draft—is part and parcel of the dissertation enterprise. It taps directly into the loneliness corona surrounding dissertation writing: only the candidate sitting in his office hour after hour, reviewing and redrafting what he has put to paper, can eventually get it right.

Your file becomes your severest critic and your greatest ally. Its contents force you to revise—and revise again—your written versions; its contents insist that matters are not as simple as you have presently put them, that certain areas need embellishment or refinement. On the other hand, the work and investment that have gone into your file over the months will yield the capability to get the writing "right" that the file-qua-critic is demanding.

SUMMARY.

1. Organization, rather than brilliance or intuition, is the most necessary dissertation-writing attribute. An extensive file is the bedrock of a successful dissertation project. The file is the objectification of organization. During its construction, the candidate practices and further develops the required organizational skills.

2. The file can be seen as a "vehicle" which one constructs and then "rides along" to the dissertation's end. To be fully effective, it must be set up at the time a thesis topic is finalized, and prior to writing the proposal and dissertation proper.

3. The chapter provides the candidate with a "starter set" of essential dissertation file headings, including assembly instructions, upon which he can elaborate according to his own peculiar project needs. The headings embrace nuts-and-bolts topics, emotional problems of the dissertation, interpersonal issues and diplomatic relations with advising and supervising faculty—all of which are expanded upon in subsequent chapters of the volume. Selected headings discussed include: a dissertation log; a timetable for various phases of the thesis; relations with proposal and dissertation committee members; contacts and arrangements for subjects and/or groups in one's experiment or fieldwork; a troubleshooter file; a serendipity/inspiration file; a devil's advocate file; a "ventilation" file; a "How'm I doing?" file; a dissertation-support-group file; a master review/progress file.

4. The uses and art of cross-filing in promoting the dissertation are considered, along with illustrative examples.

5. Tape recording is indicated as a valuable adjunct method in the building of certain files, especially "How'm I doing?"; the "devil's advocate file; "ventilation"; and dissertation-group discussions.

NOTES

1. For interesting, even exciting, accounts of how two social scientists set up files for their projects, see C. Wright Mills, *The Sociological Imagination* (New York: Oxford University Press, 1959), Appendix; and "Profile" on Robert K. Merton, *The New Yorker,* January 1961.

2. Cf., Napoleon Chagnon, "Yanamamö Social Organization and Warfare," in Fried *et al.,* eds., *War: The Anthropology of Armed Conflict and Aggression* (New York: Doubleday, 1967); Hammond, ed. *Sociologists at Work: Essays on the Craft of Social Research* (New York: Basic Books, 1964); and A. Shostak, ed., *Our Sociological Eye: Personal Essays in Society and Culture* (Port Washington: Alfred, 1977).

3. Cf., L. Humphreys, *Tearoom Trade: Impersonal Sex in Public Places* (Chicago: Aldine, 1970); and Wolf and Jorgensen, "Anthropology on the Warpath in Thailand," *New York Review of Books,* November 19, 1970.

4. "How'm I doing?" is apparently New York Mayor Edward I. Koch's daily query to constituents and city officials. "Profiles (Mayor Edward I. Koch—Part I)," Ken Auletta, *The New Yorker,* September 10, 1979.

70

5. The nineteenth-century explorer, anthropologist and poet, Sir Richard Burton, had a large part of his manuscripts destroyed (burned) by a wife enraged with their "immoral" contents and Burton's behavior. See Alan Moorehead, *The White Nile* (New York: Dell, 1966).

6. For a provocative argument for restoring certain presently lost dimensions of meaning to literature by reinstituting reading aloud as a regular exercise in university criticism courses, see R. Shattuck, "How to Rescue Literature," *The New York Review of Books,* April 17, 1980.

CHAPTER 4

The Dissertation Proposal

GETTING INTO THE PROPOSAL WITHOUT DELAY.

Timing of the proposal and dissertation effort bears stressing right at the start of the chapters devoted specifically to proposal and dissertation. One should strike while the iron is hot, that is to say, almost immediately after the final preliminary orals are negotiated.[1] "Taking a deserved rest" at this point has condemned many candidates of my acquaintance to additional years of dissertation labor, which might have been avoided if they had pushed directly on when the blood was up and the faculty familiar with and favorable toward their recent progress. I know in my own biography that an R & R year abroad after my orals, when I was completely out of touch with my department faculty, was a major contributor to delaying my thesis completion for nearly two years. In academia, leaving your university situs with matters up in the air—be it an incompleted dissertation, undecided tenure, an uncertain promotion—practically insures that the departer, upon return, will find himself a victim of the adage about what can go wrong, will go wrong.

WHY IS THE PROPOSAL SO IMPORTANT?

The dissertation proposal, known in some programs and departments as the dissertation prospectus, is crucial to, and linked with, the total dissertation-writing process in five ways: (1) Its construction is the process by which one decides definitely on the viability of a topic;

(2) It establishes a "contract" with the faculty that applies/extends to the dissertation itself; (3) It is a "trial run" for the dissertation, a "minidissertation"; (4) Its successful negotiation puts most ABDs "over the top" of the dissertation course; (5) It establishes the tone and pattern of relationships with dissertation-supervising faculty.

THE PROPOSAL AS TOPIC-DECISION PROCESS.

Contrary to dissertation mythology, the choice of topic is not an inspirational point in time, but a rather extended process, with two major phases.[2] In the first phase, one culls from various sources a list of possibles. Such a culling, remember, already assumes a basic grounding in the discipline, obtained from several years' soaking in the field. In the second phase, the ABD has to test his most compelling first choice against the criteria of researchability, contribution, originality, and potential explosiveness. The proposal is a systematic, extended exploration of one's topic, from statement of the problem all the way through anticipated analytic procedures (discussed below in the chapter). Quite literally, the candidate is saying to himself (or better be!), "I propose [intend] to spend the next eighteen months of my life buried in this topic. Here you [the "you" refers first to the candidate himself, then to his adviser and hearing committee] have numbers of pages justifying such a large expenditure of time and energy. Is my proposal convincing?"

THE PROPOSAL AS CONTRACT.

Dissertation proposals, like matrimonial ones, are accepted or rejected. To further the parallel, both are sometimes initially turned down, but second or third overtures (often with revised terms) are accepted. In marriage law, it used to be that an acceptance of a proposal was itself a contract, and either party's failure to comply was actionable by the person still willing to carry through. Domestic proposals contracts have dwindled from law and usage just when dissertation proposal contracts have emerged. The core of the dissertation proposal contract says—although not in just these words and much more explicitly in some programs than others—"We [faculty] accept your proposal to carry out a specified project, known as a doctoral dissertation. If and when said project is completed within the guidelines of your proposal, we promise to approve your dissertation."

Before I consider the most important implications/issues of the proposal as a contract, how widespread, the reader wants to know, is the contract quality of dissertation proposals within American doctoral programs? As one might expect from the discussion in Chapter One, there has been no professional research of this question about the dissertation, anymore than of half a dozen other key issues or phases. Then, too, the contract element, if studied, would emerge in numerous shadings and emphases from university to university; like our local police departments, each university, public or private, is more or less sovereign unto itself (even within the *same* state or city university system, various campus graduate schools within the same discipline will have different rules and requirements for course work, qualifying examinations and dissertations), especially in this kind of internal or domestic matter. Thus, after reviewing the following general discussion of the contract considerations in the proposal, an ABD must try to ascertain where his own college and/or program stands on the issue.

Certainly, the general idea of the dissertation as contract between candidate and graduate faculty is established. In the late 1960s, Washington University (St. Louis) sued (unsuccessfully) to take back a social science doctorate on the grounds that the writer had used unethical research methods, thus violating a vital element of the contract between him and the graduate faculty and therefore vitiating the contract; in the 1970s, Columbia University sued (successfully) for the return of a Ph.D. granted to a candidate who had plagiarized his history dissertation, again on the grounds that such a violation rendered the university's commitment to go through with the contract null and void. It should be said that dissertation contract *court law* is very sparse—probably no more than half a dozen cases on one issue or another of the thesis—but its rare formal invocation does not negate its existence or authority within the university framework; occasions when candidates have threatened to take legal action against a department (or specific members of a department) for unwarrantedly denying or delaying their doctorates are far more numerous, but almost always they are "settled out of court." I trust it is understood that I am not promoting litigation as a main-line method of getting one's dissertation approved. The occasional court's notice of dissertation disputes is presented in order to drive home the usually implicit contractual elements of a dissertation/doctorate undertaking. In all contracts, the state is a "silent partner," whose say is invoked only when remedies between the explicit contractors have failed.

An impressionistic survey of dissertation doctorate programs in reference to the contractual element in the narrower, more specific area of the proposal itself leads to the tentative conclusion that most programs recognize a contract, but to varying degrees of explicitness. In some departments, for example, the catalog, special doctoral candidacy rules and thesis committee regulations state very clearly that acceptance of a dissertation proposal (in a formal hearing) is both preliminary to and mandatory for a candidate, and binding upon the department. In many—perhaps still most—programs, the contract element of the proposal (including by just which administrative process it will be accepted or rejected) is less explicit. In less explicit departments, however, discussion with graduate faculty will usually uncover a willingness to act upon such assumptions, even though these academics are loath to construe them in "vulgar" or "mechanistic" business-type frameworks.

Certainly, then, there is enough contract background to dissertation proposals and dissertations themselves—some of it implicit instead of explicit, most of it university-based rather than court-based in terms of promulgation, interpretation or enforcement, should a dispute arise between the contracting parties—that a contemporary candidate is warranted in proceeding *as if* a dissertation proposal contract is in force once his committee approves his proposal. In the generally zero-sum model of power and authority in which he finds himself in relation to dissertation-supervising professors, the contract element is perhaps the only "guarantee" of some substance upon which he can rely.

Putting the dissertation proposal and the dissertation within the broad context of American contract law—even with the qualifications and modifications dictated by the unusual university setting and status of the particular contracting parties—gives the ABD some clout against two nightmarish eventualities that he encounters often in his dreams, and sometimes in reality:

1. As I have already pointed out, the ABD has absolutely no assurance that the men and women evaluating his original proposal and/or sitting on the dissertation committee will *continue* to serve during the several years of his project. (In some departments member-

ship is the same for both committees, in others partly the same, and in still a third category of program, completely different. Then, too, regulations are modified by personnel developments; a political science graduate department may stipulate that both committees be populated by the same faculty, but resignations may make this impossible.) What would (and does) happen if, say, the two sympathetic members of your three-person proposal committee resign from your anthropology department at Indiana University to become codirectors of the Maori Research Institute in Christ Church, New Zealand, replaced by two urban anthropologists who are, at best, uninterested in, at worst, hostile to, your dissertation critiquing the HRAF (Human Relations Area Files)?

Under contract law, parties succeeding, inheriting or buying contracts from earlier or original contractors are bound by those contracts' obligations. Major exceptions to such a rule are so-called "personal service" contracts; e.g., an opera singer sells her contract to sing in *Carmen* to someone who cannot carry a tune; the Met is not bound to let the latter ruin its winter season. Nor would Indiana's anthropology department be obligated to honor your selling your rights and obligations embodied in a dissertation proposal to a bona fide nonmatriculated purchaser. But a new Met manager, administration or even ownership would have to honor the prior management's contract with an opera singer, and the anthropology department at Indiana must honor its dissertation contract with you, regardless of changes in its personnel and their specialties.

In the instant case, the departure of the two faculty best acquainted with your topic is going to make the dissertation even lonelier than it always is, anyway, but this is a far cry from a situation where the department could renege on its commitment, citing a lack of qualified faculty to continue supervision. Most of the time when a candidate is put in left-in-the-lurch circumstances approximating this example, departments allow—sometimes even encourage and support—his acquiring an outside adviser (who may even become a dissertation committee member pro tem). Without necessarily heating up the issue by specifically citing protection in contract law, the candidate should be aware of his rights (almost always departments stress *your* duties and requirements *you* have to meet; almost never, like landlords, do they emphasize or acknowledge *their* obligations toward doctoral candidates), and be prepared, if necessary, to make demands on his department to live up to its side of the dissertation proposal agreement.

2. The ABD has no assurance that the hypotheses of the proposal are going to "pan out" in the predicted direction. There is much dissertation lore surrounding this issue: what one does if the data go astray; how a thesis committee will rule; what kind of cyanide pill works fastest. Although I want to save for Chapter Five, the bulk of discussion about how to handle "negative" or "contrary" findings with a more constructive, sanguine, less Hamlet-like response than suicide, let me note here that the contract assumptions of the dissertation proposal surround one's undertaking to *test* propositions and hypotheses which have been reached through logical, orderly and deductive canons of thought legitimated in one field or another. Neither the contract nor any (social) scientific model demands that the *results* of such testing be in a particular direction. Indeed, the very core of the intellectual and scientific enterprise is that the data be allowed to fall, and stand, as they may. There is much talk about how dissertation committees don't like—may even reject—theses in which one's own hypotheses are disconfirmed (even in the face of statements made all the time in texts and classes demonstrating that a refutation of theories represents a contribution in its own right). I know of no case in which a dissertation was turned down primarily for disconfirmation of hypotheses, excepting instances where the hypotheses were "straw men."

Toward a Contract Model of the Dissertation Proposal.

American faculty in arts and sciences are far more used to the intrusion of legal review and process into their "ivy towers" than an outside observer—and many inside students—suppose. A year does not pass in a university when several faculty do not bring grievance procedures (mediated and pursued by their teaching unions) and/or lawsuits (pursued after union remedies have stalled or failed) to compel reversals on negative reappointment, tenure or promotion decisions.

Indeed, some of the candidate's own dissertation supervisors may have been at one time or another party to one of these grievances/suits. Although faculty lose these appeals more often than not, a substantial minority win. University administrations make every effort to keep the news of such victories from the general college community;

77

most undergraduate students, and even many graduate/doctoral ones appear unaware of internecine struggles (excepting cause célèbre cases) among and between faculty and administration going on just below the surface of college life. A lesson for the ABD, if he doesn't know it already, is that his graduate faculty is rifted by many professional and personal antagonisms, most of them stemming from tenure and promotion battles that have been fought out over the years preceding his entrance upon the departmental scene.[3] If the candidate fortuitously picks two implacable faculty enemies to sit on his committee, his dissertation will be delayed in the cross fire of hostile career memories.

Curiously, the contractual/grievance model employed by faculty has not been formally or substantially extended to ABD-supervising-faculty relations and disagreements. The explanation for the near total absence of grievance procedures and a systematic view of the proposal and dissertation as a contractual relationship has to do with the anachronistic state of student-faculty relationships in dissertation doctorate programs, compared with such status relationships in other schools and colleges within the contemporary American university. The 1960s and 1970s witnessed enormous upheavals in traditional status relationships between students, faculty and administration, particularly at the undergraduate level, although graduate students, too (even some professional school students—law, medical, but rarely engineering students) fought alongside their undergraduate brothers and sisters.

When the dust settled in the 1970s, undergraduate students had made substantial advances toward "parity" with faculty and administration, manifested in many forms—from establishment of "advocacy" departments of counseling, to severe reins on professors' traditional near-totalitarian control over how much or little students might participate in classes, to no-fail and pass/fail grading systems, to requirements for full-scale, quasijudicial hearings before students could be suspended, to student participation in appointment and policy decisions, including matters of curriculum and hiring of faculty, deans and presidents.

The dust clearing in graduate dissertation programs did not give the same picture. Graduate departments are still almost medieval in terms of faculty-student relationships, especially when compared to undergraduate shops. Graduate students have more to lose than under-graduate chains; they can—and sometimes do—lose their *doctorates.* The greater stake that doctoral students have in their studies, including the dissertation, combined with the awful uncertainties about negotiating the thesis, cause these students to be meeker, more bewildered, less directed toward banding together to meet faculty in a united front. The faculty, in its turn, exploits the underdog position of the graduate students in order to maintain a status quo of nearly zero-sum authority arrangements.

The 1980s will see some movement toward emancipation of the doctoral candidate. Dissertation programs cannot singlehandedly turn back the forces of educational history. The 1980s ABD can count on more support for his accepted proposal as contractual, or quasicontractual, in nature. In practical terms, this means that faculty will be less arbitrary and more cautious about taking unfavorable action on a dissertation completed in line with the approved proposal, conscious of possible, even probable, in-university or general legal challenge lurking in the background. More court cases will surface; a few departments may institutionalize grievance procedures. The beginnings of "dissertation" law may emerge, following on the heels of embryonic "dissertation therapy" of the 1970s (see Chapter Seven for elaboration). But the 1980s are probably too soon for full implementation of a contract model for the dissertation; there still exists a very strong graduate faculty lobby for the view of the ABD as a lone figure, almost an explorer, who has to come up with a unique and mighty product—one which cannot and should not be judged or confined within narrow legalistic parameters of a contract model.

THE PROPOSAL AS "MINI-DISSERTATION."

As the candidate works on his proposal, questions about how full or complete it must or should be will keep coming up. Three criteria must be met: 1. Does it fulfill the committee's minimum demands for approval? 2. Is the writer realistically able to convert the stages of the approved proposal into the real thing? 3. Does the proposal "cover all the bases," at least in rudimentary form, of the dissertation, regardless of faculty's acceptance of it and the adequacy of its several parts? It is the latter two standards which candidates so often neglect, much to their dissertation distress down the course.

An old con maxim goes, "Don't do the crime, if you can't do the time." Don't write a Madison Avenue proposal that sounds and looks good, laced with all the current sociologese or psychologese that isn't tooled for gearing into the dissertation.[4] Even if the committee should pass such a proposal, the candidate will find himself up against a blank wall when he tries to "deliver" on a "contract" he signed without possession of an adequate "plant" or resources for production. I have seen a number of cases of candidates locked into, trapped by, an approved proposal which they never "really meant"; none of them finished his dissertation.

A thorough proposal is very nearly a mini-dissertation. Most of the time a candidate will want to write a longer version than his committee wants, or even likes. If the department is doctrinaire about maximum pages, the ABD should nonetheless "let it all hang out" in his first drafts and edit down for committee consumption, saving the longer drafts for incorporation into the body of the full dissertation. "Letting it all hang out" means exploring as fully as one can, at this time, the issues of the thesis (the parts a proposal should contain are treated later in the chapter). Although some of the issues will change—or your answers/resolutions will change—down the path of the dissertation, initial in-depth explorations in the proposal will usually stand the test of time: very rarely will one be confronted by a whole new world of objections or hurdles.

Of course, some sections can be outlined only in general form, e.g., statistical procedures; others must await the collection and analysis of the data, e.g., discussion of results. My personal counsel—and custom—is to explore even these sections in a proposal (these parts are for my eyes only). That is, I assume certain data will pan out as predicted by my hypotheses; then I run them through my statistical tools (making very sure I understand both the mechanics and assumptions of these statistics); next, I write an analysis and discussion section in line with one direction of statistical outcome. Sometimes I follow up with a devil's advocate trial run, where I assume that the data pans out in an unpredicted direction. The idea, of course, is to *anticipate* as many issues as possible, so that one isn't thrown into a panic at a later stage.

Other sections of the proposal—e.g., review of the literature, rationale for the study—can be slotted, virtually intact, into the dissertation itself. This assumes, of course, a very thorough, "mini-dissertation" job on the proposal. You will even find that one of your "alternative versions" of an anticipatively written analysis/discussion section will generally fit the dissertation as well (although more cutting and editing may obviously be necessary).

I like to see fifty or more pages to a proposal. It is all right, too, if it is wordy, loquacious, even gushy; such excesses can always be edited. One has to have a large corpus, sufficient material *to be able to cut.* An excess of pages is a minor problem, compared to too few. Terse and "economic" proposals, on the other hand, make me suspicious of a candidate's failure to sink into his subject, to look deeply into the topic's waters. I sense a continuation of the term-paper mentality being carried inappropriately into the realm of the great project.

Many faculty advisers, I know, tend to preach a limited, brief, introductory-phase view of the proposal. A tactful student can officially take this short-sighted advice but should pursue the proposal as if it were, in fact, the dissertation. If necessary, two "sets of books," or files, one for presentation to the proposal committee and another for personal, more extensive use and consumption, can be kept. "Collapsing" the proposal and dissertation will protect a candidate against promises he cannot keep and cut the completion time of the dissertation by as much as half.

There is a final way in which the proposal may function as a "trial run" for the full dissertation: although there is much variation in format, formality, rigor and composition of committee from field to field and within departments of a given discipline, today most ABDs have to defend their proposals at some kind of official hearing. Some of these hearings are very similar in style, substance of interrogation and faculty membership to the trial the candidate will face in his final dissertation defense. Oftentimes, one can get "early warning" at the proposal hearing about which faculty are going to be difficult in passing chapters of the thesis and at the final defense, and prepare accordingly. (See below, "The Dissertation Defense," Chapter Eight, for detailed discussion of strategies and preparation for the final defense, and, by implication, the proposal hearing.)

AN ACCEPTED PROPOSAL AS OVER THE TOP.

In my experience, the dissertation proposal is most often a greater hurdle in the dissertation venture than the dissertation itself. Although neither I, nor anyone else, have hard statistics on this point, I would hazard that the failure rates for proposal and dissertation are vastly different: the great bulk of nonfinishing ABDs are candidates who never negotiate an approved proposal; most completers of an accepted proposal, on the other hand, finish their dissertations in (relatively) short order.

In an endeavor where the rewards and gratification along the way are minimal, achievement of an approved proposal has to rank as the first prominent reinforcement. Candidates invariably experience a tremendous second wind upon completing the proposal. "All the months I was struggling with the proposal, I felt like I had nothing," as one of my clients put it. "Then they [the committee] approved it, and the sky opened up, and my feelings went from nothing to everything. For the first time, I felt I had something to work with. I began to believe I was going to finish the damn thing." The accepted proposal is a vote of confidence in your project by the men and women who are authorized to grant your doctorate. The candidate's internalization of this confidence generally allows him to do the dissertation research and writing in a less anxious, self-doubting mood than during the proposal, particularly if the proposal has been written in the mini-dissertation form outlined above.

Prior to the late 1960s, it was unusual to hear of committee decisions on proposals and dissertations that weren't black or white; candidates passed or failed.[5] Failure was less "final" at the proposal stage, of course—usually, one could go out and do another proposal—but *conditional passes,* although not unknown, were not frequent. By the 1970s, such conditional passes, "subject to [major or minor] revisions," had become facts of life and SOP at many major universities.[6] There is every indication that conditional passes will be common in dissertation decisions throughout the 1980s.

A proposal accepted, subject to revisions and changes required by faculty, should be construed by the candidate as a victory and as affirmative action. Even an acceptance subject to *major* changes is still basically an acceptance. There is absolutely no reason for despair when conditions are imposed, even though I have seen candidates go into damaging downspins after such faculty actions. Prescribed thesis-promoting activity at this juncture is to carry out forthwith those amendments, additions, deletions, elaborations on which thesis committee members *seriously* insist.

It is an art in itself to discern just which faculty objections and suggestions have to be incorporated in a second draft. If the candidate

82

is given a memorandum by his adviser and/or the proposal committee, summing up the hearing and enumerating demanded changes, less leeway is afforded (often a blessing, rather than a burden). But if, as is most often the case, the proposer is supposed to rely on notes from or memory of the hearing regarding points made by several members, then negotiation and diplomacy become very crucial in reworking a proposal.

In both proposal and dissertation defenses, faculty input is motivated by a number of distinct reasons. Certainly, not all suggestions made to the candidate are serious demands for amendment. Often, a committee member's critical comments are really directed toward other colleagues on the committee with whom he is conducting a long-term polemic which preceded you by years; or he is demonstrating to his colleagues (sometimes "superiors" who will make a decision on his tenure or promotion) in this semipublic forum that he is current with the field. Or he is making *pro forma* points, because that is what committee members are expected to do in this role.

Since a substantial, albeit unascertained, number of suggestions were never intended by the critics themselves to be followed through by candidates—indeed, thesis members *forget* the majority of off-the-top-of-their-heads points within hours or days of the hearing—the candidate has to separate the wheat from the chaff to avoid wasting debilitating weeks, even months, on revisions that the demanding member has long forgotten. After waiting a few weeks, the candidate has to put on his Fuller Brush Man hat at this juncture (although his heel cooling will be shorter now, since he has gained an enormous increment in status through finishing the proposal) and meet with each of the committee members individually. During these interviews, some modified version of the old army maxim about "never volunteering" should be pursued: don't "volunteer" criticisms about your proposal; don't remind a professor of his contributions to your prospective work load. If he really believes that certain changes are necessary, he will bring them up again himself. Otherwise, they can normally be quietly dropped, or at worst given very light "pen service" in your amended version.

In these one-on-one encounters, it is often possible for the candidate to challenge a professor's demands successfully, particularly if, during the interval between hearing and interview, the candidate has rehearsed a persuasive argument. A more vexing issue is that of two professors demanding contradictory incorporations in the proposal: X wants you to stress Hegel's view of history; Y insists upon Marx's. There is no easy way to solve or reconcile these demands; patient negotiation is necessary, with the candidate feeling his way as best he can between the members. One point is clear, however: one should make every effort to resolve all such major inconsistent demands at the *proposal stage*. But the peculiarly flexible nature of the proposal dissertation "contract" makes complete resolution at the earlier stage doubtful. Thus, Chapter Six deals in depth with reconciliation issues still surviving or newly emerging at the later dissertation phase.

Summing up, conditional pass of a proposal is a triumph and turning point in getting the dissertation done. Most often, the "conditions" for complete approval are not well defined or set by the initial hearing and are open to a great deal of paring down, negotiating and defusing through the candidate's initiative in individual talks with committee members and/or his adviser. It is essential for him to get a consensus among faculty about the main directions—substantive and methodological—of his dissertation, if he is not to be stalled time and again during its writing. Thus, even if a proposal were unconditionally accepted from the first hearing, it is imperative for the candidate to make the rounds of the committee members to head off irreconcilable expectations in fulfilling his dissertation "contract." Finally, even though nobody really *likes* criticism of his work, and even though the first reaction of most of us to it is annoyance, the candidate will come to value some faculty objections as contributing to a better dissertation. So to at least some extent, the proposal examination is genuinely an intellectual, dissertation-promoting stage, although that aspect usually gets lost during the anxiety-laden hour or two of the hearing itself.

WHAT TO DO ABOUT AN INVIABLE OR FAILED PROPOSAL?

A dissertation can be aborted at the proposal stage through self- or faculty determination. After putting in considerable work, the ABD may himself determine that too many unforeseen theoretical, methodological or faculty-relations obstacles stand in the way of completion.[7] Or the thesis committee may unconditionally reject the proposal—a not uncommon or especially surprising occurrence, given the tentative precontract negotiations at this point between candidate and faculty.

In the majority of terminations at the proposal stage, excepting extraordinary conditions—such as an ABD's already having devoted more than a year to the proposal, or implacable faculty hostility to a particular candidate which would be transferred to any number of further attempts—another attempt is indicated. The same advice cannot be given for someone who has been unconditionally failed on a completed dissertation (see Chapter Eight, "The Dissertation Defense," for discussion of a rejected thesis, and the distinction between a failed defense and a failed dissertation).

THE PROPOSAL AS ESTABLISHER OF "DIPLOMATIC RELATIONS" WITH THESIS-SUPERVISING FACULTY.

The writer has taken pains to warn the candidate that he cannot unqualifiedly count on faculty to be consistently interested or present during the unfolding stages of the dissertation. Perhaps some hyperbole was involved, if just to stress that even with a "helpful" or "supportive" faculty the ABD is going to find the burden of all major decisions and initiations on his own shoulders.

There *is* some measure of faculty continuity in most individual dissertation course histories: more often than not, your initial thesis adviser "lasts" through your proposal, research and writing, and defense; more often than not, at least the majority of your original proposal committee remain on the faculty and are there for your defense. Of course, their continued *presence and formal connection* with your project differ sharply from the *content* of those relationships in terms of promoting, obstructing or not affecting, one way or the other, the progress of your thesis.

The establishment and maintenance of "diplomatic relations" with relevant dissertation-supervising faculty entail an ongoing "differential dissertation association" calculus (see Chapters Two and Three for a general outline of that accounting system for interpersonal relations) which spans the four major moments of the dissertation: proposal; research; writing; and defense.[8] Accordingly, the book's discussion of the candidate's relationships with faculty must extend through a number of chapters (particularly Four through Eight), where different problematics of relationships are apt to be correlated with earlier or later moments (e.g., the farther along one moves on the dissertation course, the more likely that "maintenance" issues replace norm-establishment ones as most prominent). In this chapter, I want to alert the candidate to faculty-relationships questions that must be faced in the initial moment of the dissertation proposal.

CHOOSING A DISSERTATION ADVISER: MINIMUM QUALIFICATIONS.[9]

Most of us would have little trouble conjuring up a "dream adviser," just like we can produce on cue a pretty detailed fantasy picture of the "Mr. or Ms. Right" we seek in our personal lives. The ideal adviser would be (like the ideal scout and/or scoutmaster) loyal, true, brave, courteous, kind, helpful. But the candidate is not going to find his "dream adviser," any more than his real lovers are going closely to approximate "Ms. Right." So what should one be realistically seeking in a proposal/dissertation adviser?

The bottom-line requirement of the adviser is that he *be there* for the length of one's project. In my judgment, all other attributes are secondary (albeit sometimes very important) to this consideration. The same adviser (even a diffident one; the instance of an actively *hostile* one is another story), the same "warm body," is a crucial consistency/continuity-impelling vector through the moments of a dissertation. In numerous ways, it stamps the project as "serious" and to be "reckoned with" in the eyes of other faculty. The candidate, of course, can never be sure that his selection will remain in the program for the course of his project. But at the minimum, he should ask key probability questions (sometimes discreetly addressed to third parties, not the adviser), such as, does he have tenure? If he doesn't, is he up for it? And if so, does it appear likely he will receive it? Is he planning a sabbatical? An unpaid leave of absence? Is his health good? Is he near retirement?

The Dissertation Incest Taboo.

All other considerations are secondary, with the exception of a faculty member who is either clearly hostile to you (wishes you ill) or wants to establish a "personal" sexual relationship with you. It is most inadvisable for a candidate to go to bed with his or her adviser, or even to allow that possibility to hang temptingly in the air. The reasons for such avoidance are instrumental; they have little to do with the conventional arguments about "exploitation" of students (usually female, but by no means always; there are many cases of female faculty having relationships with male advisees) by faculty. Graduate students are, after all, consenting adults, many of them in their thirties, or even older. There is little reason to doubt that *both* faculty member and student are "getting something" from the relationship. If the student could be reasonably sure that such an intimate relationship would promote her/his dissertation, fine. And by this I don't mean that one's adviser-lover would bend dissertation requirements or write the dissertation for the candidate. Such "Blue Angel" conceptions of faculty-graduate student affairs are most naive; they happen that way in movies, not in the graduate anthropology department. By "promotion" of one's dissertation, I mean motivating a faculty member to read one's proposal and dissertation chapters with critical care, to make sound suggestions, to provide advice with key methodological and analytic questions that emerge. Unfortunately, love and passion don't generally yield such critical increments. Totally contrary to the stereotype, an adviser who loves you may do more damage to your dissertation than an indifferent one: he or she will be pushing just those kinds of romantically disorganized and nonroutine concerns that you have determined (through your careful decision to write a dissertation and construction of a file; see Chapters Two and Three) to postpone and avoid. These are the dissertation-obstruction problems of the "happy stage" of a love affair with your adviser. If—usually when—you or the adviser become disenchanted, ensuing rages, jealousies, avoidances practically insure that your dissertation will be doomed (if the adviser is, as very often happens, the "only person" qualified to supervise your particular topic) or very seriously delayed (pending your finding a new adviser). The world is more full of potential lovers than of dissertation advisers. Intersample contamination is strongly counterindicated.

The Size of the Adviser Pool.

Looking for a dissertation adviser with traits beyond the minimally required ones of continued presence and friendly detachment is affected by the *size of an available pool* of faculty. The pool of potential advisers is determined in a given department by (1) size of the faculty; (2) percentage of faculty assigned to or interested in supervision of dissertations; (3) the number of serious dissertation-writing candidates; (4) the nature of one's topic. These conditions were discussed in Chapters One and Two. In some programs a candidate will have a reasonably large (maybe three or four) potential group to pick from;

in others he may have only one, or, indeed, be put on a "waiting list." Of the four conditions, an ABD has control only over the fourth; don't relinquish that control by picking an arcane topic "in search of an unfindable adviser." Graduate faculty are less interested in what your topic is than in how you treat it from the special angle of political science, history or sociology. The dissertation is seen as training to be a general "journeyman" or "utility man" member of a given field. A sociology ABD, for example, should be able to write a thesis on homosexuality, or suicide, or homicide, or "born-agains," or Wall Street law firms with equal facility, using the conceptual and methodological tools of the sociological trade.[10] An ABD must always determine whether his proposed topic fits squarely within the category of main-line concerns of his discipline, thus guarding against extra difficulties in getting an adviser (the usual ones being quite enough) in his program.

Choosing an Adviser: Additional Desirable Qualities.

Assuming one has some leeway to "shop around" for an adviser, one can look for certain dissertation-promoting attributes, although it is certain no adviser will possess all of them. There is the added difficulty of not being well-enough acquainted with a prospective adviser to get any accurate picture of his advising potential; even if you knew him as an instructor and liked his lectures, his adviser role may be very different from his teacher function. It is advisable, then, to pursue multiple meetings with a prospective adviser in an attempt to fill in some of the blanks. Sometimes student peers can provide very useful information on advisers' styles. If you do know other ABDs who are currently under tutelage, or recent "post-docs" who did their theses under someone you are considering, by all means contact them (per the discussion in Chapter Two).

Dissertation-promoting qualities to be sought after in an adviser include:

1. At least moderately interested in your subject. Ideally, he might be someone whose own work is in the same or related area. Occasionally, a faculty member is phobic about a certain specialty or methodology in his field—an English professor detests Faulkner, a psychology teacher believes the TAT is witchcraft. One would have to be mad or masochistic to seek out the former with a proposal for "In

Praise of *As I Lay Dying*," the latter with a dissertation on "Toward Increased Validity of Projective Tests: the Case of the TAT." If on the other hand, a particular faculty member is known to specialize in one's contemplated topic, it is most diplomatic to seek him out as an adviser, if just to give him "right of first refusal." He may, in fact, not want to supervise your dissertation, may plead a work overload, but to go over his head or bypass him on his specialty is inviting trouble; he may show up at your defense with less than benign interest in your passing.

2. Reads papers and chapters within a reasonable time after submission.

3. Reads materials with a critical eye, offering ample comments and suggestions.

4. Accessibility. One wants an adviser whom one is not terrified to call for a chat from time to time, and someone who will give you an appointment to discuss key matters (like the latest submitted chapter) before the onset of another Ice Age.

5. Someone who knows his own mind, makes a decision and sticks with it. A wishy-washy adviser who continues to change his mind about key directions or thrusts in one's dissertation is a most dissertation-discouraging individual. Often, the wishy-washy adviser is very "friendly" and "personable," a "real nice guy," and students gravitate, understandably, to him, to their eventual regret.

6. Someone who "means business," who sees the proposal and dissertation—either explicitly or implicitly—as the performance of a "contract," outlined above in the chapter. It is far better to have a "grump" or even a surly person as adviser, who means business and possesses an integrity around that understanding, than a nondirective "Rogerian," an amiable person with no clear view of the "business" nature of the dissertation.

7. Someone who is respected by other faculty, preferably both professionally and personally, but at least professionally. An adviser can greatly facilitate the action taking on one's dissertation by other committee members if he has some clout in the department. Likewise, the adviser, as one's dissertation "rabbi," can protect and steer the candidate in the dangerous waters of the proposal hearing and dissertation defense, if he is forceful and has the esteem of his colleagues.

8. Someone who is respected as a "tough" methodologist. In many

departments, research specialists—often statistics and computer people—possess inordinate status and power because of the ideological aspirations of social science fields to be "just like" the hard sciences. Although it is by no means resolved that, say, anthropology's, psychology's or sociology's most appropriate or fruitful future direction is toward further quantification and empiricism, there is undeniably a current bias in that direction. Accordingly, the "research man" or "stat woman" often has the final say (the analogy—probably misconceived at bottom—is to the architects of a bridge or dam checking with civil engineers to see if the design will "go") on a given proposal.

Often these "scientific" types are not especially pleasant to deal with. They have an inclination to rewire one's thesis in a manner that takes the "soul" or "guts" out of it. On the other hand, they can be very useful in helping one write up a virtually "unbreakable" proposal contract, precisely because of their perhaps compulsive rigor. Whether one laments or praises their current entrenchment, they must be dealt with by proposal time. If such a person is not one's thesis adviser (chairperson of one's committee), every effort should be made to incorporate him as a second or third member; otherwise, the specter of his sitting on the final defense and torpedoing the dissertation (because of exaggerated deference afforded to him by less quantitative-oriented faculty members) hangs over your dissertation-writing days.

CHOOSING THE REST OF THE PROPOSAL/DISSERTATION COMMITTEE.

Selecting the other members of a thesis committee is subject, of course, to the same personnel limitations of a given department. Just how the candidate should obtain the other members varies from program to program: in some, the adviser sounds out prospective faculty; in others, the chairperson assigns faculty; in still others—probably the majority—the candidate has to go round to their doors.[11] Other members should possess the same qualities sought in the principal adviser, although because of the secondary role that second and third readers usually play, such attributes are less crucial. Perhaps most ABDs' engagement of remaining thesis committee members is a hasty affair, often arranged by telephone or letter. I have had clients who have *never met* one or another of their committee well into writing their

90

proposals. At best, one gets two people who are "lukewarm" about his project, not expecting to do an awful lot of work with it down the stretch. However, the strategies which this volume counsels make the rest of the committee more important than often considered. Central to the "contract" is getting chapter-by-chapter approval by all committee members (see Chapters Five and Six). Thus, no matter whether these faculty are assigned or selected by the candidate himself, the ABD must establish a working relationship with them early on in the thesis course. Although secondary members may not be as apt as one's main adviser to make far-reaching demands for changes (not that it doesn't happen sometimes), their traditionally passive role can create major problems by their dilatoriness about reading and/or approving one's chapters. The chances of such delays are much reduced by getting to know the other members and convincing them that you "mean business." Established interpersonal relationships also aid the candidate in preparing the defense for his proposal hearing, over which these very faculty are going to preside.

WHAT SHOULD A DISSERTATION PROPOSAL LOOK LIKE?

In keeping with the preeminent emphasis of this book, much has been said in the chapter about the human relations and emotional dimensions/significances of the proposal, those aspects of the project which are undeniably so important and, equally undeniably, never systematically examined. In any event, the bottom line is what is set down on paper. What should the proposal contain? What sections should it have? What are advisers and faculty looking for? What *don't* they want to see? What sort of writing style is required?

In addressing these questions, I have drawn on sources with which I am intimately familiar, mostly (but not exclusively) from social science, and even more particularly from my own proposal and dissertation. Aware that the volume purports to cover to some degree the entire discipline spectrum of full-dissertation doctorates, I have tried to make the illustrations generalizable to other fields. Nuts-and-bolts discussion ensues where necessary, mostly in sections about statement of the problem, and hypotheses, and in methodological and statistical design, but not, I trust, to excessive/particularistic detail. Indeed, too much "cookbook" material would be patronizing; the ABD is no fool, unprepared as he may specifically be to write a proposal and dissertation. Then, too, each project always exhibits an idiosyncratic and personalized component, demanding individual creativity in design and implementation that can never be more than partly indicated or captured by formulae. What follows is a "factoring out" of key features and sections that characterize successful/approved proposals. I also flag along the way recurrent unacceptable tacks, approaches, "wrong trees" up which ABDs often bark. Remember that my working list of proposal sections could not possibly match the diversity of formal specifications contained in particular programs. Nevertheless, I have tried to touch all the main bases of a proposal regardless of what "aliases" they may be traveling under in given university and department bulletins.

Writing Style.

In sociology, the satirical term "sociologese" has been coined by pundits to describe an unnecessary elaboration of "insider" vocabulary and style that is often unintelligible to the uninitiated. Similar ritualistic vocabularies exist in most fields, from psychology to economics to literary criticism. Although a minimum frequency of "passwords" may be *de rigueur* (consult other prior proposals in your department on this issue), a good guideline in writing both proposal and thesis is to employ a style that is accessible to the "educated layman," as well as to the graduate committee, who tend to be irritated or turned off (or themselves don't understand) by too much "insider" terminology. Certainly, if you have any hopes to convert your dissertation into a *book,* avoidance of discipline linguistic codes is imperative. (See Chapter Nine on "Beyond the Dissertation: Surviving It and Professionally Exploiting It.")

Appearance of the proposal should reflect and support its literary quality. Chapter Eight stresses the absolute necessity of a professionally packaged and typed dissertation for a successful defense, but the student is advised to establish an earlier image of seriousness and commitment with a professionally typed proposal available for faculty during its hearing.

Review of the Literature.

In my view, the review of the literature is perhaps the single most important section of a dissertation proposal, even though many ABDs

92

see it as something you "tack on" when the real work is finished. In truth, a properly executed critical review of the literature lays the foundations from which the rationale for the study, statement of the problem and hypotheses, and design of the research emerge.

Specifically, the review should accomplish four tasks: (a) establish a picture in the eyes of faculty readers of the candidate in full grasp of his subject; (b) connect the specifics of the dissertation topic with larger themes, "the big picture," in the discipline; (c) provide all-important "daylight" for the ABD's topic as an original contribution; (d) generate the end-of-proposal or dissertation bibliography.

(a) There is nothing better than a long, complete, thoughtful review of the literature in conveying to faculty the image (and reality) of a candidate who means business, in the driver's seat of his dissertation. Conversely, a skimpy review of the literature confirms preconceived faculty suspicions that ABDs are unprepared for and/or not seriously committed to the dissertation. Of course, mere length, without relevance, can bury a proposal itself; proposers will sometimes go on for pages with citations that recite the litanies of a field but are unrelated to the specific topic in hand.

(b) The candidate might see himself as film director: as his proposal film opens, the "big picture" is laid out; as the footage unfolds, the camera "pans in" on more specific locations, actors, themes, targets that will carry the picture, tell the story. The proposal writer is aiming toward a "zeroing in" on his topic, but he cannot *start* there—although many students make the mistake of beginning with very specific materials that should have been preceded by pages of introduction and gradual panning in.

Years ago, a sociology ABD decided to do his dissertation on homosexual behavior in men's rooms, so-called "tearooms." [12] The reason why he picked that exact topic (perhaps because he had access to the sample) is not crucial here; what is crucial is his "big picture" justification for this research subject.

He proposed to document numerous acts of fellatio that rest-room gays committed on each other. But the dissertation was in sociology, not pornography; how to make the transition, forge links to sociology? His review of the literature could not start with, say, observations of homosexuals in gay bars, excerpts from Gerald Walker's novel, *Cruising*, or Master and Johnson's *Sexual Inadequacy*, taking this last-mentioned team to task, perhaps for methodological shortcomings or ideological blind spots, even though there might be occasion for all these citations at the pan-in stage of discussion. All this type of literature—no matter how richly descriptive, clinically useful, "fascinating,"—is too close to sex for sex's sake, rather than sociology's, to constitute an acceptable theoretical starting point.

A classic and recurring sociological theme, starting with E. Durkheim's research in *Suicide* at the turn of the century, is that much apparently internally motivated behavior, like homicide and suicide, is at least partially determined by external social causes, structures and contexts. A newer, but certainly related, theme is that many social statuses which sociologists have usually assumed to be "fixed"—like sex and race—are, in fact, dependent upon social context: when context changes, statuses are mutable.

The tearoom researcher had to start off his review of the literature with an account of the introduction of these major themes into sociology, as well as their later stages of elaboration, including key researches in one tradition or the other. Slowly, he narrows his focus from work on "deviance" and "ascribed" (unchangeable) statuses in general down to "sexual deviance," and most specifically to homosexuality. Only with a more or less "unbreakable chain of evidence" can he present a convincing case for his sociology proposal.

Thus, this dissertation proposed to examine one kind of homosexual activity in light of two "red thread" themes in sociological theory and research. Of course, to test these particular propositions, the ABD had to observe his sample in at least one more context. Thus, the review of the literature develops, dictates, leads to an *appropriate methodology*. At a later date (having ascertained their addresses by noting their automobile license numbers in the rest-room parking lots), our ABD visited their homes in the role of census taker. He documented that the great majority of them were "happily married," "family men," lending additional empirical support to sociology's assertions that both "deviant" behavior and some "ascribed" statuses are situation-specific.

A proposal sequence has been described in which the ABD worked "backwards" (in his mental processes, not in how he put it down on paper), a person with a situation or sample in search of a "big picture." In my experience, some of this working-backwards process is inevitable; nor is there anything "unscientific" about it. I never knew

94

a case where one generated a dissertation topic by starting with permutating and combining basic postulates of a field. Through some biographical blend of elements outlined in Chapter Two, ABDs find themselves with a list of topics and samples that may be viable. A major part of determining whether they will, in fact, "go" is checking them out in a review of the literature for their solid connections/linkages with enduring large themes and research in one's field.

(c) Not only must the ABD demonstrate continuity between his project and important work that has gone before, but some input of originality as well. With this task the proposer might see himself as a running back looking for a hole in the defense, or "daylight" through which to break with his contribution.[13] The "line" here consists of the standing studies related to the candidate's proposed research. Although I have already indicated (Chapter Two) that there is nothing inherently doomed about a replication of another project (such repeats are squarely within the canons of both science and social science), faculty tend to resist the idea, unless one intends to challenge an important study whose conclusions have come to be accepted as gospel.

Imagine for a moment that historian A. J. P. Taylor had written *The Origins of the Second World War* as his dissertation. His proposal committee might have been concerned with his merely going over old ground in turning over once more the "familiar," well-documented, diplomatic, political and military events in Germany, England, France, Poland, and Czechoslovakia during the 1930s. But Taylor provided "daylight" for his dissertation with the (then) startling and controversial thesis that, contrary to nearly unanimous conventional historical wisdom, Adolph Hitler was not the prime mover of events, that his role had been largely reactive, not active. Taylor proposed to go over once more (replicate) all the key prewar historical documents and sources, but with an eye to drawing utterly different conclusions.

Ordinarily, however, "dissertation daylight" is found by going through a hole in the line, rather than knocking over a defender who is standing his ground. At the time I was selecting a dissertation topic, research in medical sociology was booming. My review of the literature indicated that the training/socialization experiences of many health professionals had been recently studied. Sociologists had done field research of medical, dental, osteopathic and nursing students. But a big hole was gaping for chiropractic students. The studies of the other health groups had documented the very-to-relatively-high prestige of these professions, already communicated to these students during training days. I took the facts that (1) no recent work had been done on a large group of health practitioners; (2) chiropractors were making concerted efforts to professionalize; (3) they were held in relatively low occupational esteem (even stigmatized) by the American public and even personally possessed discouraged occupational images; and I combined them into a "daylight" package which proposed to investigate an occupational group with the rather rare dual loading on of professionalization *and* stigma. In my dissertation I was able genuinely to compare and contrast the experiences of my chiropractic students with other groups of in-training health students by bouncing my findings off previous research case studies, as well as by conducting some original research with medical and dental students.

(d) Nothing is more dramatically and forcefully effective in summing up and reminding faculty readers, as they draw to the conclusion of your proposal or dissertation, of the enormous amount of research and thinking invested as page after page of a tightly typed bibliography. Not only should the bibliography be as massive as it is legitimate, but it should be technically impeccable in the mechanics of citation style—buttressing the picture of the candidate as totally professional and workmanlike.

Rationale for, Significance, and Implications of the Study.

Persuasive justification for one's subject should flow right out of a critical review of the literature, done along the lines indicated above. Usually, the significances of the study are multiple—some primary, others supplemental. "Contributions to knowledge" in the field (as the catalogs sometimes put it) have to be made in the areas of theory, empirical findings and methodology, although the first two are generally more primary and necessary than the third. In both "tearoom" and chiropractic student studies, participant observation was an important research tool. Both writers, in very different ways, found it necessary to amend and innovate traditional procedures in line with fieldwork conditions if the groups being observed were not to balk and act out of character because of perceived intrusions by the sociologists.[14] These methodological strategies and refinements made a contribution to the long and still developing tradition of participant observation in anthropology, sociology, criminology and psychology. They could not have stood alone as rationalizations, however: Humphreys primarily had to make a case for "tearoom trade" as further validation for the sociological perspective on deviance; Sternberg had to bring together what were formerly considered rather unrelated fields of sociological inquiry—professionalization and stigma—in the unique case of chiropractic education.

"Implications of the study" have to do with how the findings of one's dissertation might be used practically. In political science, public administration and education lingo, they often go under the name of "public policy." In many dissertations, implications have to await the outcome of data analysis to be set down fully; it will be more strategic to some theses than others to outline them at the earlier proposal stage. Many disciplines have had an uneasy time with "pure" and "applied" aspects of their fields. There was a time when anthropology eschewed "value judgments" and suggestions in ethnographies; sociology firmly distinguished between its "value-free" research findings and uses of its findings by social workers; academic psychology was doctrinaire about the intrusion of practical or "clinical" aspects into pure psychological research. But the last decades have seen increasing fusion of theory and practice, and although pockets of conservative resistance still exist, today it is appropriate, even advisable, to incorporate convincing implications of one's research into a proposal and/or dissertation.[15]

- If your social psychology experiment indicates that people are much less apt to act on their prejudices (here in terms of refusing hotel rooms to Chinese-American couples) when having to deal with minority group members face-to-face—as opposed to letter or telephone—then interpersonal confrontation tactics emerge as more effective than once-removed communications media for successfully implementing civil rights and affirmative-action programs.[16]
- If your history dissertation persuades that Hitler did not start the second world war, a policy implication for diplomacy is that the current rage for "psychohistory"—seeing nations in terms of Mao's China or Sadat's Egypt—may be misleading and should be balanced with greater attention to nations' superpersonal political, economic and military structures and ideologies.

97

- If your sociology dissertation demonstrates that the same men are straight in some groups and gay in others, then the strong potential of group therapies as change agents for sexual identities is suggested.

Statement of the Problem and Hypotheses.

What one comes to here is a formulation of the key problematic or issues which continued examination of the topic, in light of related literature and research, repeatedly yields as compelling questions. Related to this "statement of the problem" are procedures necessary to test out the truth probability of competing "answers" to the problem. Such procedures are known as hypotheses and are stated in the form of provable or disprovable assertions. To move from the abstract to the concrete plane here, let me return to my dissertation.

After a relatively short—albeit intense—time with my sample of chiropractic students, I was able to document a model of the chiropractic student under bombardment from "negative messages" about his occupational choice everywhere he turned in his life: he had heard down at the school that chiropractors were "starving"; girl friends and their parents were unhappy with his selection ("It's enough he's not Jewish, but to be a chiropractor, too!"); he was sometimes accosted at parties; the AMA continued to attack chiropractics; New York State (in 1968) continued to refuse it licensure; even classmates and faculty were "down" on the occupation. In short, the whole "rosy future" outlook documented by sociological observers of another group of health students—medical students—was replaced for my sample with a doomsday outlook.[17] Review of my field notes from the earliest weeks already shows me preoccupied with the problem, "Why do they stay on?" or, "How do they fend off the bad news?"

Although other issues were to emerge as well, the questions of why and how these chiropractic students pursued their studies in light of the multidimensional social opposition, even stigma, confronting them remained the central problematic of the dissertation. The thesis came to revolve around processes of identity management and stigma denial, themes with which some contemporary sociologists (like E. Goffman) and social psychologists (like L. Festinger) are deeply concerned.

Next, I had to propose a reasonable and testable answer to my stated central problem. Through my participant observation of the sample, I became convinced that chiropractic students (and graduate chiropractors as well) adopted a "self-over-other" defense mechanism, which allowed them to see themselves as successful "solo practitioners," "individual entrepreneurs," "heroic loners," whose especial talents and resolution would make them successes, even if the profession as a whole was "going to hell in a basket" (as one student put it to me). Later on in the thesis I was to use this "self-over-other" cultural theme of chiropractic to account at least partially for the relative lack of formal organization among chiropractors, as opposed to both MDs and dentists.

But how to "prove" the prevalence of such a defense mechanism operating to ward off intimations of an unhappy career? Hunches from "talk" I had heard in my fieldwork were not in themselves going to persuade my thesis committee. So I constructed a set of hypotheses: "The set of hypotheses which follow are essentially a series of probability statements, based on a sociological model of how respondents should score their personal chances versus their peers' chances in several crucial areas for chiropractors if the underlying theory in the research is to be confirmed. Each hypothesis is tested by a corresponding *pair* of situational questions concerning one sector (e.g., relations with family, medical doctors, success on licensing examinations) or another. One question in the pair asks the student to evaluate the chances for the typical chiropractor or student; the other question asks him to evaluate his own prospects." I then went on to list fourteen hypotheses, along with citations to the full text of the corresponding questions contained in one of the questionnaires I gave to my respondents. Here were some of them:

1. Respondents will predict higher incomes after ten–fifteen years for themselves than for the average chiropractor.
2. Respondents will predict greater success for themselves on chiropractic sections of state licensing examinations than for fellow candidates.
3. Respondents will predict that negative newspaper publicity about chiropractors in general would have more harmful effect on their fellow chiropractors' practices than on their own.
4. Respondents will indicate that their own families and friends have more fully accepted their decision to become chiropractors than have the families and friends of other classmates.

5. Respondents will indicate that they have been less subject to unpleasant social confrontations because of their status as chiropractic students than their fellow students
6. Respondents will predict friendlier relations with MDs for themselves than for other chiropractors.
7. Respondents will predict a better chance for themselves becoming members of nonchiropractic hospital staffs than for other chiropractors.

Can statement of the problem and related hypotheses really be so fully elaborated at the proposal stage of the dissertation? Certainly, the discussion of hypotheses construction and testing must be continued into the next chapter (on the dissertation per se) and spans both proposal and thesis writing itself. How refined the theory and hypotheses must or can be at proposal time is a function of (a) a particular program's demands; (b) the nature of one's topic and methodological design; (c) the researcher's relationship to his sample or subjects. At proposal time, my statement of the problem and several— but not all—of the hypotheses were already in existence, although not in finished form. Some of the hypotheses came only after months more of day-to-day contact with my sample, as I got to know all the ins and outs of their subculture.

With a "tighter" or more "rigorous" psychology dissertation experiment, for example, where the ABD conducts his fieldwork on a "one-shot" basis with university student samples, it is often possible, even required by the thesis committee, to have finalized hypotheses in position at proposal time. Already settled statistical procedures to test the hypotheses are also much more likely to be present in the experimental dissertation proposal. For most of us in other fields, both hypotheses and statistics will tend to be more open-ended, and dicier. In keeping with this book's contract view of the proposal and dissertation, however, it is certainly advisable to nail down by finished proposal time as much of the theoretical/hypothetical/statistical structure as is realistic under the conditions of a particular dissertation.

Methodological and Statistical Design.

In this final major section, the candidate must spell out the operational procedures with which he proposes to test his hypotheses. In my chiropractic student study, for example, I had to indicate the size and characteristics of my sample, dealing along the way with the question of "representativeness." My methodolological design paralleled the theoretical model I had delineated and specified in the preceding sections on Statement of the Problem, Definition of Terms and Hypotheses:[18]

Figure 4.1: Hypothesized Self-Over-Other Model of Chiropractic Adaptation

Independent Variables	*Intervening Variable*	*Dependent Variable*
Negative and Stigmatic Messages About Chiropractic ⟶ From Various Societal Sectors	Adaptive Defense Mechanism ⟶	Self-Over-Other Attitude Set re Personal Future As a Chiropractor

---

I had to indicate the ways in which I was going to "operationalize" both the independent and dependent variables; the intervening variable was not measurable, but inferred (per the logic of social science) from the demonstrated relationship between the independent and dependent ones.[19] Both independent and dependent variable measures were "complex" ones, composed of more than one indicant. Negative messages were documented by newspaper and medical articles critical of chiropractic to which students were exposed; many references to such messages which I either overheard among student and faculty talk or which were reported directly to me (I designed a system to quantify these oral references to stigma); and in questionnaire items given to the entire sample, asking them to report the frequency of exposure to unhappy news about their profession in various social contexts outside the school. The dependent variable, self-over-other-attitude set, was measured and documented by responses to a series of paired questions, introduced above, in a second questionnaire to the students.

To take one hypothesis—respondents will predict higher incomes after ten–fifteen years for themselves than for the average chiropractor—the second questionnaire presented the sample with two items:

---

1. How much would you say the *average chiropractor* starting out today can expect to be earning per year 10–15 years from now?

    (check one)

        a.____under $10,000
        b.____$10,000 up to $20,000
        c.____$20,000 up to $30,000
        d.____$30,000 up to $40,000
        e.____$40,000 up to $60,000
        f. ____$60,000 up to $100,000

2. How much do *you estimate* that *you yourself* will be earning per year as a chiropractor when you've been out in practice 10–15 years?

    (check one)

        a.____under $10,000
        b.____$10,000 up to $20,000
        c.____$20,000 up to $30,000
        d.____$30,000 up to $40,000
        e.____$40,000 up to $60,000
        f. ____$60,000 up to $100,000

Discussion of analysis of the data from these questions will be left to the next chapter on the dissertation itself, as will more detailed treatment of the trials and tribulations of questionnaire and experiment design. Let us say here only that it still remained for me to ascertain whether the distribution of data was in the expected direction at a statistically significant level, giving support to empirical existence of the Figure 4.1 model.

Even though *implementation* of the statistical design has to await the postproposal stage of collection of data, and even though the original statistical design may have to be modified along with subsequent in-the-field-dictated alterations in original hypotheses (see

Chapter Five for more on this), at least its bare bones have to be laid out in the proposal. Further, it behooves the candidate to understand the logic and mechanics of his statistical tools at the time he presents his proposal for approval. If you are going to use a Q-Sort, a semantic differential, an F Scale, a Pearsonian r, an analysis of variance, a sign test (the one I used in analysis of my fourteen hypotheses) in your experiment, be prepared to justify and explicate it in depth when the second reader on your committee begins to probe you about possible objections to its use in your research case.

Pilot studies or procedures become an issue for some dissertations, particularly those in psychology (and psychology-oriented education theses), where one has to pretest or create an instrument which will measure an independent or dependent variable. If subjects are going to be asked to play a game or do a task, it is always necessary to carry out dry runs to get the procedures straight, find out how much time is needed, anticipate "confounding errors" that subjects are likely to commit.

If you want to administer a "will to live" attitude scale to terminally ill patients for your nursing dissertation, you won't find it in the literature. You will have to construct it yourself. In that process you will have to utilize qualified judges to sort out the good indicators from the "duds" in the original larger pool of possible questions you thought up to tap the variable of will to live. Those pilot studies that yield the instruments which test your hypotheses must be conducted by the time of your proposal defense. There are sundry other kinds of preliminary testings, on the other hand, which will be carried out during the time of dissertation research. Prior to administering two finalized questionnaires to my sample, for example, I "tried out" earlier versions of certain sections of both on selected students, recent graduates and faculty, and modified the substance and/or style of many of them in accordance with the feedback I had received.

SUMMARY.

The dissertation proposal is crucial to and connected with the total dissertation-writing course in five ways:
1. In constructing it, one definitely seals his dissertation topic.
2. The proposal establishes at least a quasi or "equity" contract with

faculty that extends to the dissertation itself. Although the contract law of dissertations is in flux, varies in acceptance or adoption from one university to another, will probably never develop as tightly or explicitly in the university setting as contracts in business—because of unique, open-ended, creative, elements inherent in dissertation research and writing, and not native to the commercial world—it nonetheless has precedent and linkages in related university contexts (e.g., grievance hearings re tenure and promotion), is gaining in recognition and offers some assurance to an ABD that if he produces a dissertation substantially consistent with the terms of an accepted proposal, faculty will approve it.

3. A long, thorough, well-documented and detailed prospectus, exceeding the minimum requirements of a particular program, is recommended; such a proposal will serve, in fact, as a "mini-dissertation," much of which can be incorporated in the subsequent formal dissertation with only minimal changes: chapters or sections on review of the literature, theory, hypotheses construction, rationale for the study, and even methodology.

4. Of the ABDs who do not finish, the majority seem never to have gotten as far as having a proposal approved. It would appear, then, that getting a proposal accepted has a motivating and successful prognostic value disproportionate to its length (in terms of both pages and time) in the dissertation course.

5. Although continuity is not total, generally, one's original thesis adadviser and (usually) two other committee members who pass on the proposal stay on as the dissertation's judges. Such formal continuity says nothing about the quality of supervision, which can vary from excellent, through mediocre, to poor, with the modal experience in the mediocre/indifferent category. Guidelines for picking suitable, helpful advisers and committee members are outlined, along with a list of optimal supervision qualities to be sought after, even though the latter traits are often less than abundant in the available adviser pool of a given department.

What should a dissertation proposal look like? What elements should it contain? What are faculty looking for? The author offers a "composite" picture of a proposal, drawing on various sources (including his own dissertation), predominantly in the social sciences, to illustrate successful versions of key sections or components in a thesis prospectus. Recurrent unacceptable tacks and wrong trees up which ABDs often bark are also flagged.

NOTES

1. Some candidates may have already sketched out a proposal during the last year of course work. The same rule, in any event, applies to them: move ahead after orals on that foundation with all deliberate speed.
2. Refer to Chapter Two for an extended discussion of picking a viable topic.
3. For a harrowing account of the struggles ripping one graduate department apart (this one the sociology department at the University of New Mexico) by its then-chairmen, see R. Tomasson, "Hell in a Small Place: Extreme Conflict in One Sociology Department," in A. Shostak, ed., *Our Sociological Eye: Personal Essays on Society and Culture* (Port Washington: Alfred, 1977), pp. 266–281.
4. For a parallel overemphasis on campaigning and deemphasis on carrying out the job once elected, see Joe McGinniss' account of Richard Nixon's first successful presidential campaign, *The Selling of the President* (New York: Pocket Books, 1968).
5. Actually, pre-1970's approval procedures for *proposals* were very haphazard, rarely contained overt or even implied contract elements. In many programs, a formal proposal was not even required. A state of chaos existed, probably producing even higher nonfinishing rates for the dissertation.
6. Interestingly, in architecture there has been a decades-long tradition of candidates failing their first attempt at licensing examinations, to the extent that it is almost expected. Since most candidates pass on the next try, one suspects some element of "initiation rites" in the testing.
7. My original dissertation proposal on cultural perceptions of crime in Sweden was aborted when it fell into the hands of a methodologist who insisted on converting it from a theoretical study into a content analysis of Swedish newspapers! At that point, I had no stomach left for continuing with it. It still lies to this very day in a filing cabinet back drawer, one of the sadder uncompleted projects of my career. All academics, scholars and writers accumulate a number of similar stillborn efforts during their careers.
8. The term "moment" is used here with the connotations of both history and physics: a major period or force within a larger totality.
9. In some programs, the term "sponsor" is used instead of adviser.
10. Being a "generalist," in addition to a specialist in a few fields, is, in fact, expected of full-fledged professors. There have been many occasions, for

example, when I have been asked to "fill in" for colleagues in a sociology of the family, religion, methodology or statistics course, although none of these are my "specialties," because of the prevailing assumption that one can bring his general grasp of the field to bear on subfields.

11. In many crowded, understaffed departments, there is a "waiting list" for other committee members as well as advisers. Quite often, a candidate won't have a complete group until his proposal is finished.

12. In this composite proposal example, I draw on the research of L. Humphreys' *Tearoom Trade* (Chicago: Aldine Press, 1970), and more generally on a field known in sociologese as "ethnomethodology," which seeks to discover the taken-for-granted (unrecognized) norms by which people conduct their everyday lives. I never saw Humphreys' proposal and am "reconstructing" what it might have looked like in certain sections to meet the demands of a doctoral thesis committee. Likewise, I am making "educated guesses" about his thought processes in building a proposal.

13. Cf., basketball great "Doctor" Julius Erving's remark, "You play to daylight; sometimes it's there, and you take it." CBS, May 1980.

14. Humphreys had to assume the role of voyeur—"watchqueen"—to maintain access to his sample; Sternberg had to agree to let fledgling chiropractic students "adjust" him, as an act of faith and trust. In most participant observation studies, the researcher has to make creative, often uncomfortable, occasionally downright dangerous adaptations. Such adaptations account for the color and richness of many of these studies, but also for their frequently precarious quality.

15. Cf., Clyde Kluckhohn, *Mirror for Man: A Study of Human Behavior and Social Attitudes* (New York: Premier Books, 1961).

16. R. LaPiere, "Attitudes Versus Action," *Social Forces,* 1934. A commonsense way of putting LaPiere's basic finding, which has been corroborated in many social contexts over the years, is that folks have a much harder time turning you down when you are eyeballing them. An important implication for *dissertation-promotion policy* is that faculty are less likely to reject a candidate's proposal and/or thesis chapters if he has the courage continually to discuss the project with them in their offices, rather than by phone or memoranda. Again, I stress the importance, this time substantiated by a tradition of findings in social psychology, of regularly keeping your oar in down at the department, no matter how unpalatable the prospect.

17. In his volume, *Boys in White,* Becker had demonstrated the cheery and confident tone of University of Chicago medical students researched by him and his colleagues. (Chicago: University of Chicago Press, 1961.)

Employing a sociological pun, I entitled my dissertation, "Boys in Plight."

18. Some programs, notably psychology ones, require a formal section putting forth definitions of terms used in the hypotheses. As far as I am able to determine, most other fields have no formal rule about such a section per se, but it is, of course, vital for the proposal's and dissertation's lucidity that key hypotheses and methodological/statistical terms and concepts be predefined before being introduced in their respective sections of discussion.

19. This volume assumes a certain minimal research competence on the ABD's part. A reader who is fuzzy on the relationship between independent, intervening and dependent variables needs remedial reading in one or more good social science methods textbooks.

CHAPTER 5

The Unfolding Dissertation: Researching and Writing It

Chapter Four flows into Chapter Five, just as writing the proposal and the dissertation should be conceived of as two parts of a larger procedural unit. Although in the present chapter the emphasis is on the latter moment, the reader will see that much of the discussion of Chapter Four is, *mutatis mutandi,* relevant here as well.

Although an approved proposal is certainly an occasion for champagne, the importance of pushing on almost immediately—without resting upon one's laurels—with the research and writing of the dissertation cannot be overemphasized. By approved proposal time, the ABD who has implemented the work habits and attitudes detailed in earlier chapters of this book will have found the pace and momentum to carry him the rest of the way, provided he doesn't slacken.

There are four main components in executing the dissertation: (1) collection of data; (2) analysis and interpretation of one's findings; (3) writing the dissertation chapters; (4) presenting the unfolding dissertation to supervising faculty. Each of these involves many subissues, of which the most important, recurrent and vexing will be examined in this and the following chapter.

COLLECTION OF DATA.

How simple such a short phrase makes it all sound! So unlike the complexity, messiness and often tediousness of the real task. The methodologies of dissertation data collection can be broken down into three major categories. Non-social science dissertations, e.g., humanities and letters, generally pursue the first style of methodology, whereas social science theses range across all three approaches.

1. Research which involves on the writer's part no original collection of data directly from samples of people "out there." In one way or another, the data sources have been compiled or produced by somebody else. In humanities, letters, philosophy and history dissertations, first-order research involves perusal of primary sources like documents, original manuscripts and letters; and secondary sources such as texts, histories, monographs. In behavioral sciences, political science, public administration and education dissertations using a theoretical/methodological perspective of one or more of these disciplines, primary sources for data collection are survey, public opinion and census materials; and public documents such as legislative and administrative reports and judicial cases. The dissertation writer recollects, researches the spectrum of related data sources to pull out those ideas and facts which tend to substantiate his statement of the problem and hypotheses.

It is an interesting and much-debated (although unresolved) question as to whether such research can be called *empirical,* regardless of how thorough and exhaustive its execution, or whether that usually hallowed but occasionally scorned term is reserved for original collection on the part of a researcher. Sometimes the issue becomes not just interesting but crucial, e.g., when a department requires that a dissertation be "empirical," or involve "original research." Is, for example, an anthropology dissertation, "Contrasting Premarital Sexual Foreplay Among Three MicroAsian Folk Societies," based on computer data from the HRAF (Human Relations Area Files) "empirical"? Or can a sociology dissertation, "Differential Social Mobility Aspirations of Middle-Class and Working-Class Black Women," based on survey data from the NORC (National Opinion Research Center), be styled "original research"? There is no blanket answer to these questions. Generally, departments and programs which have gone "big" on computer methodologies and a "scientific" image would endorse such methods as empirical. Indeed, many social science departments nowadays either insist on or prefer the utilization of survey and/or census source data to the exclusion or radical deemphasis of other "contaminated" person-based sources of data collection.

2. Research which involves limited and highly structured—nonethe-

less essential—collection of data directly from living, breathing subjects or samples. This approach is characterized by a one- or two-shot, in-and-out-again gathering of data. In psychology dissertations, it is seen in experiments where student subjects are given a defined time to carry out some task, often under two or more experimental conditions. In sociology theses, it is most often found in the administering of questionnaires to groups of respondents (often classes of students). A dissertation on social mobility attitudes among black women might gather its data directly in this manner as opposed to using NORC sources (although, generally, the thesis would partake of both sources for comparative and complementary purposes).

Common to all limited fieldwork approaches are a lack of rapport with subjects and a very low risk factor in terms of permanent damage to one's methodology design. In the typical case, the candidate "borrows" a colleague's or fellow student/teacher's introductory class in psychology or sociology for half an hour to conduct an experiment or hand out a questionnaire. One doesn't know the respondents and, more likely than not—with the limited exception of returning to administer a second phase the following week—will never encounter them again. This is not to argue that the candidate must not exercise due preparation and care in designing his experiment or questionnaire (including pretesting) and obtaining his respondents—certainly, he must—but the chances of his being expelled from his fieldwork site before he collects the necessary data are very small (as contrasted with continuous collection of data from real people over a period of time: see below). If a class should unaccountably take umbrage with one's questionnaire and balk at filling it out, the researcher need only "clean up his act" to avoid a repeated reversal and take his questions to a new group. If the sample turns out to be too small or unrepresentative again, one moves on to another college class with a larger number of anonymous faces. In none of these instances of limited original empirical work is any individual setback with particular subjects fatal—inconvenient, time-wasting, infuriating, yes, but fatal, no. Its low-risk factor, combined with its genuine kernel of "real-life" research, are undoubtedly major factors in commending it to many behavioral-science candidates as an acceptable compromise between a person-disassociated dissertation based exclusively on already-gathered survey material and a person-permeated dissertation based largely on information gathered through continuous intimate interaction with

110

one's sample, entailing recurrent hazards to completion of one's methodology and, ergo, one's dissertation.

3. Research which involves long-term, continuous contact with subject groups from whom data is being collected. This fieldwork approach is most typical in anthropology but is also found with some
frequency in sociology, social psychology and certain education dissertations (those employing "participant observation" methodologies
derived from social science).

There is an enormous literature on the pros and cons of such field
studies, involving issues about whether they are truly "scientific,"
whether they are ethical (particularly if the researcher has not identi-
fied himself as such) and whether they are viable in light of high-risk
factors of expulsion from the group before the data is collected. An
ABD contemplating a field study dissertation should heed the following warnings:

a. Don't study a group which is illegal or stigmatized. In either
case, the chances of (and anxieties about) expulsion are far
too great.

b. Don't study a group whose center of (symbolic) existence involves activities and attitudes which outrage you. Your staying time in that kind of site can be counted in a week or two.

c. Don't study a group where you have to conceal your true role
and researcher identity. This avoidance is especially important if the group is engaged in illegal activities but holds even
for groups pursuing lawful ones. If, for example, the research
site for your study on "Bet with Your Head, Not Over It: A
Study of Gambling Activities of OTB Employees" is your
own OTB office where you are employed as a clerk, you had
best be prepared to change jobs—or at least branches—when
the study comes to light and your cover is blown. Nobody
likes a spy—even apart from what he or she writes—and hostile or cold shoulder reaction is the norm in these cases.

d. Don't study a group whose existence, membership, leadership
are all in doubt in terms of stability and continuity. Many
juvenile gangs, for example, of a type which Yablonsky has
termed a "near-group" because of fast-shifting and fast-
breaking changes in personnel, are poor candidates due to
their here-today-gone-tomorrow composition.

e. Don't write your dissertation about a group for which no substitutes can be made, should you be expelled. If a certain type of group is the sole representative of its kind, say, the Women's Medical College of Pennsylvania (now called Medical College of Pennsylvania) in Philadelphia, dissertation time is not the right time to field-research it. Without knowing any specific details about the college, I would guess that officials might be very sensitive indeed about letting a male observer wander about at will, fearing negative sexist publicity from his study. Even if they granted entry in the most cordial manner, they might well have second and third thoughts (as did the chiropractic college I studied) six months down the road with the ABD past the point of no return and no alternative women's medical college to turn to for study if expulsion should occur. A very resourceful, uphill dissertation *might* be salvaged along the lines of "Closing Ranks: A Case Study of Feminist Associational Reaction to Perceived External Threat," but I, for one, wouldn't want to try to write that one.

Adherence to these avoidance policies still leaves room for many field studies, although the pool is definitely narrowed. Becker did a field study of medical students, Smigel of Wall Street law firms, Montagna of prestigious accountant firms in New York City.[1] All faced certain entry and maintenance (continuing access) problems, but the groups were all both legal and very sure of themselves; furthermore, they were all replaceable: Montagna could have gone to other accounting firms; Becker to another medical college.

The reader may object that my caveats exclude many important and socially valuable topics of study. True. If you have spunk and a flair for excitement and the eye of the storm, all the more research power to you. But save your illuminating undercover participant observation of a professional auto theft ring for your first book *after* you have obtained your doctorate in criminal justice, on a more mundane topic with a safer methodology. With this sequence of projects, you'll possess sufficient salary and prestige as an assistant professor of criminology to extricate yourself from a possible charge of accessory to grand theft, stemming from your research role in a criminal enterprise!

On balance, the ABD is not advised to pursue a thesis whose primary research design calls for extended participant observation of a group upon whose continued goodwill he is dependent for collection of indispensable dissertation data (an exception has to be made in the case of cultural anthropology, where ethnographic field studies are required by some programs). *Adjunct* fieldwork, which complements the validity of primary-methods data gathered through survey and/or questionnaire materials, is desirable, when available, for adding another dimension to one's study. But hypotheses testing should not, in my judgment, depend, on a first-line basis, on the successful sustained execution of fieldwork.

Researching a dissertation within the boundaries of the first two methodological approaches outlined—using data not collected by the candidate, or employing strictly limited originally collected data—leaves plenty of room for variations by individual styles and ingenuity: e.g., it is an art all in itself to design a tight, probing, valid and reliable questionnaire or experiment. Then, too, many public policy and social science issues are best (sometimes exclusively) testable by survey and questionnaire methods, e.g., political opinion, voting preferences, demographic trends, social-class structure, the effectiveness of school systems and programs in delivering services to students.

How Much Data to Collect?

It is very important to remind oneself continually to what purposes data are being collected, regardless of method. The most relevant guideline here is whether they bear on confirmation, rejection of, qualification of proposed hypotheses. Other relevant data would be "background" materials on, for example, social characteristics (age, sex, ethnicity, social class) of respondents, or administrative rules and regulations of an organization which yielded a picture of its social structure. It is generally better to collect too much rather than too little, within the tolerance limits of one's sample—and oneself—particularly with one- or two-shot questionnaires or experiments, where the respondents will not be available to retest if holes or unexplored issues surface two months later in the analysis stage of the dissertation.

In stressing abundance of data, "fishing expeditions" are not recommended. After all, one has a set of hypotheses and procedures to draw on in pinpointing data targets. Nevertheless, hypotheses have a way of becoming altered with progress of the dissertation (see fuller discussion below in hypotheses-testing section); key questions are

113

posed in somewhat different ways; incoming data and theoretical models work back upon each other. The ratio of eventually used (in the final version of the dissertation) to originally collected data is most often not impressively high, although there is a good deal of variation among different researchers within and across disciplines.

In my study, I presented the chiropractic students with two questionnaires containing 177 items, many of them scales and multiple section questions. I was able to get nearly all of them to fill out these vast instruments because of my established, long-term relationship with them (one desirable consequence of certain field studies). I had upwards of 400 pieces of comparative data for each respondent. Certainly, I did not use anywhere near all of it in my analysis and write-up. But when the questions were originally drawn, each was included because I felt it was relevant to getting a finely detailed picture of my respondents' backgrounds and their world of the chiropractic college in a systematic and empirical way, confirming many of my impressionistic and *ad hoc* field observations. I then drew on this large pool of material to block out my thesis with a good deal of confidence that I knew what I was writing about. Many of the questions whose data did not appear in later versions of the dissertation were not "wasted" or "superfluous," since they were either stepping-stones along the way of analysis or aided in closing off theoretical deadends or analytic blind alleys.[2]

ANALYSIS AND INTERPRETATION OF FINDINGS FROM THE DATA.

The reader will remember from Chapter Four that I had presented my sample with various self-other questions designed to tap a self-over-other adaptation to the anticipated career tribulations of practicing chiropractic. Two items (see page 102 of Chapter Four) asked the students to predict their own and the average chiropractor's income after ten to fifteen years in practice. Let me continue with that example, as well as bring in others, to introduce four key issues of analysis and interpretation: determining statistical significance; handling troublesome, inconsistent or contradictory data impacting on the thesis from without (e.g., other books, studies); dealing with negative (to hypotheses confirmation) results generated from one's own data collected for the dissertation; whether, when and how to use computers in processing and analyzing data.

Statistical significance.

The self-over-other tendency was startling with the income items: the students predicted a median income of $52,500 for themselves and $28,400 for the average chiropractor. Looked at another way, fifty-two of the seventy-five in the sample predicted self-income at least one category higher, often two or even three. There were twenty-one ties and two cases where the individual predicted a higher income for the average chiropractor than himself.

Still, the final step in scientific testing of the hypothesis—that the "respondents will predict higher incomes after ten to fifteen years for themselves than for the average chiropractor"—was to determine whether the distribution of 52-21-2 was statistically significant in the expected direction. The *null* hypothesis (the nullifying or devil's advocate hypothesis, it might be instructively conceived as here) for each of my fourteen hypotheses was that chiropractic students predict their own career success to be no greater than the typical chiropractor or chiropractic student.

In specific statistical terms, the null hypothesis states that for any pair of self-other questions, students will choose the same amount of success for themselves and others, i.e., tied scores on any pair of questions, except for some error which is assumed to be random. Random error here means that students would be as likely to pick other over self, as self over other. For Hypothesis One, and the other thirteen, I employed a nonparametric statistic, the *sign test*, to ascertain whether the standing null hypothesis should be rejected in favor of my own hypotheses. In this manner, twelve of my fourteen hypotheses were confirmed, ten of them at the .001 level of statistical significance, one at the .01 level and one at .02, giving strong support to the empirical existence of the Figure 4.1 model in Chapter Four. Let me remind the reader that a .001 significance level finding means that the data distribution on a given item could have come about by chance less than one time out of 1,000, and that, ordinarily in social science, researchers accept a .05 or .01 level of significance as strict enough.

Descriptive Versus Analytic (Power) Statistics.

Whatever your hypotheses and field, you are generally going to come down to the question of using a statistic for determining significance. This is not a statistics text and does not purport to discuss the various power tools appropriate to different orders of data, and experimental and questionnaire designs. But the candidate should be cautioned against confounding in his research the related but distinct elements of magnitude, direction and significance. Suppose your dissertation in social psychology theorizes that authoritarian group therapy is singularly effective in rehabilitating drug offenders.[3] Further suppose your collected data look like this:

Table 5.1: Group Therapies and Recidivism

	Non-Recidivists	Recidivists	Totals
Authoritarian Group Therapy	60	40	100
Laissez-faire Group Therapy	50	50	100
Control Group (no therapy)	40	60	100

The magnitudes of the cell figures tilt in favor of confirming your hypotheses, although they are certainly not overwhelmingly persuasive of the efficacy of authoritarian as opposed to less directive group therapy. The direction of the data (authoritarian-receiving sample tending toward predicted non-recidivist pole) is also anti- null hypothesis. But however you operationalized the independent variables of the two kinds of therapy and measurement of recidivism, the resulting statistics in the table are all in the realm of *descriptive* statistics. An *analytic* statistic, or power statistic, as it is sometimes termed—in this particular case chi-squared—is necessary to determine whether the patterning of magnitudes and directions among and between the various cells is statistically significant. For example, it might turn out that the difference between success rates of the authoritarian and laissez-faire groups is not statistically significant, but that differences between either of these therapy-exposed groups and the control group are significant. Such results would have to lead to a rejection or modification of your hypothesis, with the "serendipitous (see below for more elaboration of serendipity) suggestion that an atmosphere of concern and support which made the addicts feel special seemed more important and efficacious than any particular therapy approach per se.

Sometimes the question of "near significant" or "approaching significance" findings comes up. One meets such phrases and discussion not only in dissertations but in journal articles and papers. Suppose an intracell chi-squared analysis of the data in Table 5.1 yields a .08 level of "significance" for the distribution of cases between authoritarian and laissez-faire results. If the writer is "pushing" the efficacy of the authority therapy thesis, there is going to be pressure for him to use the "near-significant" argument in his discussion. Social-scientifically, it is unjustifiable, since statistical significance is by predefinition a zero-sum game, just as you don't *nearly* have an orgasm or make a putt. On the other hand, certain social science departments and their research bureaus are known to take and permit certain liberties in so-called "trend" interpretations. If the candidate comes up against "near significance" with his findings, he might consult the prevailing standards of other current dissertations and methodologists in his program in making a decision about pursuing the discussion. A way around near significance is sometimes to "collapse" the data categories into fewer ones, viz., if a three-by-two cell distribution (above) yields near-significant results, collapsing it into a two-by-two one often results in significance.

The Bogy of Disconfirming Evidence

ruining one's dissertation parallels the fear of somebody else coming along and "scooping" the candidate. But there is more reality to the surfacing of negative, challenging, unexpected results during continuing review of the literature and data analysis than there is to the virtually impossible chance of a candidate really being scooped on his thesis (see discussion in Chapter Two, on this point). As a matter of fact, I never knew a dissertation, including my own, where everything turned out just as expected along the lines of the proposal. Challenges to one's theoretical model and hypotheses can come from "without" and "within," from library sources one continues to pursue even during analysis and write-up, or from the data itself. Very often the "negative data" results from pursuit of both external and internal materials. But I have never come across a case where "negative results" ensued in rejection of a candidate's dissertation, even though ABDs continue to believe that such circumstances are fatal and not infrequent. I confronted such a challenge during my own dissertation research.

In my case, the field site data were coming in nicely, i.e., analysis of self-other items were yielding strikingly confirmative results of a self-over-other tendency prediction for rosy futures as chiropractors. I was feeling quite pleased and confident. At the same time, I continued to—

what law students and lawyers would call—"Shepardize" my case: canvass all studies, literature (lawyers preparing a brief check of the latest appellate decisions bearing on their case through Shepard's recording system) related to my topic. Although I had done a good deal of groundwork for my proposal in areas like professionalization, adult socialization, stigma, I was bound initially to neglect others, whose importance would emerge only as my fieldwork, data collection and analysis proceeded. The candidate must disabuse himself of the narrow notion that data for one's study is confined to the originally collected materials yielded by his methods design; *all library literature* bearing on the problem is also data. Of course, "all the data is never in," and at a certain point one has to stop reading and collecting and write a final draft; but input should be sought after right up to the point of setting down a final version.

One afternoon toward the end (at least at the time I believed it was the end) of my data analysis, I had left my dissertation office for a Shepardizing/browsing session in the Columbia University social science library. I was attempting to find a better, more social-scientific-sounding label for the self-over-other tendency in my data. I had jotted down a list of cue words to check against the literature; e.g., egoistic, autistic, self-evaluation. Somewhere between autistic and self-evaluation, I ran across a string of psychology articles reporting that, in general, American subjects tend to elevate/score themselves over others in testing situations. Suddenly in the Columbia library I went cold. What had begun as a search for a felicitous term or phrase had turned into a thesis crisis.

Wasn't it entirely possible (even probable) that the consistent elevation of self over other in various questionnaire problematic contexts of an upcoming chiropractic career stemmed not from my hypothesized "solo" adaptation to and distancing from the negatively perceived chiropractor herd, but from the pedestrian tendency of people to rate themselves better than their peers on anything from reading ability, to friendliness, to attractiveness?

I relate this episode because sooner or later the current dissertation writer is going to experience a similar cold sweat of jeopardy to his whole project. Reflecting back on those events, I see that my crisis was unnecessarily extended and intensified because (a) I had, in understandable ABD eagerness for certainty, come to a psychological "closure" in the thrust of my thesis, putting all my eggs and energies in the basket of the self-over-other mechanism, not playing enough with alternative frameworks or keeping open to challenging objections; (b) I immediately assumed that my thesis committee knew everything there was to know about the ins and outs of psychological literature on self and other scoring evaluations and would, as one person, peremptorily raise this fatal objection to my thesis. As it turned out, the committee hadn't the foggiest notion that such an "autistic factor" existed in testing. It was *I* who informed them about it. Fortunately, after I calmed down and thought matters through, I was able to use the factor in a "serendipitous" manner to reinforce and nail down my dissertation.[4]

By stating that I self-exacerbated the crisis, I don't mean to say that one didn't exist. I had stumbled on a serious objection to my whole model, no doubt about it, and I had to find a way out. Whether or not my adviser and other supervising faculty knew about this literature was not ultimately a first-order issue. But on a very practical level, I couldn't go into a thesis defense with my rear so egregiously unprotected; even a slim chance of one of the five being acquainted with the autistic test-taking tendency and making the damaging connection, vetoing my thesis in which I had single-heartedly and -mindedly invested almost two years of my life, was an infinitely greater chance than I was willing to take. Besides, and more important, I still believed that my thesis about a peculiar self-over-other tendency operating among chiropractors was accurate. True, I had perhaps become doctrinaire about the mechanism, as heavily involved dissertation candidates and researchers in general are apt to get about their projects; on the other hand, I had given the matter intensive and long-term investigation and reflection. Confronting this issue, then, became more than covering my rear or getting my thesis "through"; its resolution meant intellectually vindicating and defending a project into which I had poured my best.

What saved me at the time, however, was not Librium or psychotherapy, or even a triggering of the autistic tendency! What saved me was my file. As distressed and depressed as I was, I sensed that somewhere in that vast pool of intelligence I had collected lay a resolution. So each day I forced myself to spend my usual time in the office, reading over my notes, memoranda on theory and methodology of the dissertation. To this day I don't know how it came to me; I simply know that the right dissertation synapses eventually got wired because

119

I kept at the file, activating connection after connection. It came to me that the only way to "factor out" the "autistic constant" in test taking was to compare my chiropractic students with other health students. If I could show that, say, medical and dental students demonstrated a significantly smaller tendency toward self-over-other evaluation on career context questions, my thesis that a peculiar self-other defense mechanism was an intervening variable in the chiropractic student case would still be viable.

It took me such a long time to come around to this "inspiration" because only weeks before I had considered the dissertation nearly done, all the data in, the analysis finished. At one level or another, I was ferociously resisting opening up questions, most certainly gathering new data with new samples. However, once I came to the realization that some comparative research was the only way out—that there *was* a way out—I gathered myself for a last research effort. After weeks of new entry and access problems, I managed to get permission to administer a short questionnaire to a few classes at my university's medical and dental colleges. I presented these health students with self-other, paired, income-prediction questions identical to those asked the chiropractic student sample. Both the dental and medical students, particularly the latter, demonstrated a startling and statistically significant reduction of the self-over-other income prediction which had been so rampant and near-universal with my chiropractic group.

Completion of my thesis was delayed some three months. But the comparative research generated two final chapters of the dissertation, including a final "implications" one, where I speculated whether chiropractic's continued "solo practice" ethic (which I had amply documented) would allow it to survive in an age where other major health professions were all moving toward bureaucratic, group-practice organization and ideology. Neither of these last chapters, of course, had been contemplated by my proposal. Yet my committee made no objection to these additions, indeed, praised them as innovative adaptations and elaborations of the proposal's theoretical and research models. This is by way of saying that modifications in methodology and adjustment, and even revision, of hypotheses during the dissertation research and analysis are probably more the rule than the exception. No matter how well one pre- or pilot researches his topic for the proposal, later intensified exposure, as well as continued reexamination of the issues, is going to force changes in one's model.

"My Own Data's Coming Out Wrong."

My challenge came from *external* data. As we saw, I ultimately stood ground with the validity of my original thesis and findings about students' individualistic defense mechanisms, although I had to elaborate and extend my methodology in its defense. I would have faced a different hurdle if my original sample of chiropractic students had not exhibited a significant self-over-other elevation in line with my hypotheses. Let us turn to *internal* challenges to the dissertation, which are perhaps more frequent than the external type of my case. What do you do when the majority of your hypotheses are either not being significantly confirmed by your own collected data, or, worse, are indeed being disconfirmed?[5]

One alternative is to play it straight: report the disconfirming results, and rely on the scientific ethos and the contract model of the dissertation and proposal, i.e., you carried through assiduously the methodology of a design the proposal committee approved. That the hypotheses were rejected makes its contribution to the field in closing off an ultimately dead-end research direction.

My sense is that such an approach washes better in a hard science experiment/dissertation—where the rigor of an ineluctable scientific logic and procedure is more seriously followed—than in social science and education dissertations, although a particular, say, psychology ABD's department may be an exception to this rule of thumb and accept as sufficient negative results produced through "honest" procedures.

The largest obstacle to getting such negative results accepted, no matter what the discipline, is the suspicion cast upon one's *hypotheses*—either that they were badly developed in relation to your specific topic and/or in connection with earlier work in the field, or, more frequently, that they were straw men. If one is disposed to defend against these objections, stand by the authenticity and logic of the original model even in the face of incoming negative results, then it doesn't do to close the dissertation on a downbeat. The writer must essay one or more explanations for the inconsistency between his predictions and the empirical results (I believe that even in the hard sciences *some* reconciliation is expected).

One reconciliatory tack to take is methodological: the measuring design and instruments used were not sufficiently discriminatory or biased the results of the data (e.g., non-mutually exclusive items on a questionnaire, scales or tests of low reliability or validity, nonrepresentative samples of respondents). The difficulty here, of course, is that you yourself designed—or at least chose among the various established measures—the research instruments for your project. Criticism of your own measures has a hollow or masturbatory ring to it; criticism of someone else's venerated measure (viz., the Likert Scale in social psychology, the Guttman Scale in sociology, the Thematic Apperception Test in psychology) as the culprit is likely to be better received but probably won't be sufficient in itself to pull you out of the negative data hole. Your committee's response may well be, "Now that you have recognized the insufficiencies of your methodology, go back and do the research (experiment) with an appropriate, valid and reliable instrument."

A strategy more promising than mere reporting of chips-fall-where-they-may disconfirming results is a "full-scale inquiry" into the causes—theoretical and methodological—for such an outcome. (How full and to what scale depends on how many of the hypotheses have been defeated: generally, if the majority of one's hypotheses are sustained by the data, "limited" explanations for the failure of certain others to pan out can be legitimately designed.) It is perfectly legitimate in both science and social science to learn by experience; tirades, especially by social scientists, against so-called *"post factum"* construction and modification of theory, measuring instruments and data analysis ignore the centrality of such reciprocal activities in scientific work.[6] Methodology textbooks, particularly introductory or "low-level" ones, often push a rigid, self-righteous and prissy research checklist model, where you (a) state your hypotheses; (b) operationalize instruments to measure the variables; (c) carry out the data collection along the prescribed operational lines; (d) analyze the results; (e) write up your findings. Nothing is wrong with this research model as an "ideal type." As a matter of fact, it is a mandatory starting point for a dissertation proposal, and, generally for research projects, pursued throughout one's career. But to insist on these steps as being the whole story—that they must be unidirectional, followed in this exact sequence, that hypotheses or methodology can never be varied once set in motion along the original lines—is mechanical, and childish. Worse, it doesn't approximate the majority of actually conducted worthwhile research where people find that they have to make changes in both their assumptions and research procedures as they come to know their subject more intimately.[7]

The ABD *should* follow the ideal-type model of sequential research steps his first time through. Initial data results will determine how he is to proceed from that point. If all or most of one's hypotheses are beautifully confirmed at this stage, congratulations, Doctor. For most of us, matters will not run quite so smoothly, and some adjustments will have to be made, including modifying hypotheses, analyzing the data in novel ways, even administering new instruments.

- Recall in the chiropractic student case that, even though the data came out "right," the writer had to add an entirely new research direction to his study, never contemplated in the original proposal, in order to defend his central hypothesis from straw man charges.
- Recall in the drug group-therapy research that the candidate had to revamp his models for both the treatment and etiology of drug addiction when it transpired that "Rogerian" group treatment was as effective as the originally favored authoritarian treatment. In this case, elaboration of the original model could be made, using the initial data pool from the three condition groups. Although the laissez-faire treatment groups were originally seen merely as a second-condition control, the finding that Rogerian groups were almost as effective in treating drug addiction as highly directive ones necessitated the researcher's examining the control data to factor out its commonalities with the favored variable (e.g., both made the addict feel special, attended to).

It is most important to drive home the point that every candidate is going to face his own peculiar crisis with his data, and that he is going to have to call upon his own ingenuity and resourcefulness to get through it. It is a dysfunctional dissertation myth to believe that "nobody else is going through this hell"—since almost every candidate is experiencing his idiosyncratic version of the crisis. It is another debilitating myth to believe, "The data's come out wrong. I'm through." The preceding crisis examples were offered as antidotes to this second

123

kind of despair, not so much for nuts-and-bolts guidelines but as an affirmation that a candidate steeped in and committed to his project will find a way, and that such a path will fall within current, more flexible paradigms for legitimate research procedures.

Nonetheless, a thorny faculty-relations issue is involved in "revisionist" dissertation research. If the proposal is construed by one's program as a contract, might not radical departures from its theoretical, methodological and analytic stipulations be interpreted by supervising faculty as fundamental enough violation to render the dissertation contract "null and void"? One must consider, first, how closely one's particular department adheres to the contract model. In any event, the charge of "radical departure" can be avoided if one initially executes the steps of the proposal as originally contracted. Having shown "good faith," one can then go on to demonstrate that realistic adaptations were necessary in light of developing conditions to carry out the *spirit* as well as the *letter* of the contract. In the dissertation case, the spirit of the contract implies that the candidate will produce a work which fully explores his topic. Such exploration often involves innovation and originality which cannot be foreseen at the time of proposal contract. There exists, as a matter of fact, support in equity contract law for subsequent modifications in performance, especially in cases of creative and artistic services. All but the least imaginative of dissertations would appear to fall within this category.

The Computer: To Use or Not to Use?

The issue whether to use computer technology in the data-processing and/or analysis stage of a dissertation is usually a serious one only in social science dissertations. Even in these areas, there are sharp differences of opinion and preference on the part of supervising faculty (and particular candidates) as to whether the computer should be a main-line or first-order methodological tool.

Certain computer services of the 1980s are undeniably potentially valuable to many fields of dissertation candidates at the *proposal stage:* increasingly, university libraries are subscribing to bibliography data banks, so that a candidate working up a comparative literature proposal for "The Concept of Time As Relative: Continuities Between the Work of James Joyce and Mario Vargas Llosa" will be able (soon, if not yet: some fields, e.g., psychology and anthropology, currently have more fully developed data banks than others) to cue a computer with key words and phrases, such as "non-linear time in literature," "early twentieth-century Irish literature," "late twentieth-century Peruvian literature," "commentaries on Joyce," "commentaries on Llosa," and within a few days and for a few dollars obtain an overview printout of the available antecedent materials bearing on one's topic. Obviously, many of the printout items will turn out, upon examination, to be irrelevant or only secondarily relevant, but almost always one finds the wheat with the chaff, especially if the cue phrases have been designed with the help of a librarian trained in this type of data-recovery procedure. Such an approach to review of the literature is immensely quicker and more efficient than traditional methods of consulting individual reference books, guides, indexes to the periodical literature of one's field. Of course, ultimately, there is no substitute for sitting down and reading the germane sources; no computer can do that for you (nor is recourse to computer summaries of materials sufficient). But the computer can zero in on key sources quite rapidly.

At later stages of the dissertation, one can use the scanning function of the computer as a "Shepardizer" to keep up with the concurrent developments in the area of one's topic right up to the time of dissertation defense. Sometimes periodic scanning will add valuable citations, even analytic suggestions.

So the use of the computer for preliminary and sustained scanning of the literature relevant to a topic, in whatever field where such a service is already available, is certainly not an issue. Controversies and anxieties arise when the computer is considered for the *main role* in a study as assembler and/or analyzer of the data. Generally, only social science-model dissertations, with elements of experiment, controls, table-partialling, correlation and the like, are amenable to computer approaches. Even within social science dissertations, the appropriateness or necessity for computer analysis will vary according to the nature of research materials (see beginning of chapter): survey data, demographic data, large-scale, large-sample questionnaire data are all good candidates for computer processing. The larger that observational data, collected firsthand, looms, the less the importance or even legitimacy of the computer; computer processing of Goffman's subtle observational studies of mental patients in *Asylums* or Nance's observations of the *Gentle Tasaday* of the Philippines strike all but a few among us as absurd.[8]

The issue of computer research in dissertation data has to be set in the ideological context of social science graduate departments. There is a "computer culture" in the air and corridors of many programs that surfaced in the mid-1960s and continues with added vigor into the 1980s. The denizens of such cultures, mostly graduate students and some faculty, appear to spend a rather large part of their days hanging around the computer room, awaiting the latest "run" on their data. An untutored listener hears much esoteric shoptalk, or "computerese." Sometimes one feels he has mistakenly wandered into a *dental* clinic, what with all the orthodontics and periodontics-sounding terminology of "bites," "bits" and "chips." Graduate faculty differ in their stance toward the computer culture. Generally, although there are many exceptions in both directions, older faculty tend to be far less enthusiastic than younger professors. Such indifference, hostility or suspicion stems from one of two sources: fear, because the older people simply were never trained in computer programming or analysis, don't care to start now and are defensive about their ignorance in this "growth" area; a sense that the prominence of computer *methods* has led to the prominence of computer, technician-like *minds,* less sensitive to the humanistic considerations which have to feed the social sciences if they are going to research social matters with any depth beyond quantitative accuracy.

A particular candidate is going to have to check out the salience of the computer culture in his program when deciding just what to write and whom to approach as a possible adviser. There are departments where one almost has to do a dissertation with the computer as a large if not exclusive research tool. If the department is computer-obsessed, probably the issue along that dimension of picking an adviser is moot. In many other programs, one finds a large computer force, with a substantial enclave of dissenters. If one is disinclined to use the computer approach for one reason or another, sufficient faculty validation can usually be found in such "mixed" departments. I would venture that few if any major social science graduate programs today are "anticomputer" in emphasis. Although I personally view this as a lamentable, in some ways pseudo-scientific, development of the past two decades, dissertation facts must be faced. The fascination and adulation that Americans in general have with gadgetry, "hardware," science, science fiction is shared, quite expectedly, by American "social scientists."

The reader will have divined that my own feelings about computers in social science and humanities research are mixed. Most certainly, it is advisable, even mandatory, for literature scanning. When I wrote my doctoral dissertation (1968) computers were still "optional," even in analyzing questionnaire data. Years before, I had taken a mini-course in very rudimentary computer procedures (e.g., counting-sorting), but little had stayed with me, nor with, I believe, my fellow students. Looking back, I see now that computers would have sped up considerably my hand cross-tabulations and hand correlation calculations for my sample. I do not believe that five computers using five "languages" would have furthered my theoretical formulations at all. My bias is still for doing sociological matters with my own hands and touch. Transfer of too many functions to the computer room sanitizes and depersonalizes social reality for me. I don't even regret doing all the tabulations and correlations myself; I liked—and continue to like— the direct contact with my subjects, even if it took more time to work through the data that way. Of course, to a substantial degree we are talking about life-style preferences and values here: I would rather drive a shift car and continue to use a mechanical typewriter because I like the feel and contact involved, the sense that I still have an important direct and physical part to play in making the machine work. Alienation is perceiving the machine as separate, independent, alien to one. I believe that computers often alienate, sometimes even subordinate, their regular users. Computer-caused "dissertation alienation" (see Chapter One for other types of dissertation alienation) is a possible, although not inevitable, outcome of the ascendancy of the computer culture in social science departments.

Like it or not, many readers of this volume are going to have to incorporate some computer methodology into their dissertation research and methodology. The two major caveats should be: 1. Don't get "swept away," and 2. Don't get terrified.

1. During the dissertation course, a particular kind of student can get "led astray" by the "fascinating" world of computer software, its whirring discs, its printout chatter. There is a whole science-fiction, "Space Odyssey" corona to the computer to which many contemporary American students are susceptible. The danger for the ABD is that he can get so caught up in the *means* of the computer culture that he forgets about its *ends* in relation to the dissertation, pursuing a kind of *Endless Summer* quest for the "perfect run." Such seemingly endless tinkering, which can keep an ABD submerged and entangled in

miles of printouts for years, is actually abetted by certain "empiricist" departments (sometimes styled "social science bureaus") where the researcher, not having developed a prior theory, is encouraged to try run after run until he "comes up with something." If the researcher, on the other hand, had a well-thought-out theoretical model to start, descent to the computer room and its rituals can lead to an orgy of running all variables against each other, in which excess the clean lines of one's original hypotheses-testing design are obliterated.

The guideline that emerges from a discussion of such hazards is: Never go to the computer with an open agenda. Use the computer for performance of specific tasks related to the completion of one part or another of your dissertation. It is equally dysfunctional to the dissertation to become a first-rate programmer for its own sake, as it is to become a grand and glorious filer as an end in itself.

2. Many students, and faculty, are terrified of the computer. Indeed, computer folks are able to get a leg up on the rest of us by exploiting that fear; they possess some powerful, specialized, "scientific" skills to which we don't have a clue. It is undoubtedly true that for most of us the uneasiness revolves around our relative unfamiliarity with higher mathematics at which we weren't much good but considered (especially during high school and early college) awesome and the summit of intelligent endeavor. The irony is that in the status order of mathematical fields, computer and statistical math rank very low! There are also very serious questions about the validity or (limited) applicability of mathematical procedures in research about people, but most of us can only intuit objections to mathematical models of social behavior, since we don't have the math that the specialists keep urging upon us.

This is not the place for an essay demystifying the computer and/or mathematics subcultures in social science, although some have been written.[9] It is clear, however, that knowledge about how the computer works greatly mitigates anxieties about it. So the doctoral candidate is encouraged to take at least one basic course in various kinds of computers and their languages. Understanding that a binary computer, for example, is, when you come down to it, only a "yes man" or a "no man," possessing a most limited and rigid "authoritarian personality," (any given computer statement is a zero-sum alternative), no matter what kind of program function it is performing, counteracts reifying or apotheosizing tendencies among the uninitiated.

But ultimately, it is really not very important for dissertation candidates using the computer to understand how the computer works; it seems unlikely a defense committee would question you on COBOL, or ASSEMBLA languages. Even if someone demanded a detailed explication of FORTRAN in relation to your computer runs on analysis of variance, the others on the defense would probably button him up. What you must understand are *the theory and mechanics of the statistic you are having the computer process,* not the theory and mechanics of the computer itself. In all but the most computer-fanatic programs, it is perfectly acceptable to take one's data to a computer consultant, specialist or technician, and ask him to run a program for, say, multiple regression analysis of your data. You don't have to have the foggiest notion of how he wrote up the program so that the IBM could understand it. Remember, the machine is just doing infinitely more quickly what we used to do by sitting down at a desk for a couple of weeks with reams of graph paper, rulers, pencils and maybe bifocals. What you must understand are the assumptions, mechanics and pitfalls of the Pearsonian r in general, and specifically in reference to *your* data. Then you must understand the meaning of all the printout categories, columns, rows, subtotals, totals from the computer. This is not the same as understanding how the computer *works*; it is knowing where to look in the computer's presentation (printout) for the results of tasks the programmer has directed it to perform. The computer will tell you what the coefficients of correlation are and which are significant. It is a wholly *noncomputer* task and responsibility, however, to evaluate the meaning of the results within the framework of your sample's size and characteristics in relation to the theory and limitations of your statistic. The thesis committee, then, may well ask hard questions about pre- and postcomputer stages of data processing, analysis and conclusions.

WRITING THE DISSERTATION CHAPTERS.

Actually writing the chapters themselves is the goal of all one's proposal construction, data collection and data interpretation. This volume does not pretend to coach dissertation candidates in literary competence per se, although some hopefully useful counsel on thesis-writing habits, attitudes and pace was offered in Chapter Two.[10] Rather, what I do here is anticipate briefly certain important questions/decisions/issues that the writer will face as he finally finds himself in the position to do the chapters: the number of chapters the dissertation should minimally include; the necessity of outlining chapters prior to writing them; readiness of a chapter or section to show to faculty; timing the writing of various chapters—which to write first; finding a typist who is not only technically competent but sufficiently adaptable to handle a long-term job which is far from ordinary or straightforward.

What Chapters Should the Dissertation Contain?

Generally the dissertation chapters should parallel the *proposal* sections, adding materials on then-anticipated, now-completed methodological implementation, data presentation, data interpretation and implications. In most instances, the critical review of the literature, statement of the problem, rationale for the study, hypotheses and methodology sections of the proposal (see Chapter Four) will be transferable (sometimes intact, more often amended, but still recognizable, due to postproposal-stage further reading, on-site-dictated modification of methodology, analysis-stage revision of hypotheses and related changes in statistical procedures). The function of a full, extensive proposal as the "grundrisse" (Marx's famous notebooks upon which *Das Kapital* was to be based) for the dissertation is once again underscored.

Outlining the Chapters.

The prolific mystery writer Donald Westlake, recently stated that he never outlines or plots his books, isn't sure where they are going.[11] Perhaps this omission explains their generally zany quality, and perhaps some fiction writers can successfully proceed without outlines (although *The Writers at Work* interviews—see Chapter Two—cast doubt even on successful fiction writing without outlining), but the ABD who doesn't outline his chapters confronts a jungle of serpentine false paths and starts which will exhaust him. The magnitude of the materials, especially of collected and analyzed data, is potentially overwhelming.

The outline for a given chapter should factor out of the myriad notes, memoranda, accumulated data, on a given part of the dissertation, the basic infrastructural posits upon which you build the chapter. These logically progressive and interrelated themes allow you to determine just which materials will now be selected out of the large total pool and used in pursuing and elaborating a major direction. Comparison of various chapter outlines allows one to determine whether the "plot" is flowing consistently, or possesses redundancies or contradictions.

I have never met a (fiction or nonfiction) writer who *likes* to outline; a little like Listerine, it is a procedure you hate to use, twice a week. Even today, I still catch myself trying to sneak out of outlining an article or chapter. The tendency is still there—especially when I am excited or eager to jump right in—to "let it all hang out" or "play it by ear," relying on existential flow to make things right. Invariably, I find I must go back, write an outline and redo the entire draft.

When to Show Chapters to Faculty?

Correctional authorities have long debated the optimal sentence time for an offender—that elusive temporal point which is long enough to do the most rehabilitative good and, at the same time, the least recidivist harm. No one knows just where that happy line falls for prisoners; nor do we know within reasonable limits of confidence how long a doctoral candidate should hold off on submitting his chapters in order to effect the most gain from the delay and the least detriment to progress and approval.

At every stage in the thesis course, this book has counseled against waiting too long, since experience has shown that substantial delays or postponements at any juncture (from serious work on the proposal soon after completion of all other course work through all subsequent stages) result in a multiplied delay in finishing the dissertation as a whole.

Still, one must show some restraint when it comes to chapter submissions to the thesis committee. It has been my experience as a dissertation adviser and editor/consultant for several publishers that the reader's attitudes and appraisal of a manuscript are disproportionately shaped by the first draft which comes to his attention. If the first impression is unfavorable, successive drafts—even substantially revised ones—never quite erase the memory or smell of the first stinker. A rule of thumb would be only to submit chapters after a second draft, or when one can state he has given it his "best shot." If one belongs to a dissertation group (see Chapter Seven), the candidate should incorporate major useful criticisms before taking a draft down to the department.

Should you submit chapters one at a time or in blocks of two or three? I argue in the next chapter that, when possible, each chapter should be approved by a majority of the thesis committee before proceeding to the next (along the lines and logic of the contract model). However, there are programs whose policies won't allow such maximum candidate-protective procedure; the ABD will be asked to hand in a couple of chapters together, or even occasionally a "solid draft" of the whole dissertation. If your department asks for all of it—or even half of it—at one time, you still have to exercise the same care for best-shot quality, must not rush through it once over lightly, in the mistaken belief that it's just a first shot: Heed the warning above about first impressions. The "whole thing" departmental preference is most disadvantageous to the candidate, spiraling his worry that he may be writing chapter after chapter of an ultimately unacceptable version of a dissertation. Short of its being firm, unbending program policy, one should make every attempt to renegotiate submission procedures with his adviser along the lines of one or two at a time.

In What Order Should the Chapters Be Written?

Many writers actually write the last chapters of a book first; this may be particularly true of mystery writers. Many *readers*—myself included—read the last sections of a book first thing off the bat: to see if the outcome and conclusions reached by the author are interesting, startling or valuable enough to warrant following through 200 pages of development. With dissertations, one almost has to write first (at least one draft of) the chapters dealing with data collection and interpretation (see detailed discussion above), not just because these are the "meat" of the thesis, but because execution of these dissertation components will restructure the content and format of other chapters and sections—e.g., critical review of the literature, statement of the problem, hypotheses, rationale for the study, even though these latter topics officially precede methodology, data-processing, analysis and interpretation, and "discussion" in chapter order. My preference, dictated by the "hydraulics" of the parts of the dissertation system, is to rework chapters on the bibliography and theory—after all, the proposal, if done properly, was a first draft of these chapters—after doing a first draft of the "meat" chapters.

Writing Versus Submission Order.

The questions of writing order and submission order are distinct. If one is lucky enough to have an enlightened and reality-oriented dissertation committee, it is advantageous to submit the methodology and hypotheses-testing chapters first; if the faculty approves these infrastructure chapters, there is no way, short of an intervening decline into senility, that they are going to fail you on superstructural chapters, such as critical review of the literature. The reverse is not unfailingly true; many a negotiator of preliminary chapters, including the one on theoretical models, has been brought up short by faculty rejection of the central procedures and analysis chapters. Enlightened committees being rare birds, the candidate is most likely going to have to submit the chapters in standard *seriatim* order. Notwithstanding, substantial drafts of the central chapters should precede redrafting of the other chapters, if the latter are to make consistent sense in the final draft of the entire dissertation.

Finding and Keeping a Suitable Typist.

Even the most proficient of amateur typist dissertation writers will want to have those versions of chapters shown to faculty professionally typed. Additionally, candidates who write in longhand may want intermediate versions typed up to get a better sense of how they flow. Thesis typing demands special technical and emotional skills. Manuscripts, especially social science ones, are apt to be filled with tables, charts, figures, diagrams, graphs that require enormous care in getting rows and columns of figures in the right places. The nature of dissertation research and writing practically guarantees that the candidate will have to make *changes* in materials already submitted to and typed up by one's typist. The ABD should make it quite explicit to his prospective typist that sudden alterations, sometimes eleventh-hour ones, can be expected. Although one's typist is not on twenty-four-hour duty, there is an on-call requirement to dissertation typing (e.g., your committee is scheduled to read your data-analysis chapter tomorrow, and you've discovered two sections which simply must be changed and retyped today) not involved with most manuscripts. If the typist is not willing to live with this changing—and often overtime and irregular-hour—situation when you spell it out, you must look elsewhere.

The other consideration with a dissertation typist is, parallel to the bottom-line requirement for one's adviser, that he/she is staying put in your location for the working period of the thesis—anywhere up to two years. It is most unsettling and delaying to project completion to change typists in mid-dissertation, since the initial typist will have

133

learned your whole style of abbreviations, editorial markings, grammatical and spelling quirks, which the second typist will now have to learn anew.

I recommend "shopping around" for a dissertation typist, not in the sense of getting the best price, but finding a sanguine combination of technical, attitudinal and stable-residence qualities. Money should be very little object here, since the project is so vital to the rest of one's working life.[12] Actually, a good dissertation typist can sometimes transcend his/her official role and function as a help agent and friend in times of dissertation distress or frenzy (see Chapter Seven). Unless you are absolutely strapped for money, I advise *paying* someone to do the job, rather than having it typed as a "favor" by a friend, lover, secretary or spouse. These various unwary acquaintances and intimates are not going to put up with the peculiar demands dissertation typing will make on them, so your thesis may be delayed, and/or your friendship jeopardized.

Often, the best way to get the proper typist is by referral from a friend or colleague who has done his dissertation or a similar long manuscript. I contacted my dissertation typist in that fashion. For the following six or eight months I lugged myself and chapters up five floors to his Greenwich Village apartment. But his competence, availability and even input into the manuscript (questioning here, editing there) were worth the foot-pounds and dollars expended. Sometimes the working relationship forged in the fire of dissertation writing develops into an extended one, where the typist/colleague handles subsequent books (this was not the case with me and my typist, since he went on to become a child psychoanalyst!), dispensing with the hassles of writer and typist having to get to know each other with every major new project.

SUMMARY.

There are four major components in executing the dissertation: (1) collection of data; (2) analysis and interpretation of one's findings; (3) writing the dissertation chapters; (4) presenting the unfolding dissertation to supervising faculty. This chapter deals with the first three components, and their most important subissues.

(1) The candidate has a choice between three general data collection approaches:

a. procedures which involve no collection of original data on the ABD's part, e.g., using library sources or survey data;

b. research which involves limited and highly structured data collection from subjects or groups, e.g., administration of questionnaires to classes or experiments to college student subjects;

c. long-term continuous collection of data from groups, e.g., participant observation.

The advantages and disadvantages of each approach are considered. The hazards of using participant observation as one's primary dissertation data collection method are detailed; the candidate is advised to opt for some combination of a. and b. approaches.

Some standards for determining just how much data to collect are offered, with an argument for gathering too much material rather than too little, since a filtering and sifting process inevitably occurs from the time of initial collection to eventual selection of those data for inclusion in the later dissertation drafts.

(2) The author considers with the reader how to handle four problematic issues/situations, most of which he will confront in his analysis and interpretation of the data:

a. determining whether one's hypotheses are confirmed by the evidence at statistically significant levels; herein of the difference between descriptive and analytic (power) statistics; and the concept of "near-significance";

b. handling troublesome, inconsistent or contradictory data impacting on one's dissertation from "external" data sources; herein of the uses of "serendipity" to extricate oneself;

c. dealing with hypotheses-disconfirming results from "internal" data, i.e., one's own originally collected data; herein of controversial postproposal, during-research hypotheses revisions, and additional data collection not indicated or foreseen at proposal time;

d. whether, when and how to use computers in processing and analyzing dissertation data; the author offers a demystification of computers and an analysis of computer subculture norms and ideology to calm the typically frightened, uninitiated ABD as he approaches the machine room.

(3) Important questions and strategies involved in actually writing the dissertation chapters are considered:

   a. just what chapters should/must the dissertation minimally include;
   b. the necessity of outlining chapters prior to drafting them is underscored;
   c. how to determine when a chapter is "ready" to show to faculty;
   d. scheduling the writing of various chapters—which to write first and which subsequently; herein of the difference between order of writing and presenting to faculty;
   e. the importance of patiently contracting with a typist who is reliable, emotionally adaptable and flexible enough for solid performance on the long-term and often odd-working-hours dissertation.

NOTES

1. Howard Becker et al., *Boys in White: Student Culture in Medical School* (Chicago: University of Chicago Press, 1961); E. Smigel, *The Wall Street Lawyer: Professional Organization Man?* (Glencoe: The Free Press, 1964); Paul Montagna, "Bureaucracy and Change in Large Professional Organizations; A Functional Analysis of Large Public Accounting Firms," unpublished doctoral dissertation, New York University, 1967.
2. Collected data not incorporated in the dissertation can sometimes find a place in articles or books subsequently spun off. See Chapter Nine.
3. For the past two decades, one influential school, Synanon House, has insisted that narcotic addicts are best cured by exposure to a firm, patriarchal, family-type therapeutic community. Cf., L. Yablonsky, *Synanon: The Tunnel Back* (Baltimore: Penguin Books, 1967).
4. I understand serendipitous data to refer to unexpected findings in research. Often, they initially appear contrary or inexplicable in relation to one's paradigm. But often, too, they can be turned to one's advantage.
5. Note the stress on *majority*; in my study, twelve of fourteen hypotheses were confirmed, two rejected in favor of the null hypothesis.
6. Cf., "Isaac Newton and the Fudge Factor," *Science,* February 1973; Robert Merton's discussions of the interplay between theory building and research data, as well as his praise for serendipitous analysis (both of which themes contradict, in my view, his attack upon and rejection of

what he terms *post factum* theory building). *Social Theory and Social Structure* (New York: Free Press, 2nd ed., 1968).

7. Hammond, ed., *Sociologists at Work: Essays on the Craft of Social Research* (New York: Basic Books, 1974).

8. E. Goffman, *Asylums: Essays on the Social Situation of Mental Patients and Other Inmates* (Chicago: Aldine, 1961); J. Nance, *The Gentle Tasaday* (New York: Harcourt Brace Jovanovich, 1975).

9. See, for example, R. Bierstedt's vintage demystifying critique of S. Dodd's mathematical models of society, in "Real and Nominal Definitions in Sociological Theory," In L. Gross, ed., *Symposium in Sociological Theory* (Evanston, Illinois: Row, Peterson, 1959).

10. Somehow or other, the candidate must bring to the dissertation project a minimum level of writing ability. Absent this, the case is futile. Most ABDs clear this hurdle. It *may* be possible to improve beyond bare competence by consulting books such as Zinsser, *On Writing Well: An Informal Guide to Writing Nonfiction,* 2nd ed. (New York: Harper and Row, 1980).

11. *New York Times Book Review* section, April 13, 1980.

12. By this point, the candidate has so much time and money invested in the dissertation project that hesitating or obsessing over an indispensable expenditure of, say, $500 is myopic. Besides, the IRS may allow typing and xeroxing costs as a deduction for job training (check the current regulations).

CHAPTER 6

The Unfolding Dissertation: Diplomatic Relations with Your Committee

Relations with faculty, as one's dissertation unfolds, can be the most anxiety-creating component of the process because the candidate has the least control over this element. Earlier chapters have had much to say about the generally unsatisfactory and often haphazard departmental conditions under which one selects, or is assigned, a proposal/dissertation committee. Naturally, the problems emergent from such selection circumstances at the proposal stage tend to continue into the dissertation stage, although now, necessarily increased contact with second and third committee members may actualize or exacerbate difficulties and conflicts which were latent at proposal time. The candidate faces two basic sets of dissertation negotiation issues: 1. those with the committee/department as a whole; 2. those with individual members of his committee. The first set involves structural conditions and strategies that almost all candidates will face—normal, inevitable bases everyone has to touch, inevitable hurdles one has to jump. The second set often gets us into the psychological context of the "abnormal": here, contract negotiation and general human relations skills which stand the candidate in good stead for the first set of issues are of limited use; most often, the candidate has drawn a particular kind of "problem professor" through chance, and dealing with him/her effectively may require psychotherapeutic skills which most ABDs don't possess. Because these second-set problems are so idiosyncratic and tinged with psychopathology, they are much less amenable to general suggestion or solution.

ISSUES WITH THE COMMITTEE AS A WHOLE.
Keeping in Touch Down at the Department.

I have noted a tendency on the part of dissertation writers to cut down—or off—their communications with their committee and department. Immersion in the thesis necessarily creates a sense of going it alone, a reluctance to show it or share it with anybody before it is done. Such commendable unswerving attention to the materials of the dissertation per se has, however, to be tempered with action along the contract and diplomatic fronts of the dissertation course.

It is absolutely essential that the candidate present his unfolding dissertation, preferably *chapter by chapter,* for approval to as many committee members as possible (again, preferably to all of them, but always to the adviser and second most interested faculty member). Remember that the collected and analyzed data are most probably going to dictate important changes from the original proposal's theory and methodology. Assuming the contract model is explicitly—or, more often, implicitly—in effect in one's program, the "other party" must be consulted when the candidate is introducing alterations in his performance. The ABD has to go into the defense with all chapters having been "initialed" by his committee.

What the candidate wants, then, is a reasonably prompt and careful reading of his chapters. Under the best of conditions, faculty's response to these needs is problematic, but nothing is better calculated to ensure compliance with neither of them than a low to nonexistent profile down at the department. I realize that many ABDs are most reluctant to "make the rounds" of their committee for reasons outlined in earlier chapters. There is no getting around the need for a certain minimum of face-to-face meetings with the adviser and committee members. On the other hand, some of one's lines of communication can be sustained/supplemented by progress letters, notes or phone calls.

The particular importance of the departmental secretary as a conduit for getting through to the chairperson and other faculty is rarely recognized. Like court clerks and bailiffs in the judicial system, he/she is often the real manager of everyday program business. I have known

139

departmental secretaries to make or break an ABD's thesis by reliably and sympathetically conveying messages from him to the "boss," or "forgetting" about them. Departmental secretaries are also important—even determinant—in scheduling times for defenses and even arranging which faculty (sympathetic or hostile) end up hearing one's dissertation. Without being unctuous (but not embarrassed either; it's part of "taking care of business" and protecting oneself) about it, the candidate should make a reasonable effort to get on friendly terms with the departmental secretaries and administrative assistants.

Being Pulled in Different Directions.

It is not uncommon for different members of one's committee to prefer or even demand that the dissertation stress different areas or, worse, treat the data from irreconcilable perspectives adhered to by one or another professor. Elaborating other areas is not so devastating a demand to comply with as writing a thesis from contradictory angles.

You might ask whether the dissertation proposal wasn't designed to head off just these kinds of dilemmas. Proposal approvals often *do* avoid the worst of them. On the other hand, second and third members tend to read and even hear the proposal (at the hearing) with less than the keenest attention and interest (recall the manner in which they are recruited).

Postproposal appointments with individual members may be helpful in bringing out contradictory demands of faculty which were incompletely voiced at the hearing. Even so, it is in the nature of faculty attitudes toward dissertation supervision that the first time other-than-adviser members of a committee really take the work in progress seriously, read it with care, generate objections to it may be when the candidate starts bringing full chapters around. Perhaps only then do many faculty believe the *candidate* is serious about it. In any event, such "delayed reaction" on the part of the other members is all the more reason for making sure each chapter is presented in turn to all members before drafting the next one. It is usually pointless to argue that postproposal faculty objections violate their end of the contract, because of the peculiarly "flexible" nature of this type of contract. Only in the (very rare) case where a committee member completely reversed his endorsement and rejected the proposal—rather than demanded changes—would recourse to legalistic interpretation of the proposal be called for, and probably decided in the candidate's favor.

Before dealing with "irreconcilable demands" about how he should write his thesis, a candidate must ascertain whether the demands are truly mutually exclusive and, even if they are, whether both faculty members "mean business" with their required lines of thesis inquiry. For example, in sociology almost all substantive fields in which a dissertation might be written can be approached from the "functionalist" or "conflict" perspective, institutional interpretations which have been conventionally construed as contradictory in their assumptions. Since most graduate faculty subscribe to one version or another of these two positions, it is not uncommon for an ABD to feel torn in two directions by committee members of opposite functional/conflict persuasions. However, recent sociology has witnessed the emergence of a "hybrid" model which posits institutional structure and process as determined by both cooperative and conflictive moments.[1] This accommodative paradigm has extricated many a recent political science or sociology ABD from a theretofore genuine thesis dilemma.

If the demands of two thesis supervisors are truly irreconcilable, then one has to look to how committed the faculty members are in sticking to or enforcing the implementation of their positions in one's dissertation. Mention has already been made of offhand, casual critiques and suggestions—most of which are quickly forgotten—"thrown out" at the proposal drafting and hearing stages. Getting to the bottom line of committee members' requirements for a dissertation involves the aforementioned round of postproposal appointments, where a candidate has to probe subtly, prod gently, particular faculty's recall of points raised earlier, objections, suggestions for inclusions. I say subtly because dissertation annals are filled with stories about candidates' "volunteering" for months of extra research and writing. If, after this round of reinquiry, one of the members backs off from his position, or neglects to mention his earlier insistence on, say, a functionalist approach, while the other faculty member continues to be outspoken in requiring a conflict perspective of theory and methodology, this particular problem *may* be laid to rest. It is always possible, on the other hand, for the functionalist advocate to raise again his objections at a later point in the dissertation, for example, after he sees the first chapter. If the dilemma reappears, one has to pursue a strategy of *role-partner confrontation*.

Resolution Through Role-Set Analysis.

Chapter Two contained an extensive discussion of the ABD's critical social relations, summarized by Figure 2.1. Let us recall and further elaborate here the *student* status of that configuration:

Figure 6.1: The Role Set of the ABD's Student Status

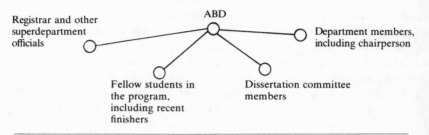

Figure 6.2 presents an enlargement and differentiation of an ABD-thesis committee segment of the role cluster where role conflict and strain are present:

Figure 6.2: The ABD and His Thesis Committee

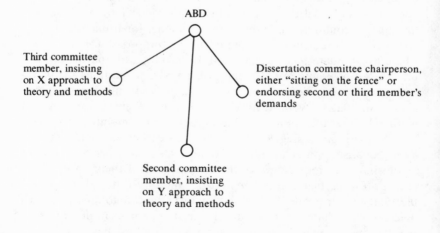

Robert Merton had devised strategies for minimizing or defusing contradictory demands made on a status incumbent by his role partners.[2] When possible, compartmentalization of interactions with various partners is useful: e.g., a young woman dates various men on different evenings; presidential candidate Lincoln talks abolition to Pennsylvania voters, and protection of slavery to the Georgia electorate. Another strategy, possible in some contexts, is to heed some role partners and relatively ignore others: faculty tend to invest more time and interest in publishing and research roles, for example, than in dissertation supervision, after a calculation that the latter activity counts for little in career mobility.

But neither compartmentalizing or avoidance of some role partners' demands are going to work for an ABD if he has already gone "one-on-one" with his several committee members and determined that two or more are adamant about his pursuing contradictory approaches in his dissertation. Given this type of situation, Merton suggests the approach of throwing the *incumbent's problem into the role partners'* laps. Indicated strategy is the ABD's presenting the dilemma before the entire committee. The argument runs that it is unconscionable for a committee to place a good-faith candidate in an impossible middle, not of his own doing, especially after his proposal has been passed. By laying the entire issue out on the table in the presence of all the role partners, it is hoped that the depth and pain of the dilemma will be seen by everybody. There may well be a fight among the committee, but resolution, at least for the candidate, of the issue should result. Such resolution may entail the resignation from the committee of the member whose position lost, but, given his continuing hostility, his departure is desirable.

The ease with which committee-member role conflicts can be resolved depends on the stance of the adviser. If he takes Y's or X's side, just from the social-psychological principle of "two-against-one," capitulation by the odd-person-out might be predicted, particularly since colleagues are generally (but not always) deferential to the position of the primary dissertation adviser. If one's adviser is diffident or undecided (either generally or on the specific controversy), matters get stickier. In such a case, the candidate must persuade him that he is more comfortable in writing the dissertation from one angle rather than the other and calmly suggest that it is, in fact, the adviser's duty in the role set to facilitate the dissertation by supporting the candidate's endeavor. How successful these final negotiations will be is too often dependent on the "personal relationships" between candidate and adviser to suit this writer, but with this particular thesis snag, matters sometimes boil down to such personality factors.

If all strategies, including confrontation of role partners, fail to resolve the issue, the only place left to go, it seems, is the department chairperson. Such recourse should be taken only after it is very clear that all other remedies have been exhausted. One danger is wounded *amour propre*: academia is unfortunately filled with prima donnas; "going over the head" of this type of supervising faculty member may result in his continual sniping at your dissertation effort in large and small ways for the next year. The other danger is closing ranks: the chairperson may be bureaucratically opposed to "departure from channels" and refuse to intervene. Nonetheless, for some small minority of ABDs, there will come a time when "going to see the man," with all its possible backfires, is the only path left.

Faculty Demands for Unanticipated Revisions.

Sometimes the problem is not inconsistent demands from faculty role partners, but one or more dissertation committee members insisting that the candidate revise his thesis, often in ways to which he is strongly opposed and/or which will require months more of research and writing time. It is in the nature of the flexible proposal/dissertation contract that one must be prepared for at least some modification requirements on the part of faculty; after all, I have tried to indicate that the candidate *himself* will probably see the logic and need for alterations as the research and analysis of his data proceeds. The difficulty becomes acute when the writer's changes are not coincident with those demanded by faculty.

The candidate is tightrope walking—at both the proposal and dissertation stage—between alienating his committee by entertaining no version of the dissertation but his own, and becoming servile (and hopelessly confused) by bending to every whim or suggested change in direction thrown out by one committee member or another. Although the following discussion urges capitulation if matters come to either that or indefinite suspension of concluding, an ABD should certainly stick to his guns until it becomes quite clear that the committee is not buying his arguments. In my experience, committees will often accede, even against their own views and objections, to the candidate's preferred treatment of basic issues, if they perceive him as on top of the material, and if he persists in a dignified and firm manner.

Although I won't repeat them here, one must follow indicated procedures (see preceding section) for establishing (a) just how new and/or conflictive faculty demands actually relate to the current version of the dissertation; sometimes they can be accommodated or incorporated without excessive difficulties; (b) just how serious and mandatory the committee's demands for change are.

After the candidate has completed the calculus of determining just what revisions simply "won't go away," they should be slotted into primary and secondary/tertiary categories of importance. The latter category, no matter how such changes irk one as silly, capricious or just plain wrong, should be completed forthwith. It is dissertation-destructive to take any kind of stand on matters that do not go to the heart or guts of the dissertation and/or require relatively little extra work. If you are planning to derive a book or a number of articles from your dissertation, you can note that these materials will be excised from the published versions.

Primary required revisions are of two types in terms of their emotional consequences: (a) "affectively-neutral" revisions and/or additions in methodology or theory. A faculty member may insist upon inclusion of another control group, or more elaborated discussion of an alternative theoretical model, or execution of additional statistical procedures in the analysis of the data. I have in mind here various operations which may require substantial library or field research—some of which the candidate may well believe are not necessary—but which are still generally "resonant" with the central themes of one's own draft. In my judgment—after one has made very sure that such changes are unconditionally expected—these types of primary revisions should be carried through without a whimper, sustained by the knowledge that one is generally "home free" on their completion.

(b) "affectively-laden" revisions and/or additions. One of my acquaintances wrote his sociology dissertation on bureaucracy under a leading "authority" at a major eastern university. His theoretical paradigm was a Marxist/conflict one; the adviser's was a hard-line anti-Marxist functionalist view of bureaucracy. It took three drafts and almost four years for my friend to finish. He knew all along that the adviser would veto the Marxist versions (the first draft was polar Marxist, the second one, "temperate" Marxist) but felt that to write the dissertation which the adviser would approve would be to cut the theoretical and ideological guts out of it, and to "sell his soul" through such a capitulation. I have no doubt that the approved third draft contained the adviser's rather than my friend's sociological voice on bureaucracies (although the distance between the two in this particular case was perhaps an extreme, atypical illustration of student-adviser "dissertation dissonance.") I would take issue, however, with the need for so much self-questioning and agony of four dissertation writing and revising years, and certainly with the *dissertation myth* that he had "sold his soul," a feeling which still continues to bother him years later.

Lying behind the dissertation myth of "selling out" is an exaggerated notion of the importance of one's dissertation. It is related to the myth of the dissertation as perfect, or as *magnum opus*. People's souls are simply not consigned to the devil, or even purgatory, for the "misdemeanor" sins committed against others, self or conscience in writing a doctoral dissertation. My friend had lost sight of the only reason for writing a dissertation: to get a doctorate. The dissertation became a "symbol" for him of progressive political identity, righteous opposition to the oppression of dissenting students by Establishment faculty and Lord knows what else. During the three years that he held out, he was consigned to insecure part-time teaching positions; wiser in my view to have given in, and then, with the credential problem behind, to write a streak of books pursuing the polemic. In fact, he is now writing such books, but three or four long years later than they might have been produced.

No more than the observer in the "tearoom" could my friend convincingly plead shock, surprise or indignation at the "goings on" of his adviser. Indeed, he had been the adviser's fair-haired boy through much of his earlier course work, and even qualifying examinations. While, as I have pointed out, faculty do have a way of cutting students loose as soon as they become ABDs (which *is* grounds for legitimate shock), they rarely change their theoretical and ideological stripes. Certainly, this particular ABD knew in depth the functionalist views of bureaucracy held by his adviser. Put in this context of preknowledge, the earlier drafts seem almost like kamikaze dissertation missions.

In my current view of "dissertation ethics," the inherently relatively

146

minor social and human-relations consequences of doctoral research exercises, combined with the *self-chosen, insider, and achieved status of the ABD,* relegate "soul-searching" to the categories of dissertation diversion and dissertation self-sabotage.

ISSUES WITH INDIVIDUAL COMMITTEE MEMBERS.

With just a little bit of bad luck, the student is going to run into at least one of the "bad apples" depicted below, where faculty conflicts and differences about the dissertation can get "personal." However, one has to be very careful before reaching a judgment that the essence of a difficulty with a faculty member stems from specific "chemistry" between him and the candidate. The odds are against a personalistic interpretation in large-enrollment doctoral programs, since, as we have seen, faculty are skeptical or reluctant about getting involved in students' projects; they doubt serious student intentions, and proposal and dissertation supervising score few points for faculty careers. *Dissertation paranoia* consists largely of misinterpreting the general skepticism, cynicism, indifference or even outright hostility that graduate professors often develop toward ABDs as more specifically, even exclusively, focused on a particular candidate. Of course, it is not pleasant to be the target of even generalized negative and dysfunctional attitudes and actions, but if Professor X is a bastard to *all* his advisees, one deals with the problem in a different manner than if one is being singled out. For example, the possibility of a successful protest to the chairperson is greatly enhanced if five ABDs will attest to disturbed behavior or maltreatment on the part of the same faculty adviser (although when the chips are down, doctoral students rarely will take the chance of uniting in protest for fear of being ejected from a program where faculty have nearly all the power).

But whether your "bad apple" exhibits character aberrations in general or with you in particular, there is no easy management of the problem. The offending character trait should be considered in terms of the differential dissertation association calculus; if, for example, the thesis committee member is heavily into S and M in his leather-lined den at home but is able to tear himself away from such fantasies long enough to critique your analysis of variance helpfully down at his bare-walled office, go right on by his extra-dissertation deviance. Sometimes character aberrations of graduate professors can actually be very *useful* to the ABD: I have found methodologists (as a group, certainly with exceptions) to be startlingly fussy, overcautious, compulsively self-doubting types. Psychoanalysts would call them "anal." On the other hand, if one can get past all that, these people are excellent for designing airtight, fail-safe experimental designs.

Unfortunately, there are other faculty members whose personality problems cannot be defused as irrelevant to the progress of a dissertation or used to promote its progress actively. Here I can only signal some of the most common types of "problem professors," whose socio- or psychopathologies can be most disruptive to a dissertation. The ABD should be on the lookout for such faculty and avoid them from the start if possible; otherwise, make every effort to replace them as thesis committee members if matters have gone too far. To attempt a list of specific tactics for avoidance or replacement would be doomed to banality, since the variations for particular interpersonal contexts and conflicts between problem professors and ABDs are so enormous. The ABD must weigh the variables of his own role relation with his unwelcome partner, set in the larger frame of departmental politics, in deciding how to solve this stubborn and unfair (unfair even within a general context of unfairness) obstacle to dissertation completion. Here is a "Least Wanted List" of dissertation problem professors:

The "Young Turk" Professor,

who has recently received his doctorate. Anxious to identify himself with his new faculty reference group and put distance between himself and the old student peers, this type of junior faculty member can break one's dissertation chops in a manner less frequently found among older, somewhat more compassionate faculty veterans. Socialization to the new collegial group may involve, in his marginal, immature view of matters, being "tough" with the graduate students from whose ranks he has recently departed. His career aspirations and hang-ups can easily translate themselves into your dissertation hang-ups and delays, produced by his hypercriticisms.[3]

The "Career ABD" Professor,

who himself took a decade to write a thesis—often because *his* angry adviser had preceded *him* with a ten-year-long effort—and at some level wants you to live through the same hell he (and his predecessors) did. Such a dissertation delayer may well not be in touch with these feelings and couch his thesis-advising neurosis in authentic-sounding rationalizations, such as "soak in it some more," or "these things can't be rushed," which are certainly sage enough counsel up to a point—which he always exceeds. There isn't much an ABD can do with this type of entrenched character disorder. If such a professor ends up as your adviser, you must make every effort to replace him.

The Sadistic Professor,

who uses his position of faculty power to ventilate upon an ABD personal and career rages in a manner that entails little risk of being censored or sanctioned. This is a most virulent type of problem professor who can conceal much of his pathology under catch phrases like "demand for rigor," "upholding of standards," and the like. With such a man or woman the candidate has to take action, either by joining with fellow students similarly tortured, or by denouncing him to other professors and/or the chairperson.

The Sexist Professor,

(man or woman) who converts the dissertation into a flirtation, emptying conferences of any value for furthering the thesis. Obviously, there are degrees of unacceptable and dysfunctional behavior in this area. Like American society in general, academic society is overwhelmingly sexist in climate. A female ABD is bound to be exposed to a certain amount of patronizing and manipulative behavior from male thesis committee members. Some women recently reported hostile and thesis-delaying behavior on the part of male *homosexual* graduate faculty. The cross-combinations of intergender sexism are rather numerous in late twentieth-century academia. But sexist banterings, pseudo-chivalry, "dirty jokes" and innuendos, as annoying and offensive as they undoubtedly are, are not in and of themselves threatening enough to the thesis to cause a search for new committee members. An ABD has to have a thicker skin than *this*, whether dealing with faculty, respondents or groups being researched. It is only when the sexual dimension (or tension) becomes the *core* of the role relationship between ABD and faculty member, occluding attention to the dissertation, that a change must be made.

Feminists may be unhappy with my position here, but this book is

149

concerned almost exclusively with completing the thesis: deep-rooted sexism is still a fact of graduate university structure and hierarchy. Parts of it (like pseudo-chivalry) can actually be exploited by a woman. Time is probably on the side of feminism, but I believe the feminist ABD has to suspend her struggle for that ongoing cause during two years of the dissertation struggle since the latter will demand every bit of her energy, strength and interest. Writing her dissertation within a context of sexist faculty-student relations is not "selling her soul," contrary to some conventional rhetoric on this point. Two years later, she can return to the battlefield with the added ammunition of the doctorate in hand.

The "Hamlet-Complex" Professor,

who doubts every version of your thesis, often rejecting his own earlier endorsements of which research tacks to pursue. This type of faculty member can delay and frustrate a candidate to desperation with advisory approaches such as, "All the data is never in," or, "The question can be looked at from virtually an infinite number of angles," or, "On the one hand this, but on the other hand . . ." or (maddeningly), "Let's go back to square one, for argument's sake. Suppose you started with X model instead of Y. What kind of data would you collect then? [this after four months of data collection along lines of model Y] Have you given that alternative some thought?" Generally, such men and women are neurotic doubters in their own lives and projects.

It is true that doubt and skepticism (as texts on the logic of scientific inquiry constantly point out) are part and parcel of scientific advance, and neurotic doubting can hide behind these venerated scientific cautions, up to a point. But there comes a time when one has to take a chance (all science is ultimately based on probability; not certainty, but assumptions), go with one thought-through version of theory and related research, and rest one's case. Otherwise, dissertations would remain forever locked in your office desk with you as the only reader. Faced with a neurotic doubter on your committee, the best strategy is to use his doubts as long as they pose legitimate objections or critiques to your dissertation direction; but when the point of usefulness is passed, then one must take a firm stand against getting sucked into the professor's vortex of infinite uncertainty. Psychotherapists have found

150

that doubters (fundamentally persons with low ego-image) respect, even welcome, limits and lines drawn by others. The candidate has to say, "Enough is enough," politely, but with strength and conviction.

The "Passive-Aggressive" Professor,

who superficially presents himself as "friend" of the candidate but contradicts that goodwill by large and small acts of dissertation sabotage. Often he "promises you anything" but gives you nothing, or worse. Passive-aggressive professors don't like students and/or specific role obligations, such as dissertation supervising. On the other hand, they feel guilty about such role aversions. *Passive,* indirect aggression is the compromise between hostility and guilt. It surfaces in behavior such as unreasonable delays in reading one's unfolding chapters, or violation of a promise to support your dissertation's stance in negotiations with other committee members. In dealing with the delays and even perfidies of such professors, the candidate's best weapon is exploitation of the guilt component of this neurosis. When push comes to shove, the passive-aggressive's need for conveying a socially conformist, norm-abiding image will generally prevail over his indirect aggression (at least long enough for you to get him to read your materials).

The Jealous or Envious Professor,

who senses, sometimes accurately, that you are already, or potentially, cleverer in the field than he. Thus, you are perceived as a threat to him, and every possible action will be taken to head off your completion. As with several of the previously noted hard-core neurotic types, there isn't much constructive reasoning together to be achieved with a green-with-envy supervisor, and whenever possible one has to replace him, or at least relegate him to a back-burner committee status.

Problem Professors, Candidates' Problems and the Psychoanalytic Subculture.

In actual cases, advising professors often possess more than one dissertation-destructive trait. For example, continued dissatisfaction with successive drafts of your work may stem from a combination of a professor having spent ten years in the dissertation-writing salt mines

151

himself, combined with a compulsive self-doubting neurosis; one could have a psychoanalytic field day speculating on the reciprocal causes and effects of neurotic doubting, perfectionism and a history of ten years down in the dissertation dumps. Whatever the problem, the ABD's major effort must be spent on eliminating or minimizing it. Elimination of such a problem professor is the preferable course; it dispenses with the need to practice "psychotherapy" where the need to practice dissertation writing is already quite demanding enough. If one has to "live with" a nonreplaceable problem professor, the candidate willy-nilly gets caught up in some "lay" psychoanalyzing and psychotherapeutic "cooling-out" techniques.

I have noticed that in some fields students *and* faculty actually seem to expect—even *like*—some of these interpersonal problem processes, particularly in psychology. Many of my psychology doctoral candidates (most often those in some version of a clinical program) appear to see their dissertation difficulties as rooted in the "father complex" or "passive-aggressive" neurosis of their advisers as in any matters to do with the substantive and methodological issues of their experiments. I suspect that the culture of clinical psychology is a kind of "intervening variable" in a few selected fields of dissertation course and negotiation, although ABDs may overemphasize it, to the neglect of the objective issues of their projects. Beyond psychology programs, it is my strong but undocumented impression that ABDs in *all* fields are overrepresented in the population of psychotherapy patients.[4] To what extent they are in therapy because of the dissertation problem is also very difficult to determine. It may also be that graduate *faculty* are overrepresented as an occupational group as patients. All this is by way of saying that a significant minority of ABDs and professors may well be wrapped up in the "cult of personality," whatever the field of dissertation, and that such involvements spill over to the student-adviser relationship, producing a measure of both the interpersonal difficulties I've outlined, as well as suggesting potential resolutions.

My own view is that such "hidden-agenda" extra-dissertation interpersonal processes, where both students and faculty see themselves "working through" emotional blocks, are dangerous to a candidate, since they tend to root success of the thesis in the shaky ground of personal friendships and "understandings" (which, as we have seen, are subject to radical reversal, change and even disappearance), rather than in compliance with the proposal and dissertation contract. The "psychoanalytic factor" is most salient in elitist programs, particularly in the northeast (most particularly in New York City, the seat of psychoanalytic sub-culture and practice). Looking to the rest of the nation, I believe ABDs are less likely to encounter it; even when present, its urgency or prominence for successful negotiation of the dissertation course will probably be comparatively small. Even in psychoanalytic culture departments, the ABD should make every effort—albeit avoiding pariah-like labels of "not being in touch with himself" or "hostile"—to put the dissertation project back on the clearer tracks of his proposal contract. That is, unless he too is caught up in notions of the dissertation as encounter group or therapy. If such is the case, my experience predicts an additional dimension of dissertation *tsures* diabolically conducive to ABD anomie.

THE "PANZER DIVISION" ANALOGY OF AN UNFOLDING DISSERTATION.

Let me conclude the two chapters on the struggle to write the dissertation in perhaps appropriate martial fashion. My advisees find the "dissertation army" analogy useful:

Figure 6.3: Assault on the Doctor's Degree, Earlier Campaign Phase

COMPLETED DISSERTATION

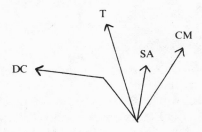

The dissertation army is composed of one's various major files. The goal of the struggle and campaign is to reach completion and defense. No matter how closely strategists study Clausewitz, some divisions always move ahead of or straggle behind others. For example, in the ABDs' battle for the dissertation (see Figure 6.3) his theoretical elaboration (T) and sustained contact with committee members (CM) may forge ahead of his statistical analysis (SA) of incoming data, and his data collection (DC) might not simply be behind battlefield schedule but actually deviate from the dissertation scheme. As "general" of all the "divisions' of the file, the candidate must keep deploying and repositioning divisions and maintaining supply lines (i.e., here input into various files), so as to end up with the following alignment of his dissertation army:

Figure 6.4: Assault on the Doctor's Degree, Later Campaign Stage, Nearing D Day

COMPLETED DISSERTATION

Without pursuing the metaphor excessively, ultimately the arrows/thrusts (see Figure 6.4) represent chapters of the dissertation developed out of major files.

SUMMARY.
Presenting the dissertation to the faculty can involve two basic kinds of problems: 1. structural issues with the committee as a whole, that most candidates face, one way or another, as a matter of dissertation course; 2. difficulties with a particular professor that take one into the realm of psychology, and often abnormal psychology.
The first category of issues prominently includes:

a. prompt presentation of unfolding chapters of the dissertation to faculty for prompt critique, suggestions, requests for revisions and approval;
b. managing and reconciling conflicting thesis demands made by different committee members, as to which theoretical and/or methodological directions to develop;

154

c. responding to requests for revisions, including how to determine which faculty demands, made by which faculty, are "ne-
gotiable" and which are "firm";

d. managing ethical or emotional qualms about having "capitu-
lated" or "sold out" in making faculty-required revisions
which go against the grain of one's political ideology, or
against strongly held convictions about what the dissertation
has genuinely demonstrated.

The second category of faculty-presentation problems concerns individual committee members who exhibit some kind of character disorder or neurosis which spills over to and contaminates the thesis
advising, supervising, or judging relationship.

A list of "least-wanted" professors is presented, along with some
brief analysis of probable etiologies of their disorders, and general
advice for freeing oneself from their dissertation-detrimental clutches.
On the least-wanted roll are: the "young Turk" professor; the "career
ABD" professor; the sadistic professor; the sexist professor; the
"Hamlet-complex" professor; the passive-aggressive professor; the
jealous or envious professor.

The candidate is cautioned about the dissertation hazards of involving himself in a psychoanalytic subculture, present in some departments—particularly psychology ones—which make "virtues" out of
some of the disorders displayed by faculty and convert substantive
issues of the dissertation into elusive and mutable "personal" and
"psychogenetic" ones.

In the last section of the chapter, a "Panzer division" metaphor of
the dissertation's "assault" on the doctor's degree is represented by
two final figures.

NOTES

1. Ralf Dahrendorf's "Toward a Theory of Social Conflict," *Journal of
Conflict Resolution,* 11, 1958, was a seminal article in developing the
hybrid model. Such a position was at first vigorously rejected by the
powers-that-be of functionalism (e.g., R. Merton) but eventually accepted as mainstream. One is tempted to suggest that this hybrid model
arose as much to resolve the conflicts of sociology ABDs caught between
two supervisors on opposite sides of the functionalist-conflict paradigm
as to resolve the contradictions in sociological theory per se!

2. Robert Merton, *Social Theory and Social Structure,* 2nd ed. (New York:
Free Press, 1968).

155

3. Recall my earlier suggestion (Chapter Four) that recent graduates of one's doctoral program are a good source of support and information for the ABD. But the reference was not to such people who are superordinates in *your* doctoral program. As "young Turk" assistant professors across town, they may be devils; in the role of until recently "student peer" in your program, they may be helpful angels. The paradox exists only when one doesn't take into account the two different social status contexts that are operative.
4. See Chapter Seven for a discussion of whether psychotherapy is effective in helping dissertation depression.

CHAPTER 7

Down in the Dissertation Dumps: How to Get Out

THE DISSERTATION WAVE.

Figure 7.1 schematizes the dissertation course as a "wave," with the writer sometimes down in the dumps, or troughs, of one or more of the "three Ds"—dissertation depression, doubt or desperation—and sometimes riding the crests of relative elation or satisfaction with the project.

Figure 7.1: Troughs and Crests of the Dissertation Wave

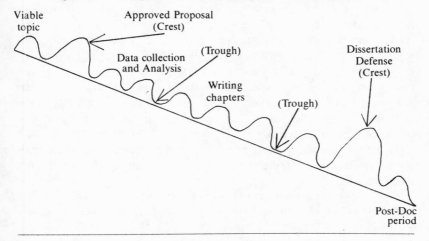

There are two vectors to the dissertation wave's course; one undulates, the other moves steadily downward. The most striking crests are achievement of an approved proposal and successful defense of the thesis, with selection of a viable topic, completion of major data collection and their corresponding analysis, and completion of various dissertation chapters other important high points. Troughs are the between times; when, for example, the data isn't panning out the way you hypothesized, you feel overwhelmed by what's left to be done, you're having trouble with your thesis committee. Note the *trough* trend—Post-Doc—at the end of the dissertation rainbow. Contrary to dissertation mythology, all problems are not vanquished by successful finishing. The book will have more to say about the dangers of post-dissertation depression and defeatism in Chapter Nine, which deals with surviving and professionally benefiting from a thesis.

The downward sweep of the wave figure is designed to convey an image of dissertation momentum building which generally makes successive stages easier; however, one has to stop way short of any assertion that matters are a "slide" from accepted proposal phase onward; there are too many instances of a candidate becoming trapped in a deep trough of fieldwork crisis, data analysis problems, a contrary chapter on discussion of the experiment, to talk about principles of increasing ease in the dissertation course. Trends, certainly; laws, no.

DISSERTATION DUMPS: NORMAL OR PATHOLOGICAL?

Before examining specific dissertation depressions, discouragements, desperations, doubts, let us consider for a moment their clinical connection. Not infrequently, dissertation writers exhibit symptomologies resembling or even duplicating clinical pictures of the neuroses—such as anxiety and hysteria—and even some of the psychoses—such as depression or paranoia. ABDs deep into a thesis will often report that they feel on the verge of a nervous breakdown, or that they are "going crazy." A reader unfamiliar with dissertation course and moods, including a pre- or new ABD, may protest that I am surely exaggerating matters with talk of neuroses and/or psychoses as dissertation-related or even caused. But those in the soup know differently.

Most candidates experience one or more very painful classical symptoms of various clinical syndromes. In my experience, however, these psychopathological symptoms are paradoxically normal and predictable for the dissertation course. It may be true that a certain small percentage of ABDs are "round the bend" before they ever get their hands on a proposal and data analysis, and that such tasks exacerbate a preexisting emotional condition, but I believe that the vast majority of emotional disturbances exhibited during dissertation days date their origins within the thesis period and from the unusual stresses of the course. An analogous situation exists with prison homosexuality: most released prisoners return to preincarcerated heterosexual behavior upon release. One can talk about temporary or condition-based homosexuality. In the same way, one can discuss the "temporary insanity" of the ABD, with the assumption he will be his old nonsymptomatic self when the defense is done. On the other hand, we know that unusually traumatic and prolonged isolating social contexts (e.g., concentration camps, prisons, "reeducation"/brainwashing, solitary confinement) can permanently alter detainees' psyches, particularly if they are not deprogrammed upon release. There is the very real danger that some portion of the lonely, traumatized dissertation writer population may carry dissertation pathology beyond completion into their postdoctoral lives. Accordingly, this chapter identifies the most prominent dissertation emotional disturbances for the reader; offers some etiological light within the framework of the dissertation condition; considers a range of agents, strategies and therapies for heading them off at the start, coping with them once they beset a candidate, or making sure their presence doesn't continue beyond completion of the dissertation.

A CLASSIFICATION OF DISSERTATION ANXIETIES AND DEPRESSIONS.

Candidates' dissertation-caused or -activated anxieties and/or depressions manifest themselves in one or more of three spheres: negative and gloomy feelings about the dissertation itself, particularly about its doubtful outcome; a diminishment of self-esteem; a real or believed deterioration in relationships with significant others, for which the demands of the dissertation are blamed. Within each of these large areas we can list more specific problems. For each we can then further inquire as to whether they are primarily *dissertation myth-derived*: *candidate caused,* through deficiencies in work habits,

159

filing, or motivation; or almost *inevitable consequences* of the structures and processes of the dissertation course. Strategies for overcoming or containing them will vary according to etiological category.

Doubts About the Dissertation Itself.

- "I picked the wrong topic." As we have seen earlier, there is almost no such thing as the wrong topic, particularly at the Chapter-Four stage of the candidate's dissertation, when so much groundwork and prior committee approval and validation (e.g., accepted proposal and earlier chapters) have already been won. *The wrong topic myth* has to be clearly recognized as just that. Recognizing this, the candidate must make every effort to put this type of self-sabotaging anxiety out of his mind.

- "The data's come out wrong." Chapter Five took pains to point out that when one is talking dissertation and research data, "right" and "wrong" are not terms which accurately describe the realities of analytic procedure. Almost invariably, at least some of the data does not pan out according to initial hypotheses and model, and one must revise and often reenter the field with new measuring instruments. A candidate suffering from "wrong data" anxiety or depression has overbought the myth of the *a priori dissertation,* which introductory methodology texts and formal departmental guidelines most often push.[1] What is necessary here is a restructuring of attitudes toward acceptable/prevailing scientific procedure, with an emphasis on serendipity and the revisionist models outlined in Chapters Four and Five of this book.

- "Nothing comes; I can't write another word; the well's gone dry." Periods of blockage are inevitable in long-distance writing, but the intensity of depression and despair will be aggravated if the ABD suscribes to the *myth of the easy dissertation,* that others are gliding right through with no blockages. A negative self-fulfilling prophecy is often seen in blocked periods: the more one bemoans stoppage, the more pronounced it becomes. The only way out here—a procedure which requires much courage—is to put in the daily time at the office whether the juices are running or not. If you've laid the groundwork with your files, it's virtually impossible that your dissertation well of ideas is truly exhausted; immersion in the files will—a few days sooner or later—prime the pump once more. The absolutely *worst* possible path is to lay off the thesis, take some kind

160

of R & R; upon return from a three-week break, in my experience, the trail will be colder than ever.

- "I can't see the end; I'm overwhelmed by what's still left to do; I'm never going to finish the damn thing." There is no gainsaying that the dissertation is a very long project with many hills to ascend. One might liken the experience to that of explorers who, expecting the source of the Nile over the next hill, reach its crest only to find another hill, and so on. But the analogy really doesn't hold, since the ABD has a "map" for his dissertation course in the form of proposal and file which expeditionary forces don't possess. The "map" allows him to look ahead and see the dissertation course as finite and finishable.

The *myth of the perfect dissertation* may be aggravating matters here. No dissertation, or, for that matter, no book, is ever "perfect," or absolutely finished. All successful doctoral candidates and book writers can think of ten important changes they would have liked to have made within days after a project's final defense or press date. But ten changes later, the dissatisfaction would be renewed. I often suspect that after, say, two drafts of a dissertation, further revisions don't make a thesis better, merely different. One is reminded of Camus' character in *The Plague,* who spends his life rewriting the first sentence of his novel—endless versions of horses trotting down the Champs Elysées. Candidates with relatively low ego-strength are peculiarly vulnerable to the "neurosis" of compulsive "disserta-.ion revision," (beyond the bounds of necessary changes in hypotheses in line with emerging data), too eager to pursue self- or faculty-suggested "new angles" past the call of duty and dissertation. In some cases, such ABDs may have a low self-esteem problem, which denies their deserving the doctorate: compulsive revisions can ensure the validation of such unworthy ego-images.

- "I've left something out." The candidate is haunted by the fear that faculty is going to jump on just the one study, experiment, dissertation, monograph which challenges his thesis—and which he has accordingly either downplayed or omitted from his presentation—and is consequently going to reject his 335 pages *in toto.* The truth is closer to faculty rarely knowing the details of the specialized issues of a dissertation and the candidate being the world's expert in the area. Certainly, *something* is always going to be left out, but that a particular deletion will be pounced and focused on by a wrathful faculty is a manifestation of dissertation paranoia.

- "I've been scooped." Belief that another ABD has beaten you to your "exclusive" is an erroneous transfer of either journalistic or hard science hazards to social science, arts and humanities fields. I have detailed at some length the virtual impossibility of another candidate's even coming near your model and methodology in the disciplines to which this volume is addressed, even in the improbable event of the titles of two dissertations being very similar: as we have seen, there is enormous room—indeed, need—for variety, multiplicity and even replication of studies within most topics. Lying behind "I've been scooped" anxiety is sometimes the *myth of the ultimate or definitive dissertation,* which says once and for all everything worthwhile and possible about a given area or topic.

Bewildered and Negative Feelings About Oneself.

- "What have I got myself into? I must have been crazy to take such a job on." It is common for candidates deep in a dissertation to suffer second thoughts about the soundness of their initial judgment in undertaking the thesis, especially when the current dissertation mood is "no end in sight." This uncertainty about the thesis decision is bad enough, but people show a marked tendency to generalize it to questioning their decision-making competence in other areas of their lives—areas in which, prior to the dissertation course, they may well have felt confident and secure.

Part of the process of restoring faith and credibility in one's judgment is to dispel the "no end in sight" mood by a return to proposal and file "maps" (see above). Consider as well how antithetical the decision to write the dissertation was to any kind of spur-of-the-moment, "inspirational," "off-the-wall," or "crazy" choice. Chapter Two depicts in detail the full range of extremely rational and deliberate *planning* that antedates the proposal and continues into later phases. When a candidate is in mid-dissertation doldrums, he has to "get back to basics," remind himself that a whole history of dissertation development—involving countless days of proposal writing, negotiations with faculty, questionnaire design, file building, field work, memorandum writing, chapter drafting—preceded today's urge to rip up Chapter Three because the last section just won't flow, and that he will survive and vanquish a day's or a

162

week's frustrations and doubts. Getting back to basics also involves reviewing the *reasons* for which one undertook the dissertation. At the start, they were substantial and deliberate; then, too, the candidate (especially if he read this volume) went into the vast project with his eyes open. Unless one's life circumstances have changed substantially since the initial decision a year or eighteen months earlier, the validity of the reasons for pursuing the dissertation should be up-to-date, still in force, compelling.

- "Why do I continue to torture myself?" A candidate caught in the no-end-in-sight trap may shift his self-critique from his possessing poor judgment to his being *masochistic*. Candidates' friends and relatives, seeing him in long struggle, often offer this kind of pop psychology diagnosis; indeed, a candidate's analyst may come up with this type of interpretation! But diagnoses of the ABD-as-masochist, whether made by the candidate himself or others, are almost invariably wrong. Masochism is the intentional imposition of pain upon oneself. Psychoanalysts see it as self-punishment for a range of sins and guilts, more often imagined than real. Dissertation writing, on the other hand, is the intentional imposition of a large project upon oneself. Psychoanalysts and others would do well to see it accurately, as goal-directed self-growth, commitment to aspiration. It is true that *pain* is common to both masochism and dissertation writing, but the contexts, uses and symbols of that pain are entirely different in the two situations. But it would appear that some psychoanalysts "buy" the ABD patient's fantasy version of the infinity of the dissertation; from that empirically erroneous perspective it is easy enough for a misdirected and misinformed therapist and his candidate patient to spin a clinical picture of the patient-as-masochist, torturing himself by continuing with work he will never complete.

It is crucial that a mid-dissertation-depressed ABD see his pain as functional, not masochistic, no matter what outside observers believe. Essential to the pain-as-functional perspective is rejection of the myth of the dissertation as endless. The masochistic trap, especially when pursued and elaborated with "professional help," inaccurately and diabolically converts a rational, noble, realistically obtainable and even heroic enterprise into a garden-variety neurosis or psychopathology. If an ABD catches himself in masochistic diagnosis, he must shake it off; if friends suggest it, he can laugh it off; if his analyst takes this tack, he must cut him loose. Pursuit of the *dissertation-as-masochism myth* in therapy is indeed masochism itself: blaming and criticizing oneself for untold work on a futile project (the entire analysis is masochistic because the assumption of futility of the project is dead wrong). In my judgment, an ABD who gets sucked into this direction of "therapy" is lost: every session in the dissertation office is subsequently seen as "throwing good money after bad."

It alarms me to speculate over the number of dissertations sabotaged by analysts pursuing the masochist interpretation. The danger is greatest when the therapist himself has not written a full dissertation (i.e., psychiatrists, MSWs, counselers with various non-doctorate credentials). Lack of familiarity with the unique world of the dissertation—including its immensely deliberate and planned nature, the multiplicity of tasks involved, the extensive filing system required, the thoroughness of the initial decision/commitment to write the dissertation, the predictable, chartable crests and troughs of the course—makes it very likely that an analyst will misinterpret "normal" dissertation responses in the context of "neurotic" or "disturbed"—here, specifically, "masochistic." His reference points are from a world where people's everyday activities simply do not include a project as rigorous, demanding, hazardous and solitary as a doctoral dissertation.

- "If I ever finish, I'll never write another thing in my life." One hears such threats often enough from ABDs. Should such pronouncements be taken seriously? I have seen enough cases of "burnt-out" candidates who never mount another serious piece of work in their field to dismiss such intentions merely as fleeting dissertation delirium. In certain dissertation disciplines—notably clinical psychology, where the candidate practices full-time psychotherapy upon receipt of his doctorate—additional long projects are not normally part of the career; the psychology ABD's last-ditch view of the dissertation may be motivated at the time by frustration or desperation, but it is also realistic and legitimated by career norms. For the rest of us, it is a very dangerous attitude, susceptible to self-fulfilling prophecy, since part and parcel of our English, political science, history or sociology trade is to continue writing articles, monographs, books.

It is paradoxical that an exercise presumably designed to launch a career can, not infrequently, stunt or destroy it.[2] Persons who get trapped in the burnt-out view of themselves are suffering from lack of dissertation perspective. They are usually victims of some admixture of the *dissertation-as-perfect, dissertation-as-magnum opus* and *dissertation as home-free myths.* An ABD already in the grips of cynicism must remind himself of the professional scheme of things: the dissertation is the *first* in a series of written projects he is going to have to (and, one hopes, want to) produce as professor of literature, anthropology or educational sociology. Although the most immediate, and often humiliating, supervisory strictures of adviser and thesis committee will be absent in later works, other enforcers of standards replace them, e.g., referees for journal articles; editors in publishing companies; senior faculty members, judges for fellowships, travel grants, research grants. Regard your dissertation as your debut, not your swan song. Regard many of the objections that supervising faculty raise as an introduction to the rules of your discipline's game, rules which you may as well get used to, since you will confront them time and again in the following thirty years.

- "Bob and Carol finished, and I'm the dummy who's left behind." ABDs often begin to question their abilities as well as their judgment during the dissertation, particularly when they begin to compete with program cohorts in terms of finishing dates. One has, first of all, to keep dissertation mortality rates in mind: if Bob and Carol finished, chances are high that Ted and Alice didn't. More important, dissertation writing is not really a "group sport," but much more like an individual one. As we have noted, programs do not set a quota system for how many degrees they will confer: if you show up a year after Bob and Carol with an acceptable dissertation, you won't be closed out. If the dissertation is any kind of competition at all, it is one with *yourself,* on the order of a marathon, where, with the exception of a few stars, the goal is simply to finish.[3] Behind the self-devaluation related to peer group comparison and competition may very well lie adherence to the *dissertation as home-free myth*: Bob and Carol have made it, can rest on their laurels, are above the struggle. The reality is, of course, quite to the contrary; the dissertation stage is the *least competitive* one in an academic career. Upon receipt of the doctorate, buyer's market competition is awaiting one in faculty appointments, promotion, tenure, publishing contracts and grants. In the sweep of a three- or four-decade career, the fact of some peers finishing the dissertation a year or two sooner or later than others is not very significant, no matter how maddening it may seem at the time to the "left-behind" ABD. Again, putting the dissertation phase in the wider context of a long career, accompanied from start to finish by new projects, tests and challenges for *everybody* in the field, should help the candidate avoid the self-flagellation of dissertation envy over earlier finishers, in favor of renewed attention to the development, at one's own rhythm, of one's own thesis.

Negatively Affecting Relationships with Others.

● "I'm becoming an ass kisser." There is no gainsaying that the realities of faculty-candidate dissertation politics entail for almost all students a certain amount of kowtowing and self-effacement. Attention to the strategies for presentation of dissertation self—outlined in detail in Chapters Two, Four and Six—will protect against the worst of quasi-feudal graduate faculty liberties and/or abuses. The successful candidate has a fierce desire for completion, combined with a realistic intelligence about the social context of the dissertation. He should not allow the anticipated situation-specific need for subordinate role playing to be generalized into any revised and deprecatory evaluation of self as "ass-kisser." So long as his relationships with friends, family and fellow workers outside the dissertation zone are not altered toward the temporary accommodative pattern maintained with faculty, one's general integrity, in my view, remains intact.

However, the candidate should not delude himself with the inaccurate consolation that upon finishing his doctorate, the days of ingratiation are necessarily over: hierarchical, bureaucratic academia is characterized by wheelings, dealings and power plays. Often, the comportment of an untenured assistant professor toward senior faculty is indistinguishable, in its tenor of subordination and humiliation, from that of an ABD toward his thesis committee. Ultimately, as Merton has suggested, occupational contexts and pressures can shape, or reshape, personality, and the temporary self-effacement of dissertation politics can become, over time, a permanent posture in dealing with both academic colleagues and with others outside the career zone. A certain undetermined number of professors do develop the accommodative seed of dissertation days into a way of life.

166

- "It's coming between me and Jack/Jill." Dissertation times are trying ones for family and love relationships. There seem to be two ways in which the dissertation can cause rifts between intimates. The ABD's devotion to the dissertation—his time spent in the office, at the library, in the field—drastically reduces the time spent theretofore with others. He becomes an absentee spouse, father, lover, locked in his office, or grudgingly spending Sunday afternoon in the park with the family, but preoccupied with how his computer runs are going to pan out on Monday. Secondly, during the course of the dissertation, the ABD changes certain of his fundamental values and perceives himself to have "outgrown" a spouse or lover. This type of dissertation disruption is discussed in Chapter Nine. Of course, in some instances, the two disruptive patterns interact and reinforce each other: an ABD who believes she is growing apart from the previously shared *Weltanschaung* of her husband buttresses this perception by spending radically less time with him, "away" on dissertation business.

I think that tensions around ABD role absenteeism are more common than serious estrangements from previous values, although the latter must not be minimized (often, value conflicts remain latent for a long period, are not so blatant as physical withdrawal of a person). There are no terribly good ways around the reality of dissertation withdrawal from loved ones. The book has stressed the necessity for a large block of time reserved for being alone with the great project. Family and lovers, not similarly engaged with their own task, are almost certain at times not to "understand," even when they generally profess support and concern for the ABD's success.

In certain serious respects, living with an ABD wrapped up in his thesis is like living with a handicapped or "problem" person (e.g., an alcoholic). Support and information groups have been formed by and for close relatives of many of these problem categories (e.g., spouses of alcoholics, disabled persons, released mental patients). These groups parallel those formed by the "problem" persons themselves. Later in this chapter I discuss possibilities and prospects for ABDs banding together in dissertation therapy/support groups. An important adjunct to that development (still embryonic) would be establishment of groups for ABDs' mates and lovers. That such plans sound farfetched or even facetious to some readers reflects, I believe, general ignorance in the United States about the plight of probably 100,000 ABDs each year, struggling to write a difficult and lonely dissertation with little or no support system provided by graduate education programs. In the absence of such group developments, ABDs must take other tacks to familiarize intimates with the contours of their projects, if dissertation-caused differences and rifts are to be prevented from escalating. Books already exist about *How to Live with an Alcoholic* and *How to Live with a Schizophrenic.* The present volume might profitably be given to dissertation spouses for information on "How to Live with an ABD."

- "The dissertation's breaking up that old gang of mine." In a less intense vein, dissertation disturbances of friendships parallel those for intimate relations. Through the process of differential dissertation association, the candidate will be spending less time with certain acquaintances, because of the across-the-board reduction of socializing during dissertation writing, combined with a discovery that some friends are nonsupportive, uninterested or even, in some cases, detrimental to the project. In a sense, people's attitude to your heavy involvement in the thesis, curtailing time spent with them, becomes an unintentional test of their true feelings for and understanding of you and your aspirations. At dissertation's end, some of the predissertation members of your friendship network may be absent.[4] On the other hand, *new* friendship bonds may be formed, particularly with other contemporary dissertation writers.

A subcategory of problem here might be the changing nature of the ABD's relationships with and feelings for his fellow employees. Involved again is the general issue of the candidate's simply taking some of his capital out of almost all his roles, from family to friends to work. Beyond that, however, depending, of course, on the nature of the job and its degree of intellectual isomorphism with the dissertation, a candidate may wake up in mid-dissertation to the fact that he doesn't have "that much in common" with his fellow employees.

Dissertation estrangement from some friends on or off the job, through current recognition of theretofore latent intellectual and philosophical differences, should not be the cause for self-blame or critique along the lines of a candidate feeling "traitorous" or that he has "taken on airs"; although it is not uncommon for people to whip themselves with these self-recriminations. Attenuation of friend-

168

ships are always *triste,* and sadness is an appropriate response. But there is every reason to believe that one will meet new friends, probably find another kind of employment as well, more empathetic with the postdissertation self, values and interests.

Reification, Alienation and the Dissertation-As-Enemy.

Whether candidates are disturbed by problems with the dissertation itself, self-image or dissertation-precipitated changes of relationships with others, an underlying attitude seems to be that the dissertation has taken on a life of its own, beyond the control of its creator (à la Dr. Frankenstein's monster: I have, in fact, heard advisees exasperatedly use this specific literary image to describe their feelings about their theses. Indeed, with some changes in Mary Shelley's plot, we might recast MD Frankenstein as *ABD* Frankenstein doing a dissertation in biochemistry or physiology!). Whether the dissertation stubbornly won't come out right, overwhelms one with its demands, deflates one's self-image, diabolically fouls up relationships with lovers, families, friends or work, the sense of it "being out to get me" is there.

People have, apparently, a universal tendency toward reification—assigning too much power to abstractions—in most spheres of human activity, from economics to religion to family organization and, inferentially, to doctoral dissertations as well. Reification is characterized by amnesia about who created social products. Forgetting that we frail imperfect humans forged them in the first place leads to a sense of powerlessness, rage and a misconception that such products are timeless, immutable, and demanding in perfection beyond our abilities to comply. When a candidate reifies his doctoral dissertation, he is vulnerable to all these dysfunctional attitudes toward the thesis that accompany reification in any other area. The only way to get on top of a "runaway dissertation" is thoroughly to refresh one's memory about the personal origins of the proposal and Chapters One through Five. This is accomplished by once again immersing oneself in the dissertation file, to trace the project's genesis and development up to the present time in your own notes, memoranda, questionnaire construction, cross-filing.

WHOM CAN I TURN TO?

The remainder of this chapter is devoted to a consideration of various resource persons—counselors, self-help strategies and dissertation-writing peers—to whom a candidate might resort in times of the dissertation-directed, self-directed or other-directed emotional pains outlined above. In light of his own dissertation situation, a candidate will have to appraise which resource—or combination of resources—is likely to help him and be *available* to him.

Technicians: Methodologists, Statisticians, Computer Programmers.

Particularly in the social sciences, dissertation candidates have recurrent difficulty with the methodological, statistical and computer aspects of the project. In my view, the major cause of these problems is the quality and/or scope of graduate courses offered in nuts-and-bolts areas. All doctoral candidates are required to take four or five such courses, supposedly to prepare them for methodologically designing their theses. But the course sequences are more often than not uncoordinated with each other, or pay excessive attention to small, isolated, discrete techniques and studies in and for themselves, rather than pointing toward their utility or relevance in an upcoming thesis. There is, as best as I can make out, a near absence of anticipatory socialization for the methodology and statistics of the dissertation, and a graduate student can get an "A" in all of these courses and still face the dissertation as a methodological illiterate.

As noted earlier, consultants are usually available for a fee to provide the instruction that was owed a candidate in his course work: how to design a methodology and statistics tailored to his thesis. Although such "outside help" should be sought only as a "last resort," that stage comes rather quickly for most candidates, since other remedies—particularly program-affiliated methodologists—often prove unsatisfactory. That is, such methodologists are most reluctant to give time, attention and advice to the specific details of one's methods, statistics or computer runs. Remember, the formal assumption holds that the ABD learned all those nuts and bolts in the "stat-meth" courses; why should the experts be bothered to repeat such instruction? After one or two tries down at the department, the ABD gets embarrassed—by faculty's adherence to the counterfeit stand that such matters were already taught, and thus deficiencies are the candidate's fault and hence his responsibility for removing—and looks elsewhere for guidance. It is an open question whether faculty should be informed of resort to extradepartmental technicians. Certainly, they know that perhaps a majority of social science candidates use them, but straitlaced departments probably would prefer to let sleeping methodologists lie: the self-serving image of the ABD going out and designing his dissertation completely on his own, equipped with a full complement of appropriate skills taught him in his courses, is then preserved. Under some circumstances, I could even envision a scenario where a program or committee out to "get" a particular candidate might seize upon evidence of his use of various consultants (and it is entirely possible that an ABD might want two or three for various stages of the methodology) as evidence of "cheating" or not writing his own dissertation. In most instances, the resort to consultants is par for the course in social science work; faculty engage in it all the time, usually acknowledge such advice at the beginning of published research papers. But a kind of "double standard" exists for faculty and ABDs in this area. Just how stringent those standards are, and where lines are drawn for legitimate versus illegitimate dissertation aid and comfort are hard questions, but the ABD consulting outside technicians should keep possible disclosure difficulties in mind, and probably his mouth buttoned.

For whatever help you go to your technician, it is imperative to get him to explain the metatheory behind a method or statistical tool he employed, exactly what the statistical tests demonstrated in terms of your hypotheses, what the limitations of particular employed instruments are in relation to reliability and validity.[5] If you don't fully understand the first or second time around, keep at him. This is what you are paying him for out of your hard-earned coolie-wage adjunct professor salary. The last thing you need is a replay of the impatient methodology professor down at the department. Although the defense committee won't want an explication of FORTRAN or a mathematical proof for Chi-squared, they may well want to probe your grasp of the hazards of Chi-squared with small samples, or your handling of the reliability issue in your use of the Q-Sort or semantic differential scales.

Sympathetic Professors.

As I have indicated in earlier chapters, the sympathetic, interested professor—be he adviser, thesis committee member, departmental chairman or other faculty person—is an unreliable, rare, and generally highly problematic commodity in the dissertation-help stockpile. You might get delivery on one; then again you might not. If you do, he may run like a Packard but just as easily turn out to be a lemon, or get "recalled." By all means give this direction several tries—you probably would, in any event—but be cautious, just as "the other side" is careful and noncommittal. Even if you "connect" with a helpful faculty member, take his aid on a day-by-day basis, utilizing it for what it is contemporarily worth, but keeping in mind Chapter One's accounting of faculty unreliability, departures, absenteeism and even hostility when it comes to helping with dissertations. A calculus of dissertation politics also dictates that the candidate be careful if the sympathetic professor is not a member of his committee. For many hierarchy-obsessed faculty, extended consultations with such a professor might be considered as "going over my head," or "not going through proper channels," even though the indignant complainer hasn't lifted a finger to help, either substantively or emotionally, with the project. At all costs, avoid *addiction* to any faculty help, since your "supply" can be cut off at virtually any time through a multitude of circumstances over which you have no control.

Another danger here is that the sympathetic professor can stray into the murky waters of psychotherapy. A dissertation-depressed candidate may or may not benefit from therapy at this point (see section below), but it should *never* come from a faculty member in one's doctoral program. With the exception of some cases in clinical psychology programs, he is unqualified and might unwittingly exacerbate dissertation problems by introducing "red herring" suspicions about your emotional stability to thesis committee members. Faculty are all too ready to account for dissertation delay in terms of individual psychopathologies of candidates, since this approach allows them to ignore the roles of program structural deficiencies and absence of support systems in depressing, debilitating and delaying dissertations, conditions for which *they* are responsible.

Sympathetic and Supportive Students.

Dissertation dumps is a time when the candidate's self-esteem is low; often, he is being "dumped on" by his graduate professors. During 1968, when I was doing both the fieldwork and analysis of data for my dissertation, I was also teaching sociology part-time at Queens College. In that period I hit my deepest troughs with both a fieldwork crisis and then an analysis one, where the validity of my empirical findings came into question. On more than one evening I built my lectures in Introductory Sociology around my research traumas with my chiropractic student sample and site. In a very personal and immediate way I was able to show my students what "doing sociology" really meant, including the hazards, dilemmas, pains and triumphs along the way from fieldwork to analysis. In a certain real sense, one class in particular functioned like a kind of group adviser or sounding board for me, making suggestions how I might handle one or another type of obstacle. At a certain point in the course, this particular class began to anticipate eagerly my account of how matters had fared in a given week. I believe I managed to convey all of the traditional areas and issues of an introductory course in a very unusual, alive and engaging manner; those semesters, with my own research and career on the line, may well have been my finest teaching hours.

And *both* parties got something valuable: I gave my students a rather unique course, and they in turn led me toward solutions—sometimes, while lecturing, "daylight" would come to me—and a renewed sense of self-worth. When *I* doubted that I could finish the dissertation, or that the thesis was worth finishing in any event, *they* rushed in to affirm confidence in their professor and the importance of his project. Just when my graduate professors were taking me down a peg, about my dissertation in particular and, inferentially, about my sociological competence in general, my students gave me back my sense of being a good teacher and my conviction about the "rightness" and "deservability" of getting my doctorate to become a full-fledged professor. It was a most moving experience. I recommend sharing dissertation research with one's classes to any ABD who is teaching subjects that lend themselves to legitimate exploration through the vehicle of the dissertation. Sometimes a number of courses so lend themselves: I could certainly have centered sociology courses in methodology, medical sociology, social psychology and perhaps deviance around my research of semistigmatized chiropractic students confronting a medically oriented society.

Of course, one must take care not to give an excessively ego-oriented or maudlin presentation; it is important to give a full account of the theories and facts of the research problem, as well as the emotional aspects. But presentation of autobiographical materials as one important element alongside more objective features appears increasingly in social science research.[6] I have repeatedly contended in this

173

volume that perhaps the sharpest pain of dissertation writing is its generally lonely and unshareable quality: friends, spouses, lovers, work colleagues, families, cocktail party guests, often even advisers and committee members, don't want to hear about the thesis. But in one's students, there exists a captive and potentially interested and caring audience with whom one can share one's "obsession."

Self-help Techniques.

Certain train-yourself activities can be very useful in inculcating the "pack animal" set of the dissertation routine. Nobody is going to finish a dissertation who doesn't have an attitude of getting back to it day after day, month after month, regardless of how well things flow or get bogged down in the office during a given period. In my experience, the endurance, tenacity and long-range rhythm developed from the pursuit of the long-distance category of sports such as running, swimming and skiing (cross-country) can often be transferred over to the motivational rhythm and long-range drive vital to sustaining dissertation performance. I realize that many ABDs cannot or will not entertain such self-help counsel because of already demanding work and family schedules, physical limitations (although age is certainly not necessarily one of them) or plain distaste for taking up sports which they feel are boring and/or tedious. Enough, however, would be interested and aided to justify a brief discussion.

I can relate my own writing projects, including my dissertation, to my regular pursuit of long-distance running over the past fifteen years.* In running, if you persevere, you get to a point—within limits—where you could run indefinitely: the finish of your daily—say, seven-mile—run isn't much on your mind in the fifth mile as any desperate sort of goal (maybe years ago when you started running it was), since you've long since developed the conviction that you'll be running distances like this three to five times a week for many years to come. You become comfortable within your run, the more you see it as just another segment of a lifelong activity. The reader, of course, knows me well enough by this chapter to recognize that far from advocating the dissertation as a lifelong activity, I believe it should be finished

---

* The reciprocities I have personally experienced between writing and running are no doubt among the reasons I entitled the first chapter of this volume "The Loneliness of the Long-Distance Writer."

from proposal to defense in a maximum of two years. But remember that the dissertation is only the first of many "runs" or projects for the typical ABD. To get into a long-distance frame of mind and perspective during dissertation time can create an invaluable career mood that equips one with a confident, receptive and engaged attitude toward new long works over the following thirty years.

But the existential mood developed in long-distance running can help not only with subsequent projects, but with the dissertation itself. The more I give myself up to my run, let myself merge into and participate with the paths of Central Park, the more effortlessly I flow and finish. Each time I begin to brood about *The Finish,* my pace is broken, the run becomes a burden. And so it seems to be with writing a dissertation: the more the candidate is immersed in his files, flowing with his fieldwork, humming along on his office typewriter, deep, deep in the very stuff of the dissertation and conversely, less preoccupied with the magical/mystical *Finish* date, the faster the thesis is going to move ahead to completion. Obviously, this running/writing illustration is not designed to devalue the booklong insistence on organization and planning as fundamental to dissertation success. The point to be made—which many dissertation finishers and professional writers would affirm—is that, perhaps paradoxically, when one has planned and outlined, and planned again, what has to follow is, as Philip Roth might put it, a "letting-go," a self-absorbed merging with one's dissertation materials.

Psychiatrists and Other Types of Psychotherapists.

Many dissertation writers are in one type of therapy or another, although it is impossible to know what percentage entered at the time of—and principally because of—dissertation depressions and anxieties.[7] The general question, in any event, is how effective is psychotherapy in getting a candidate back in motivated harness to finish the thesis. All I can do here is point up some issues which cut across the multitude of individual and group schools and approaches in which a candidate may be involved.

The greatest dissertation danger in psychotherapy is the tendency of analysts to relegate immediate dissertation griefs of the candidate to a secondary or symbolic dimension, insisting that sessions be spent on the "underlying," "psychogenetic," "developmental" processes, often dating back twenty or more years, which, they claim, account for the

ABD's present emotional discombobulation about Chapter Three of his thesis. I am not arguing for a total abandonment of psychogenetic character development interpretation, but for a redress of the balance between the role of biographical process *and* contemporary objective difficulties with the project. It may well be that you are resisting finishing the thesis because you don't want to face adult roles (prolonged self-infantilization), or because your father's perfectionist standards have penetrated and paralyzed your sense of self-esteem and worth ("I can't write anything good enough"), but, not withstanding the presence of such hang-ups, the data coming out contrary for five of your eight hypotheses is not to be casually dismissed as "secondary" or "transient" by an analyst who wants to "get down to the root of the problem."

When the data is coming out wrong, or one is in danger of being kicked out of one's field site, or the second reader is making the candidate's life hell with psychopathic or sadistic vacillation, that *is* the root of the problem, and any therapist who won't turn all his interest, concern and support to those matters on their own terms and in and for themselves is dissertation-destructive. Time enough when the immediate realistic dissertation crisis is past to get back to the extirpation of a twenty-five-year-old Electra complex. Recall my insistence in Chapter Two about the need for pushing the dissertation to the center of your life. Upon accomplishing this very difficult rearrangement of your life-style and priorities, the last thing you need is an analyst or fellow group therapy members misdirectedly trying to push it to the sidelines again by insisting you are acting "obsessively" or "compulsively."

Some years ago I wrote a series of articles on the radical criminal trials of the early 1970s.[8] One striking theme was how the radical defendants insisted that their lawyers be not only competent, but politically radical like them so that they would truly understand the nature of the struggle. It may well be that dissertation writers need analysts and/or fellow group therapy members who are "like them," having written or engaged in the process of writing a full dissertation.

A person looking for a "like me" therapist to work with during the dissertation course will not actively seek first time around an MD psychiatrist or MSW. The two largest categories of therapist remaining are Ph.D.s certified as clinical psychologists, and "Ed. Docs" who have received certification. At least these last groups have ordinarily

176

written full theses. Even so, one has no guarantee that after fifteen years out in practice they are still "up" on the world of dissertation requirements and regulations. This selection *caveat* is by no means airtight. One can hit upon a psychiatrist who happens to be a researcher and writer as well, who will treat substantive dissertation difficulties at their face value; or one can have bad luck with a Ph.D. "Rolfer" who only dimly remembers his dissertation days and insists upon attacking misalignments of your cartilage and faciae instead of those of your data. Still, as a pretty good rule of thumb, therapists who themselves wrote dissertations are less apt to go off the deep end of misinterpreting the range of dissertation-based woes outlined above as psychopathological and psychogenetic-based disturbances, and more apt to deal with them forthrightly and intensively, as predictable byproducts of the unique dissertation-writing structural context and its unusual demands.

People in psychotherapy are notorious for forgetting that therapists are *their agents.* An ABD who *knows* that what's bothering him the most is his repeated inability to write an acceptable version of his proposal on "Economic Theory in the 'Young Marx' " cannot continue with an analyst who purports to "know better" than he about what his "real" problems are. Now, analysts can refuse to deal with substantive thesis difficulties for two different reasons. First, they can psychoanalyze, symbolize or deemphasize the dissertation, in the manner just depicted. Second, very commonly, they can claim lack of competence: "I've got a Ph.D. in psychology. I don't know the young Marx from the old one." I believe the ABD has to terminate with the first kind of reluctant analyst. Matters are more complicated with the second. Even though the therapist might not be able to help with the specific details of a field outside his own training, one can certainly capsulize for him the gist of the problems encountered, which he should be able to grasp and connect up with the general model of dissertation writing that he pursued in his own case. Some dissertation dumps have less to do with substantive issues of data and analysis, and more to do with feelings of reduced self-worth and deteriorating relations with others. If the latter woes are preoccupying a patient/ABD, a therapist must be willing to bring them to the center of the analytic hour, working on them in and for their own right.

But the world of the ABD is so unusual, the origins of dissertation pathologies so often misunderstood, that even the most sympathetic and eager-to-help therapist, not abreast of dissertation writing, may fail to provide satisfaction. This is another way of saying that conventional psychotherapy may not be effective in treating dissertation difficulties, may even be dysfunctional to progress. My own counsel to the ABD in—or seeking—conventional therapy is to practice once more the calculus of differential dissertation association and ask questions like, Did the analyst write a thesis himself? Is he current with dissertation-writing requirements? Does he have any other patients who are writing dissertations? Has he indicated a willingness to put my dissertation difficulties at the center of our work together? Will he read my dissertation materials, or at least some sections of them? Does the therapy group he wants me to join have any members who are also writing theses? Of course, the ABD is the final judge, but I would counsel that if he gets more than one "no" to the above questions, he should seek help elsewhere for emotional problems related to the dissertation. Because ABDs have been encountering too many "no's" to these kinds of questions from conventional therapies and therapists, some of them have turned for help to a new field, "dissertation therapy."

Dissertation Therapists.

I have no idea how many psychotherapists, psychoanalysts and counselors do dissertation therapy, either as a speciality within a larger general practice or exclusively. When I began this work in the late 1970s, I knew of no other persons in New York similarly engaged (although undoubtedly there must have been at least some others of whom I simply had not heard). More recently, one meets the odd psychologist with a dissertation patient or two, or reads an occasional counseling advertisement (e.g., in the *Village Voice* or *New York Review of Books*) for individual or group professional dissertation counseling/therapy.

No attempt will be made at this point to outline how dissertation therapists operate, first, because the "sample" of us is so small that I would, in any case, only be relating how *I* work; and secondly, because the entire *volume* is precisely a booklong description of what I do. Hopefully, if you read the book, you won't need a dissertation therapist! Indeed, accurate alternative titles for the book might be "The Portable Dissertation Adviser," or "The Portable Dissertation Therapist." I have tried to distill for the ABD the most useful dissertation writing and surviving wisdom I have accumulated with advisees and clients over the past twelve years.[9]

Even though dissertation therapy might reasonably be thought of as a "growth industry," given the meager or unsatisfactory resource/ support persons and systems presently available, there are several reasons why, in my judgment, only limited growth will take place:

1. The speciality demands of the practitioner a formidable combination of psychotherapeutic, generalist intellectual, methodological, editorial and human relations skills (of which the exercise of some contradict the exercise of others) which can be developed only over a long period of time.

2. Within the already limited pool of potential dissertation therapists, the rewards (monetary and otherwise) are probably perceived as too uncertain or not large enough, given the demands of such work, to lure many recruits.

3. The work is inordinately time-demanding. Unlike "straight" therapy, one must spend about two hours reading the client's materials for every hour of personal consultation.

4. Fees must, accordingly, be medium to high, putting the dissertation therapist beyond the budget of perhaps most ABDs.

5. Dissertation therapy is draining. Even if one is lucky enough to get interesting dissertations, serious, regular, critical attention to them cannot help but take energy and creativity away from one's own projects.[10] I have discovered that my maximum number of clients at any time is three; beyond that very small sample, I am drained, unable to give my best to additional ABDs, or to my own writing.

6. The dissertation therapist has no power. In a sense, the dissertation therapist is the adviser the ABD wishes he had down at his program, the adviser he can't get, except for the rarest of cases, for all the structural reasons outlined in this book. But the dissertation therapist has no connection with the committee and department (in fact, the client may be anxious that his consultations are confidential, unknown to anyone, most particularly his program). If dissertation therapist and client together work up a dissertation proposal which the therapist thinks is acceptable, how do matters stand if the official adviser and/or committee turn it down? Obviously, the therapist cannot intervene; he has no standing. The specter of such a rejection (which sometimes happens despite the best efforts of therapist and ABD) is always in the minds of seasoned thesis therapists and forces them to take

caution in accepting candidates whose projects or capacities they doubt. The tendency of the client to become very dependent and trusting toward the thesis therapist, combined with the brute fact that he has no control whatsoever over the decision-making processes of the candidates' thesis supervisers, puts the dissertation therapist in a perpetually vulnerable position.

7. The dissertation therapist as doppelgänger. There he sits in his Eames chair, in the shadows, unknown to the program committee, "control running" his ABDs. The "legality" of dissertation therapy is not entirely clear. How would the candidate's program construe his consultation with the shadow adviser? Would it be construed as cheating—the doppelgänger therapist as ghost writer? I suspect that certain departments would take dissertation therapy in stride, seeing it as a cross between an ABD consulting a technician and psychotherapist (which in a general way is not too far wrong), whereas others would see it not unlike the illegal term-paper-writing enterprises that have flourished on college campuses.

Clients are referred to me by psychologists, other clients, psychiatrists, but I have not had a referral, inquiry or objection from dissertation-supervising faculty or doctoral programs. Whether such silence implies ignorance that therapists like myself are working with some of their candidates, recognition and tacit approval, recognition and disapproval—tempered with guilt about faculty-created conditions causing the need for outside support services—I cannot say. But added to the feelings of powerlessness and uneasiness about the dissertation therapist role is an uncertainty about its "legitimate" status in the eyes of those supervising faculty who must ultimately decide the client's dissertation fate.

For one or more of the above reasons, then, one would not expect a growing pool of dissertation therapists to be available for ABDs in trouble in the 1980s; (and the ABDs visiting the extant ones will continue as a tiny percentage of the whole). *Leaderless peer group dissertation therapy,* however, to which we will now turn, seems to me a much more promising direction for helping large numbers of contemporary dissertation writers in distress.

Fellow Doctoral Students in the Same Boat.

The 1970s witnessed both a marked shift in traditional psychotherapies from individual to group forums and an unprecedented wide-scale use of group process in many kinds of consciousness-raising movements (e.g., women's, men's, gays' groups). Recently, there have been reports of the group context being used with dissertation writers: a faculty-directed group in a school psychology doctoral program in New York; a psychologist-directed private group for doctoral candidates in Manhattan; a leaderless group of dissertation writers in social psychology at Brandeis; a sociology group at New York University. I have indicated my skepticism about the efficacy and/or widespread availability of either conventional psychotherapists or dissertation therapists for helping with dissertation problems. With all the yet-to-be-solved obstacles in creating viable dissertation-help groups, certain of their subspecies emerge as potentially the most effective "external" support resource for the most number of ABDs. Although they began among psychology candidates, there is no reason to limit their development to that field, especially since the most effective support groups do not operate on a psychotherapy model.

Should a dissertation group be directed or leaderless? If directed, what kind of person should be the facilitator? If leaderless, of what should the membership and format consist? Since dissertation groups are in their infancy, answers to all these questions and the issues they entail are empirically "up for grabs." My own experience as a group leader or member (with prisoners, alcoholics, in general private practice, as member of a men's C-R group) is considerable, but I have never conducted dissertation groups *per se* (occasionally, a person in a general group has been an ABD); nor do I believe that many others in the early 1980s have had long-term, in-depth participation, either as leaders or members, with several dissertation groups. My observations and suggestions, below, about the formation and process of such groups involve "educated guesses" extrapolated from my familiarity with dissertation difficulties and professionally directed and self-help groups in general.

If the group is led, who should do the supervising? Much depends upon the *goals* of the group. In one New York school psychology doctoral group, candidates under the direction of faculty prepare specific dissertation sections to be presented at scheduled meetings of the group. All members are candidates in that particular program. This arrangement seems ideal for nuts-and-bolts aspects of the dissertation: since group leaders are also the duly authorized thesis supervisors, their acceptance of your production in the group is virtually identical with approving sections of your thesis. But program-mandated groups of this sort can probably be counted on two dissertation-typing hands. Beyond their scarcity, they do not lend themselves to exploration and ventilation of the *emotional* dimensions of the dissertation course, their tone and direction being almost exclusively rational and "instrumental." Supervising faculty, after all, do not see their role here as therapists, nor the groups as therapeutic or consciousness-raising ones. Most certainly, they will not tolerate "personal" attacks on *them,* a venting of pent-up rages that every ABD worth his salt has accumulated.

Finding a suitable leader who is not a supervising faculty member, especially for dealing with emotional issues of the dissertation, involves the problems discussed in preceding sections. If the leader is a psychiatrist or clinical psychologist, he is apt to misinterpret dissertation-specific hang-ups within the inappropriate framework of conventional nosology. If the leader is a dissertation therapist, the same difficulties outlined in the preceding section about his position, potential and status in working with individual candidates stand for his working with dissertation groups.

As the situation now stands, and can reasonably be projected to continue for years to come, supervised dissertation groups, of either the substantive nuts-and-bolts type or emotional-support category, will not be available to the great majority of ABDs as a mainstream support resource. Depending upon the nature of the group, particularly the difference between instrumental/goal or affective/emotional priorities, the reasons for lack of access run the gamut from failure of most departments to offer work-in-progress groups as part of their doctoral programs, to unavailability of proper and competent leaders to run therapy-oriented dissertation groups, to graduate students' well-known limited cash flow.

Guidelines for Forming and Sustaining a Dissertation-Support Group.

In the face of these realities, *leaderless* peer dissertation groups appear to be the subspecies most likely to flourish and survive. What follows is a "program" to guide ABDs in setting up their own dissertation-support group. Remember that my guidelines are general and largely untested in this particular sphere. Particular groups will undoubtedly have to tailor their procedures and development along the lines of their own needs, memberships, emerging experiences. There is no absolute "right" or "wrong" manner in which to proceed. The bottom line is that members' dissertations should be pushed along to completion; the only reason for the group is dissertation progress. My program is offered, like my suggestions for setting up a dissertation file, as a "starter set" to get a group going. Feel free—in fact, expect—to alter, contradict, elaborate on it in ways which will enhance its dissertation-promoting function. Be forewarned that group construction is a difficult task which demands persistence and motivation. Special obstacles exist with a dissertation group, since all members are initially programmed to have little patience, interest in, or time for anybody else's dissertation problems. On the other hand, the special tenacity and motivation that ABDs possess (otherwise they wouldn't be ABDs pursuing such a momentous project) may serve them in good stead in making a self-help group work. If you are suffering with your dissertation and have exhausted other avenues of aid and comfort, certainly it is worth a try to reach out to your *compañeros* in the dissertation struggle. Although parts of the dissertation agony may indeed, as I have argued, be basically "unshareable," the size of that irreducible private portion is undetermined; it may be smaller than I, or you, think.

Specific Considerations.

Members should be recruited among dissertation writers in the same general field, although not necessarily from the same program. Although all ABDs face some common problems in negotiating the dissertation, there are too many peculiar discipline-specific hurdles to expect anthropology, history and comparative-language ABDs to work together to mutual benefit in a dissertation group. If nothing else, lack of training in others' fields would be a great barrier to communication and aid. If members are all cadres from the same *department,* one has the double advantage of their sharing not only the discipline but the specific subculture of program requirements and faculty sociometrics in which they must negotiate their dissertations. But drawbacks to exclusive intradepartment membership might be: potential for excessive, dysfunctional rivalry among program "siblings"; reluctance to discuss faculty-specific gripes for fear of *soplones)* (squealers: see below for more on confidentiality agreements in dissertation groups); possible disapproval or suspicion of the group by conservative faculty, who might construe it as protest, or even cheating. Cross-departmental groups have the advantage of bringing to attention different angles and ways out of or around common discipline dissertation problems, to which a department-centric group might be blind. Members might also feel less reluctant to speak out in cross-department groups.

Since both kinds of groups have certain credits and debits, group formers will have to weigh their relative merits in terms of the circumstances of their own programs. The recruitment process will vary from feeling out peer ABDs (who were perhaps study group members from pre-ABD stages of the program) to advertising in college and local newspapers.

An optimum maximum size should be four or five members, since particular people will not want to wait more than four weeks (even getting self-obsessed and possessed ABDs to wait that long will be a problem) for their night, and because members will not be able responsibly to keep up with issues and developments in more than three or four other theses. On the other hand, less than four is undesirable, since the number of potential relationships, or advice pathways, among members is drastically reduced. Table 7.1 gives the reader some guidelines for manageable lower and upper limits to dissertation group size. Keep in mind that if you want to end up with a permanent group of four or five reliable candidates, initially you have to contact seven or eight, since a couple will probably drop out after a few meetings.

Table 7.1: Increase in Potential Relationships with an Increase in Group Size

Size of Group	Number of Relationships
2	1
3	6
4	25
5	90
6	301
7	966

Source: W. Kephart, "A quantitative analysis of intra-group relationships," Hare (ed.) *Handbook of Small Group Research,* 2nd ed., New York: Free Press, 1976, p. 218

Meet weekly on a round-robin, home-and-home basis in each other's dissertation offices. When the group members come to your office, they will reinforce your sense of legitimacy and commitment to the often isolated and cut-off-from-others dissertation project. They may also give you valuable suggestions for streamlining your office or filing system. You will probably feel rather proud when the group comes to you and sees how you operate. That pride is a mighty dissertation motivater. On the other hand, visiting other members' offices is heartening as an antidote to dissertation isolation: "Hey, I'm not the only person in the world holed up in a home office with a big file, trying to write something nobody around me understands." What is created by these visits is a shared sense of professionalism and pride about dissertation writing which works against the low self-esteem that ABDs often develop. Meeting in each other's home offices also helps to dispel dissertation myths, sometimes suscribed to by families, spouses, lovers, that their ABD is some kind of a kook/loner, the only one in the world on this mad venture. Here they have before their eyes a *group* of persons all taking the dissertation business most seriously. Group visibility may take some of the "heat" off: hubby may not complain so much the next time you demur from a Friday night out on the grounds of dissertation business in the office.

All group members must be provided with detailed abstracts of everybody's dissertation in progress. And members must pay unswerving attention to studying them just prior to a particular member's "night up." If the group is delinquent in this vital "homework," the group is sure to break up, starting with the departure of the first person for whose presentation they have failed to prepare.

If a member intends to discuss specific substantive problems of his work that are not explicit in the abstract, he should provide members in advance with a description and summary of the gist of the problem.

Any particular week's meeting should be reserved for one, or at most two, candidates to present their work in progress and related difficulties. It is preferable that members of the group be at different stages—from proposal, to collection and analysis of data, to writing chapters, to preparation for defense—rather than, say, all beginning or just about completing. Those farther along can anticipatorily socialize those at an earlier stage. On the other hand, the relatively fresh and undiluted enthusiasm that beginners bring to the group can be helpful to tired or discouraged mid-dissertation members, who often have lost sight of how far they have come and are reminded now by seeing how far the beginners have to go.

On a given person's night, the problem may be focused primarily on substantive issues of the dissertation itself, a member's self-feelings or interpersonal difficulties related to dissertation life. The presenter will find that a surprising amount of advice and support will surface, angles on and solutions to the difficulty that the presenting member never considered. Although discussion will range near and far, two rules, sometimes difficult to interpret or enforce, must be held to: all discussion must be related to the task of completing members' doctoral dissertations; *the group must not do psychotherapy,* if for no reason other than the fact that the members are not trained therapists. Since emotional problems related to the dissertation will frequently occupy the group's attention, it is very easy to stray into psychoanalytic and psychotherapeutic waters. Most leaderless support groups formed around one problem or task—e.g., men's, women's, minorities', gays' consciousness-raising groups—quickly come to the psychotherapy crossroads. Those groups which take that path almost always deteriorate into internecine pop-psychiatric warfare and disband. A theme common to most of the C-R and many of the "deviant" (alcoholic, drug-addiction) support groups is that the psychogenetic misinterpretation of their problems and behaviorial patterns is foisted on them by other groups, obscuring the structural, sociological conditions they face, in whose context their speciously "sick" or "disturbed" behavior is actually rational and appropriate. This is the tack the dissertation group must take when it approaches a given member's "dissertation psychopathology." Instead of seeing a candidate's difficulties in personality and personalistic terms, the group must closely analyze the very real dissertation pressures under which a member is operating, as well as explode the dissertation myths under which he or others may be laboring in labeling him, say, "masochistic" or "obsessive." (Consider the ease with which an uninformed psychotherapist could misinterpret the absolutely essential need for an intricate and complicated filing system and religious time in the dissertation office as "obsessive-compulsive behavior.")

Members must make every effort to attend all meetings (like the dissertation itself, meetings that facilitate its progress must become a top life priority) and "put away" preoccupations with their own theses when other group members are "up." As I have already noted, the inner-directed set of the dissertation writer is going to make total focusing on the other person's project very tough, at least in the beginning. If, however, members are able to reach the "takeoff" plane, they will discover what all successful C-R, self-help and support groups find: "It's your night even when it's not your night." In a given session, nonpresenters who are involved and listening attentively will hear about *their own* dissertation problems being wrestled with by their peers. Indeed, the similarity of thesis difficulties, both in substantive and emotional keys, and in etiologies is precisely why support groups are able to work.

Presentation schedules will occasionally have to be altered to help a particular member who is facing a critical dissertation problem. Perhaps a member must meet with his thesis committee the following week for a hearing on his proposal, or the final defense has been pushed ahead two weeks, or her husband is threatening to leave her on grounds of adultery, citing the dissertation as corespondent.

Role playing is very useful in many dissertation crises contexts. If the group member doubts his oral performance capacity with faculty, the other members can take the roles of proposal hearing or final defense faculty and subject the candidate to a full-dress (and full-time: the group should devote the, say, two hours of the session to the member) rehearsal. Devil's advocate questions should abound; with this particular kind of "psychodrama," it is helpful if at least some of the others in the group are in the specific program with the protagonist, since they will have insider intelligence about the personalities, quirks, theoretical and methodological preferences, as well as interrogation styles of his committee members.

Jill's marital rift with Jack can also be handled with role-playing, where other members take the parts of her husband and children. I believe that both-sex groups work best, since many of the interpersonal dissertation problems center in one way or another around disrupted relationships with loved ones of the opposite sex, or with families. It is very important to have both men's and women's points of view about issues like role absenteeism or reduced sexual enthusiasm available when candidates confront a "home revolt" along these lines.

Upon unanimous agreement, the group may sometimes invite outsiders to attend. Guests would generally be of two types:

Intimates, usually spouses or lovers, of a member who is experiencing home difficulties because of disagreements over the obtrusive dissertation. Bringing in a spouse or close relative to get "both sides of the story" has numerous precedents in many self-help group therapy and marriage-counseling settings. Often, when the relative/outsider sees his beloved ABD defended and supported by three or four other men and women facing similar difficulties, there will develop a willingness to reach some accommodation or compromise during the dissertation course. Not that the fellow member will always come out smelling like a rose! A female group member may go along, at least part of the way, with an irate "abandoned" guest wife and insist that the dissertation-writing husband can make significant adjustments in his schedule to effect *rapprochement* without stalling the thesis' progress.

Guest speakers who have somthing special or unique to contribute. Such persons might be a member's acquaintance who is a specialist in the methodology and statistical analysis of the group's field, or a recent dissertation finisher, or a "sympathetic professor."

All dissertation "victories" and rites de passage—*be they acceptance of a proposal, completion of chapters, setting of a date for the final defense—should be formally acknowledged by the group.* All such milestones should bring a shared celebration, if only a toast with wine. Every within-course victory is an enormous motivater not just for the particular member achiever, but for all other persons in the group as well. Each success reinforces the conviction that the dissertation group is effective; which reinforces commitment to and involvement with the group; which leads to further victories—and so an upward spiral emerges, with all members being carried nearer to completion.

Since sensitive "personal" material is going to come up repeatedly, the issue of confidentiality should be discussed from the start and agreed upon. How far to go with confidentiality is a tricky matter. May one confide in lovers and spouses, for example? I have found that people invariably do, no matter what the strictures of their vows, so mum's the word, except for close family. There will undoubtedly be times when particular supervising faculty, perceived as the instant dissertation completion obstacle, either by the candidate himself or other members, will be commented on and analyzed in—putting it discreetly—less than sympathetic terms. The danger is that a group member will be reluctant and or afraid to speak out about a faculty member if he fears that such comments will get back to a particular professor or department, threatening his own or other group members' position in the program. There is no foolproof, airtight guarantee against information being leaked. One could like awake nights thinking up *unintentional* permutations of ways in which "slanderous" materials could get out. But beyond exercising reasonable care, such sleepless nights would be exercises in *dissertation paranoia*. Obviously, you don't spill your guts about problems with *anybody* in the group, be they problems with family, spouses, friends, dissertation professors, on the first few nights—or even during the first months—of meetings. Usually, over time—after it becomes clear which people have signed on for the long haul—groups develop a strong subculture of commitment and trust, especially when members see some progress toward goals. I think it is relatively rare and unlikely that "snitches" would remain long-term members of such groups. In any event, an informer would jeopardize his own program position as much as anyone else's in the group. Needless to say, any member found "telling tales" must be expelled from the group, and this should be understood from the first sessions.

Don't abandon the group without giving it your best shot. A group worth its salt always takes time to gel. Essential dissertation-completion attitudes are patience and endurance. Practice, indeed develop, those traits by sticking through the troughs of the group's development. The group instrument that will emerge will almost certainly cushion some of the blows of the dissertation course and speed up its finish.

Being Your Own Best Dissertation Friend.

Some of the resources delineated in this chapter for coping with dissertation disturbances will work better than others for particular people. My own belief is that leaderless dissertation support groups are likely to be the most effective of the change-agents involving help from other persons. But I have to reiterate my caution that the candidate cannot rely on the certainty of *any* of these outside agents coming through to save the day. Even with a good support group, one must never turn off, or even idle, his own dissertation motor; the group could have a major disagreement and disband tomorrow. So the chapter ends where the book began—with the insistence that some irreducible part of the dissertation is always going to be private and that one must be fully prepared to go it alone. The most reliable (because you have complete control over it) and probably most effective "therapy" in times of dissertation trouble and despair is staying with your file, spending prescribed time each day in your office, soaking in the project. Here we confront once more the existential loneliness of the long-distance writer. If the candidate has the courage to live through it, the "insurmountable" problems will be solved and one day become dissertation lore to pass on to the next generation of candidates, including perhaps one's own ABD son or daughter.

SUMMARY.

1. The dissertation course is conceptualized in Figure 7.1 as an undulating wave with troughs of depression and doubt, and crests of enthusiasm at points of completing major phases, such as the proposal, especially difficult stretches of analysis or sticky chapters. The overall direction of the wave is downward, in that each successive stage from proposal completion onward is generally easier (although not without the possibility of at least temporary serious reversals further along) because of accumulated momentum, success and motivation.

2. An argument is advanced that most "disturbed" or "psychopathological" behavior exhibited by candidates during dissertation research and writing stems from "normal" response to excessive, "abnormal" dissertation pressures, rather than from deep-seated, prethesis personality problems. There is, however, a danger that dissertation-precipitated disturbances can persist beyond the end of the thesis if preventative measures, outlined in the present and in the final chapters, are not exercised.

3. Dissertation-caused anxieties and/or depressions are focused in three spheres: (a) negative feelings about the dissertation itself, particularly its doubtful outcome; (b) a diminishment of self-esteem; (c) a real or believed deterioration in significant other relationships, in which the demands of the dissertation are seen as the culprit. A listing of these disturbances is followed by an inquiry as to which are dissertation-myth derived; candidate-caused, through deficiencies in work habits or motivation; or predictable consequences of the structures and processes of the dissertation course.

4. The common and dysfunctional tendency of ABDs to reify their dissertations, converting them into objective enemies, is analyzed.

5. The second half of the chapter offers an extensive inventory and appraisal of various resource persons, facilitators, counselors, self-help strategies and dissertation-writing peers to whom or to which a candidate might turn in painful, emotional times described in the text. These include: technicians; sympathetic professors; one's own supportive students; self-help techiniques, particularly long-distance

sports; psychiatrists and other psychotherapists; dissertation therapists; and support groups of fellow dissertation writers. A thorough evaluation of the effectiveness of psychotherapists and dissertation therapists is conducted, concluding that dissertation support groups are potentially more effective and certainly more available to large numbers of ABDs than either of the other two resources. Guidelines for forming and sustaining an effective dissertation support group are provided.

6. The chapter concludes with the author's assertion that, even though dissertation groups may prove particularly helpful, the candidate's best and most reliable resource in times of dissertation dumps is the accumulated wisdom and "capital" of his file. He is commended to immerse himself in it on a regular schedule, even when matters seem blackest or most circular; solutions will emerge. Once again, the inevitability of the ABD's having to go at least some of the painful distance alone comes to the fore.

NOTES

1. One wonders when *methodology textbooks* will give doctoral students a more accurate picture of the revisionist and reciprocal nature of theory and research as American high school *history books* have begun to explode sanitized, storybook versions of American history. See, Frances Fitzgerald, *America Revised; History Schoolbooks in the Twentieth Century* (Boston: Little, Brown, 1979).

2. See Chapter Nine for elaboration of strategies to prevent postdissertation self-destruction.

3. The only situation in which time becomes a factor is where an ABD delays so long, he plays out the total allowed (usually ten years) program matriculation time. Even then, extensions are usually granted.

4. In a classic study, Merton and Lazarsfeld demonstrated that friendships have a minimal chance of surviving the explicit recognition of deep differences on basic issues and values. "Friendship As Social Process: A Substantive and Methodological Analysis," in Berger et al., eds., *Freedom and Control in Modern Society* (New York: Van Nostrand, 1954), pp. 21–54.

5. For an elaboration of what the ABD has to learn from his consultant about the theory of statistics as opposed to the mathematics and machinations of particular statistics and computer programs, see Chapter Five.

6. See A. Shostak, ed., *Our Sociological Eye: Personal Essays in Society and Culture* (Port Washington: Alfred, 1977).

7. Let it be clear that I am focusing on explicitly recognized dissertation

doubts, difficulties, anxieties. If an ABD, God love him, is not particularly bothered by the dissertation, these sections on therapy and the dissertation are not for him; and primal scream, Rolfing, transactional analysis or Sullivanian approaches may be just right for whatever extra-dissertation ill ails him.

8. D. Sternberg, "The New Radical Criminal Trials," *Science and Society*, Fall 1972.

9. What I have attempted to do for dissertation writing in this volume, Martin Shepard tries to do for psychotherapy in his *The Do-It-Yourself Psychotherapy Book* (New York: Wyden: 1973).

10. The theses are often more interesting to the *therapist* than the writer, since the former approaches them afresh, unweighted down with the history of tediousness experienced by the candidate.

CHAPTER 8

The Dissertation Defense

THE DEFENSE: FORMALITY OR SERIOUS LAST STAGE?

In dissertation subculture, the defense is painted in two contradictory ways: 1. It is a "piece of cake," a mere formality, where the thesis committee more or less "rubber-stamps" a foregone acceptance of the dissertation. Under this view, the defense is rather congenial, almost festive, and the ABD, past the serious part of initiations, is heartily accepted into the fraternity of doctorate holders in his field. 2. The defense is a threatening, grueling two or more hours of adversary proceedings, where the (usually) five faculty members lean toward stopping the ABD from entrance into the fraternity unless he fights like an intellectual tiger.

It is difficult to know for certain which of these two contexts more closely approximates the mood and meaning of the "typical" defense of the 1980s. Much, as we have already seen in the book, depends on the specifics of particular programs and the individual relationships that an ABD has with faculty. When I defended my thesis in the late 1960s, the mood at New York University, at least in social sciences, was "piece of cake." And yet I was apprehensive about the defense: so much had not gone as expected at prior stages that I was not ready to believe in the "in-like-Flynn" model. Then, too, two additional, non-thesis committee members were assigned to my defense. One of these persons I wasn't acquainted with; the other had a reputation as being very difficult with candidates. It was also unsettling that so few candidates came up each year; surely, I thought, with only six or seven doctorates awarded (with over one hundred people at one or another stage of doctoral studies), the defense must be a formidable checkpoint. Years earlier, my preliminary comprehensive orals had been an ordeal, and it just did not seem logical that at this final point the relentless faculty would lie down and die.

It should be noted that my predefense intelligence was not very reliable, since so few got through that the pool of successful candidates to question was small, and at the time I was writing, all of my ABD peers were atomized and isolated from each other: we formed no dissertation consciousness-raising or support groups which might have collectively acquired a better picture of how serious or rigorous the defense was likely to be.

MY OWN DEFENSE ORDEAL.

It turned out that my defense was the very devil itself. Each man had his own copy of my 400-plus-page dissertation, although I had no idea how closely the two non-committee members had studied it. We sat around a long conference table, with me at the head (or *foot*, as I certainly experienced it more accurately an hour into the hearing). For a while things went well; I fielded questions about the sample, methodology and fieldwork quite handily. Then the "spoiler" turned his guns on me. He singled out one section of my hypotheses testing and began his own dissertation on how it was faulty, or wrongheaded, or didn't prove what it was supposed to prove. I do not remember just what the objection was, most certainly because of traumatic amnesia. I do recall trying desperately to understand his argument in order to make a coherent response, but failing. To this day I don't know if the other committee members understood either, or pretended to understand to save face or to avoid a picture to me of a faculty divided. I do know that this fellow began to turn the defense against me. I remember the frustration and despair that hit me, the sweat of fear that drenched my shirt: Here I have devoted my life for nearly two years to this dissertation, here I know more about chiropractic student culture than any man alive; and this son of a bitch, picking out three or four pages of my 422, is going to sink me! I remember also thinking about my wife's celebration party for me that night, to which she'd invited probably one hundred folks, and how mortifying it was going to be explaining what happened to me when they arrived to congratulate me. It is not the profoundest piece of advice, I hope, that I offer the reader in this volume, but still a self-protecting one: Don't schedule a defense celebration party for the same night as the defense.

Again, I'll never quite know why the "spoiler" didn't succeed. Perhaps the others felt he was picking on me or were irritated that he took up so much time with points they didn't grasp. The three committee members knew how I had put my heart and energy into the project, knew I grasped the subject better than my interrogator, regardless of his superior debate style and my momentary intellectual paralysis. The close contact I had maintained with my committee, showing them chapters of the dissertation as I went along, probably saved the day. Somehow we got off the sticking point and moved rather desultorily through half an hour more of questioning.

Then, as the custom is in these matters, I was asked to step outside while they made their decision. The fifteen or so minutes I waited in a corridor or empty classroom seemed like hours. With every passing minute I was more certain they had rejected my thesis, or at least my *defense* of it (more below on this distinction). After an eternity, my adviser came out and said, "Congratulations, Doctor." By that point I was more flooded with relief than joy; I actually cried. Afterwards, the defense committee took me for the traditional success drink. The spoiler did not attend. Although nothing very substantive was mentioned, I knew it had been a near thing.

At least it had been a near thing in having my dissertation accepted unconditionally. I know now that the worst that could have happened would have been the committee's insisting I make certain changes to satisfy, in this case, the one unrelenting member. I understand now that ultimate full acceptance had never been in jeopardy—I had simply done too much competent sociological work for them to have turned it down—but my lack of information about other than zero-sum defense outcomes, combined, I believe, with the faculty's own informal *ad hoc* procedures about passing, failing or conditionally passing dissertations at that time, caused me much grief, most of it squeezed into the two-hour defense and subsequent fifteen minutes of waiting for the jury to come in.

Shortly after my defense, I began hearing about people who passed subject to "major" or "minor" revisions; I have since known of several cases where a candidate was failed outright and irreversibly (at various universities). It would require a study in its own right, and in any event there is no data available, to inquire as to whether dissertation defenses in general have moved closer to the adversary model over the past couple of decades. But my comments in this chapter about preparing intellectually and emotionally for the defense are in line with my booklong abiding point of view in dissertation matters: Assume that the defense committee is out to torpedo you, that you are going to have to go it alone on the defense with no allies on the committee. Preparing your defense in line with these assumptions, you will come to the hearing with your best possible case. If the defense turns out to be congenial and uneventful, what a pleasant surprise—but never count on it.

PREPARATION.

The old medical joke about the operation being a success but the patient dying has its dissertation analogue in the thesis being a success but the defense a disaster. At first look, it appears that the mere researching and writing of the dissertation is itself a most adequate preparation for a little two-hour defense (what are two hours, after all, compared with two intensive years?) with five people, none of whom know half of what the candidate does about his subject. And yet, paradoxically, it may be just that excessive expertise, relative to faculty, that can backfire (as in my case) with a professor who wants to make it clear who's boss.

A candidate must prepare for the defense in *three* areas: 1. total mastery of the substance of the dissertation; 2. "packaging" of the dissertation for the social ritual of the formal defense; 3. cultivation of a set of self-protective and realistic attitudes about the defense which will carry the ABD through both the predefense period and defense itself with relative equanimity. The operative word in preparation is *defense*—taken very seriously and literally—of both the dissertation and the sensibilities of its writer.

Readiness on Substantive Issues.

Regular attention to one's devil's advocate file (see Chapter Three) right up until the time of the defense is an optimal approach for keeping at one's fingertips the most difficult or probing questions examiners are likely to put. Devil's-advocate-file exercises should be supplemented with devil professor role playing in the candidate's dissertation group.

Packing the Dissertation for the Defense.

The defense candidate has to keep in mind that the faculty's approach to the dissertation is far different from his own. The ABD is obsessed with it; whereas total faculty man-hour attention to it probably hasn't amounted to one week's time in the candidate's office. All his wrestling with details of data-gathering, slightly variant statistical approaches, tedious assembly of bibliography and footnotes, proofreading couldn't interest them less. As outrageous as it seems, from the amount of blood, sweat and tears shed by the candidate, my sense is that the defense committee readers go right on by about 75 percent of the material.[1] What, then, do they tend to focus on? They look to the big picture, to a sense of what the dissertation is contributing to the field and to it's original elements (see discussion in Chapter Four). The candidate's packaging preparation should be in these areas.

An important and almost universally neglected aspect of packaging is the two- or three-page single-spaced *abstract* that University Microfilms requires at the beginning of all dissertations. Programs vary as to whether that abstract has to be included at the time of the defense, or whether one can write it up after a successful defense. My counsel is to make it the first item that hits the defense reader's eye: a terse yet complete overview of the dissertation, including the statement of the problem embedded in the key concerns of the discipline, a conveyance of its contribution and originality, the hypotheses developed from the problem, the methodologies employed in gathering and testing hypotheses-related data, the major findings, discussion of the results and implications of the study for the field. The abstract should lift the central themes from each chapter, condensing each into no more than a paragraph or two.

Dissertation defenses have a "shotgun marriage" aspect to them. They almost always seem to be set up a day before the spring term is over, with half the faculty packing their suitcases for the next day's summer trip to Formentera. It becomes a very real problem for the candidate to get the five required warm bodies together for the two hours. Usually, three of them have to be the thesis committee, with the other two from the department or a "sister" department (say, an

197

anthropologist attending a sociology defense). More often than not, mere chance (along with a little help from the program's secretary) as to who happens to still be in town and available on June 31 at two in the afternoon—rather than any logical connection of a member's interests or specialities with the candidate's thesis—determines who sits in the fourth and fifth defense chairs. Certainly, one cannot gear any extensive preparation to these latecomers to the dissertation scene. It may well be that, given the structure of their general university obligations—in which serving as fifth reader of a dissertation can hardly place in the top rungs of priority—combined with the fact that they may not receive your 300-page, 30-table dissertation until a few days before the defense (there are true and not infrequent stories about defense members seeing the thesis for the first time when they sit down at the examining table), the abstract is the *only* part of the dissertation they read! Under these circumstances, the need for and utility of a clear and convincing abstract with some clout should be very apparent.

Aside from orienting, impressing and maybe pacifying eleventh-hour faculty arrivals at the dissertation, repeated revision of the abstract by the candidate throughout the dissertation course puts the 25 percent the defense hearing will concentrate on at the top of his inventory. To repeat my advice from Chapter Three, once a month throughout the dissertation course, starting with the proposal stage, the candidate should sit down with a tape recorder and recount, off the top of his dissertation head, the story of his thesis. Any given oral abstract should then be played back to test its credibility both to the candidate and the awaiting reference group, the defense committee. At a number of points, the entire series of monthly abstracts should be chronologically played back, so that the ABD gets a sense of the development and the stages of his project. After ten or twelve of these, telling one's dissertation story to the committee that final afternoon should be almost second nature. If one should happen to get rattled during the defense, long-term recital training should ensure carrying it off anyway.

Appearance of the dissertation is another aspect of packaging for faculty that is often neglected (although in a minority of cases it is *overdone*). Although an IBM Selectric-typed dissertation won't carry a word-salad dissertation, the average reader wouldn't throw it aside anywhere nearly as quickly as a less elegantly typed version. With borderline dissertations (which the author most definitely does not counsel settling for) a beautifully typed thesis might even win the day. In any event, the final draft of the dissertation which the committee uses should be professional typed (as should the final version of the proposal). The cost of three-to-five hundred dollars is a most justified and necessary expense. It makes absolutely no sense for a candidate to have given years of his life to a dissertation and then balk at spending a few hundred bucks to have it presented and packaged with style. As a matter of fact, one's dissertation *deserves* a first-class presentation. If you are reluctant to have it typed up properly, this should give you some signal that perhaps the thesis isn't yet up to par.

A first-rate abstract and professionally typed version of the dissertation have postdefense professional uses as well: universities sometimes ask professorial candidates to include an abstract and even, for people under serious consideration, a copy of the entire dissertation in their application papers; if you want to adapt your dissertation for publication as a book, you must have a professionally typed version to send around to interested publishers.

The point here is that all readers of the dissertation, from defense committee, to employers, agents, editors or publishers, get a sense of how the candidate *himself* views the quality of his project as reflected in its physical representation. Our trade, after all, is practised with and mediated by typewritten documents; there is no getting around this central fact of modern scholarship. When a candidate pays scant or sloppy attention to this norm, his faculty readers have a tendency, not without a certain justification in this context, to label or prejudge him, and *a fortiori,* his dissertation, as "unprofessional."

THE DEFENSE STATE OF MIND.

Until quite recently, patients signed their consent to operations without surgeons informing them of the procedures or risks of particular surgery. Patients awaited surgery in ignorant terror. After years of malpractice lawsuits by operees demanding, but not being awarded, damages for "complications" from operations, the courts evolved the tort doctrine of "informed consent," which holds that it is the doctor's duty to describe the operation, including what could go wrong, before the patient can give his permission. In most doctoral programs, it is the responsibility of the candidate to start the defense's wheels rolling; of course he needs the permission of at least his adviser, who presumably has made a judgment that the dissertation as it now stands is either acceptable or has gone about as far as it can go within its present framework of development (the distinction between the two will be discussed in a moment). In some ways, the typical ABD facing his defense is like the patient facing his operation, particularly under the old model of "uninformed consent," in that he has neither a clear picture of what will likely transpire nor of what could go wrong. In such a state of defense darkness, we have the breeding ground for predefense terror, during-defense paralysis and shock, and postdefense depression and outrage.

"Uninformed consent" is most likely to characterize those ABDs who have failed to gain approval of successive stages and chapters of the dissertation from crucial committee members, have failed to pursue the contract model of the dissertation (in many programs the during-dissertation supervision and validation guidelines are still so vague that a candidate can go ahead with the bulk of his thesis unscrutinized by faculty); have refrained from joining any kind of dissertation support group. Keeping in close touch down at the department and keeping in close contact with dissertation-writing peers is a synergistic process which anticipatorily socializes the ABD to his defense, reduces the "great blank" (A. Moorehead's term for uncharted Australia) of the final trial. But since many ABDs, either by personal decision or structural laxity of their program, continue to shy away from regular interaction with faculty during the dissertation course and/or refrain from joining with other students in the same boat, defense terror and shock are likely to continue. However, the following pages attempt to spell out the options open to the committee and some of the dynamics of the defense hearing, to alert and prepare the unwary ABD.

If a candidate has pursued the contract model to the full, he has relatively little to fear, since the three supervising faculty have accepted the thesis at least in its general thrust, and they constitute a majority of the defense committee. Any subtraction from three-person prior approval—say, one member sitting on the fence about the validity of your methodology—greatly increases the chances of defense obstacles. The opposite-polar case is going in without *anybody*'s approval. It sometimes happens that even when a candidate keeps in contact with his committee, these faculty will not make a commitment at a given point, want to "wait and see." Such reluctance may not be delinquent or dilatory on the part of supervising faculty; they may feel the product is a borderline "hard" case. In such an event, unwilling to take a firm stand, they may prefer to "throw it into the lap" of the final defense committee of five. This is a position of extreme jeopardy for an ABD, almost a Russian roulette model of the defense, where one has no allies and the moods or caprices of any of the five can push the group decision in one direction or the other. I believe that if an ABD follows the "game plan" outlined in this volume, his chances of finding himself on such an end-of-dissertation spot are, if not impossible, at least quite slim.

DEFENSE COMMITTEES' OPTIONS AND THE ALL-OR-NOTHING MYTH.

Head-in-the-sand ABDs approach the defense with the *all-or-nothing myth* (which may have some *reality* in their particular cases if they have assiduously avoided faculty approval of the basic outline of their thesis): "either they grant me my doctorate 'at five in the afternoon' or they flunk me." I have already noted that the trend in defenses is toward passing with revisions required. Different programs use various terminologies, but there are five categories of defense result: 1. Unconditional pass, with no revisions, except changes in typos, or semicolons and commas. I believe the frequency of this outcome to be on the wane. 2. Conditional pass, subject to minor revisions, larger than commas and spelling. A candidate might be asked to run another set of tests on his data, or elaborate on a critique of certain theories, or further develop implications for the study in the last chapter. I believe that this second category may today be the modal one. 3. Conditional pass, subject to major revisions, where whole chapters or sections of the dissertation have to be rewritten, reanalyzed or even re-researched. This third pass is not an insignificant number and is growing. 4. Occasionally a candidate, through nervousness or speaker's block, fails his *presentation,* even though the faculty *passes his dissertation,* with or without revisions. The author knows of several cases of just such a mishap. This type of failure was always cured, either by another defense or by some innovative faculty approach, viz., with a particularly formal-group-shy candidate, individual professors contrived to examine him about his dissertation over lunches and dinners. The departure (at Harvard) from the conventional examination was justified on the grounds of the dissertation itself being outstanding.

201

5. Complete failure of the thesis, where the committee judges that no amount of revision will cure defects in the thesis because its core is unsustainable. People who fall into this last category are truly dissertation tragedies and often never recover from the blow. The final section of the chapter addresses coping with this situation.

Candidates should make every effort to ascertain the range of options for their specific program, and further, if possible, what the "percentages" are in terms of where recent prior defenders were allocated, along the option spectrum. If one is not in constant touch with faculty and ABD groups, he may well have to go in to the program chairman and ask him outright. Obviously, inquiring about the empirical distribution among the formal categories is a much more delicate matter, perhaps better pursued among fellow students (although student grapevines, as opposed to dissertation support *groups,* can be notoriously or hysterically misleading on this score).

The point is to replace the terror of the all-or-nothing myth with a quite different pre-, during and post-defense attitude which accepts any outcome from numbers one through three as a victory. (Even the rare fourth outcome is usually only a temporary setback.) Certainly, one is trying for a number one, but the odds (and each department has to be checked individually to get accurate ones) are more in favor of a conditional pass, with most often minor—but not infrequently major—revisions. The outcome of the defense, then, parallels the outcome of the proposal hearing, where I argued (in Chapter Four) that approval subject to changes was still a major victory. I realize that a conditional defense pass is existentially more of a letdown, coming at the end when one smells victory, than a conditional proposal pass, so much earlier in the game. But, again, by this point the ABD has waited and worked so long that "running the few more miles" (see the analogy between dissertation writing and long-distance running developed in Chapter Seven) of the revisions should be taken in stride. The momentum to negotiate the revision "gun lap" will only be lost if the candidate goes in with all his eggs in the unconditional pass basket.

DEFENSE DYNAMICS AND ALIGNMENTS.

The favorite defense-lore story has to do with how, either unintentionally or by the candidate's design, two or more of the defense committee become involved in a lengthy debate with *each other* over some point generated by the dissertation and forget about questioning the student. At the end of two hours, he emerges as unconditionally passed without being especially examined. This is a kind of counter-vailing myth to the defense horror story of a candidate being mer-cilessly battered by a unified and relentless faculty five for a couple of hours. Although both versions are apocryphal, they both touch upon the theme of intracommittee relations and interaction during the de-fense. How should the candidate perceive the five persons facing him over the defense table in a manner calculated to expedite a successful defense? As a committee of the whole? As a tightly knit group with a common perspective? As a temporary aggregate of individuals with no shared view?

We have already seen that the administrative procedures for com-mittee formation almost guarantee that the five will not be one group, in the sense of having shared an antecedent developmental history centered on concerns of the candidate's dissertation. For defense pur-poses it is best, and most accurate, to break down the five into one *group* composed of the three long-standing dissertation committee members (although not necessarily united in attitudes, interests or level of concern about a dissertation: the adviser might be highly involved, the other two thesis committee members only nominally engaged) and two last-minute visiting firemen *individuals,* with prob-lematic connections both to one another and to the "Gang of Three." Dissecting the committee in this initial fashion does connect in some sense with the "divide and conquer" defense tale recounted above.

I believe that in almost all cases—unless one has special credible intelligence to the contrary—the candidate should "play" to the thesis committee group within the defense five. The ABD has had by this point an involved experience with the three, beginning with a hearing on his proposal (not unlike the dissertation defense, in many respects) and continuing through the research and writing of the dissertation, where all along, if he pursued the contract model of the thesis, he kept them current with unfolding developments. The last two members of the defense committee share none of this dissertation history: in a fundamental sense, the group alignment is the candidate plus his the-sis committee, against the two *pro-tem* faculty judges, notwithstanding quite different official demarcations. The latter two may well not even have *read* substantial parts of the dissertation.

This structural realignment of groups within the dissertation defense doesn't yield inevitable or universal increments for all candidates. Specific circumstances of programs and peculiar relationships with one's committee have to be weighed. If the committee has been hostile for two years of supervision, the candidate's being part of the "in group" here will not protect him from their pursuing that animosity into a trying defense. If the committee has been indifferent to his project, "in-group" status will not provide much protection against overzealous attacks from the last two faculty, although the tendency of even disgruntled members of a group to unite against a "common enemy" sometimes accrues to a defense candidate. Thus, the author does not mean to counteradvise the original defense rule of thumb that the candidate should expect the hearing to be an adversary one. It is nonetheless true that in those cases where one has had a "good" regular relationship with his committee (probably a minority situation, and, in any event, open to the hazards of subjective misevaluation by the candidate), he can anticipate the majority of the final committee to be in his corner.

In my own case (see above), I went into my defense with my thesis committee on my side, although this unity developed only after prolonged negotiations, accommodations, stages and struggle over a year and a half of my dissertation course. The fourth member was a person known to be tough, and perhaps a "hatchet man," but I had never taken a course with him, so I had no specifics with which to work. I had never met or known anything about the fifth man. Even had I been inclined to do so, there was no time to "case" the final two, since there couldn't have been more than a two- or three-week interval between their appointment to the committee and D day. As matters transpired, Number Four tried, and almost succeeded, in torpedoing me. He was aided by his collegial reputation for being quite brilliant. What saved me was the dissertation-specific group realignments, where my thesis committee (but not with alacrity: they let me roast for an hour) eventually took my side, even against their esteemed colleague.

Although one's historical experience with his committee may allow him to rely on a generally sympathetic stance toward his dissertation, this does not imply an easy defense; one still must prepare thoroughly with devil's advocate training geared to anticipating the most difficult queries which the three are most likely to pose. For reasons outlined above, no preparatory time should—or usually can—be devoted to the final two faculty. It is always possible that the defense examiners will get off on a tangent and dispute/debate among themselves, leaving you without much more to do than look engaged or impressed, or that the member whom you dreaded most gets replaced because of illness with Ms. Milquetoast, or that because it's a beautiful summer day outside, the board okays you in an hour and a quarter to get to the beach. Still, anybody who comes in without preparing for and expecting very hard questions does so at his dissertation peril.

DURING THE DEFENSE: WHAT TO EXPECT AND HOW TO COPE.

The normal format has the candidate seated at one end or another of the table in some type of seminar room. I believe it is important to *rehearse* the scene when possible. Most often, you can learn from the departmental secretary a week or two in advance exactly *where* the defense will be held. I was able to do this. Go to the room during a vacant hour and sit down just where you'll probably be asked to sit during the actual defense (one way to insure this seating on D day is to get there earliest).[2] Then run through the story of your thesis, exactly as you've done with your tape recorder for the file (it might be a good idea to tape this version as well, for listening to prior to D day). It may even be possible to get your dissertation group to come down to the examination room and role-play the committee.

Although we don't have a situation where the candidate can really be in control, small doses of student direction can be carved out. For instance, it is important to be physically comfortable during the defense. You might very well want to ask faculty for permission to remove your coat if it makes you feel tight or restrained. Or you might want to provide yourself with a pitcher of water to guard against getting dry during the session. If you are comfortable using a blackboard in making points—either through employing it in lectures and/or dissertation office work—try to get janitors to move one in for your defense. I have always found the latter group of grossly undervalued university workers to be very decent and accommodating in helping me with stage adjustments.

Usually, faculty will ask you questions on a round-the-table basis, with each member posing an uninterrupted series and segment of questions, and the adviser acting as moderator and "anchorman." It is putatively his job to make sure matters don't get out of hand by particular faculty interrupting each other's questioning time or taking over the meeting. Advisers/facilitators have varied success in this role; generally, the more involved your adviser is with you, the better he will do in this respect. The round-robin format tends to break down in most cases after the first hour or so, with a concomitant increase in cross-fire questions.

Remember that some inquisitors are more equal than others—normally the Big Three—and that it is correspondingly more crucial to give satisfactory responses to thesis committee members. (I maintain this, notwithstanding the—I believe—unusual turnabout of questioner importance in my own defense case.) Remember, too, that to pass you do not have to respond adequately to *every* question; I've never attended a dissertation where candidates didn't flunk at least a couple of questions (which is not surprising considering that *dozens* of questions are usually posed). You do have a very important and reliable ally sitting in the room, not in a chair but on the table: *the dissertation itself*, with all its completion, presence, facticity, embodiment of long-term thinking, research, analysis and conclusion. It is *prima facie* evidence and expert witness to your qualifications for the doctorate. If the going gets rough or the defense seems to be going against you, try to get the committee and your rattled self back to basics: open up your 300-page tome and remind them—if necessary by reading chapter and footnote—what the defense is at bottom all about: the written document of your researched dissertation. You may not speak so well, you suggest tactfully, because of the pressures of the defense situation, but let the faculty focus on the permanency of your research, rather than on the transiency of a nervous oral presentation.

What does a candidate do if he suddenly goes plain blank, most likely because he sees the tide going against him? I suggest excusing oneself from the defense for a few moments to visit the loo. Often, with some cold water in the face and five minutes' respite, you can come back and turn it around. But won't the committee think it strange? Maybe, maybe not. After all, students are constantly excusing themselves from classes to visit the bathroom; we professors often take a five-minute break during a lecture and leave the room; nominated Cabinet members excuse themselves during Congressional confirmation hearings; in your own defense, members of the committee may themselves drift in or out, or come in late, or leave early. Even if your committee should consider your departure a bit unusual, and even be onto why you took the break, so what—if the alternative is sitting there and suffering the sinking of your dissertation ship? Coaches have always known the effectiveness of a "time-out" for stopping the momentum of the other team. It is most possible that a defense time-out can break the faculty momentum against you; on your return a whole new area, with which you feel more confident to deal, might be broached. If during the last hour you acquit yourself with competence, nobody is going to weigh your mid-defense break seriously in voting whether to pass you (indeed, most will have forgotten it).

AFTERMATH.

If you are fortunate enough to win an unconditional pass, aftermath is no more than correcting some spellings and grammar (if that), and filing the appropriate number of finished xeroxed copies with your department and the registrar/recorder office. Passes subject to minor or major revisions entail further minor to major substantive dissertation work, and, in the case of passing subject to major changes, another decision about how and when to continue.

If you pass subject to minor revisions, get right on the case. No momentum should be lost here; usually, you can satisfy amendment requirements within a month or two. Precisely as with a proposal passed subject to revisions, make the rounds of the defense committee to "nail down" exactly what they really insist on being altered or elaborated. Remember from our discussion in Chapter Four that some of the suggestions and objections offered are soon forgotten by the questioners; the art of discovering how much they remember and how much they have forgotten is treated there.[3] Sometimes the adviser is delegated by the others to sum up required amendments and police their implementation. If this is program procedure, it is an easier route for the candidate, since the other four defense members will generally sign a final OK without perusal of the changes upon the assurance of the adviser that matters have been altered in accordance with their defense wishes. With the adviser supervising all revisions, the trick becomes to negotiate with *him*, in terms of what he recalls as the salient objections.

Whether he has to make the rounds of the entire defense committee or consult mainly with the adviser, the candidate is guaranteed a more sympathetic reception from faculty than at the much earlier stage of discussion of proposal revisions. Now he has gone through the fire of the defense and is nearly one of them. The candidate should keep in mind this definite and favorable change in his professors' perception of his status and prestige when he sits down at the revision bargaining table. I believe this attitude change applies—although perhaps with more reservation—even to the candidate passing with major revisions. It would be very difficult to draw precise and satisfactory lines between passes subject to minor versus major revisions. Certainly, there is some overlap in the middle, and some programs might go one way or another in a borderline case. Minor revisions generally go to secondary and tertiary matters of substance and methodology: one is asked to elaborate on a theory, thicken a bibliography, further refine the statistical workup and analysis of one section of data. But although changes are a good deal more than cleaning up some preposition-ending sentences or a sloppy abstract, the defense committee has accepted all the major components of the dissertation, and the candidate is "home free." Major revisions, on the other hand, speak to the committee's dissatisfaction with one or more primary components of the thesis: they may be dubious about the theoretical framework; or they may believe the testing of hypotheses was too thin; or that the analysis and discussion section was weak or unconvincing.

The diplomatic procedures for determining just what changes are "nonnegotiable" is the same with this conditional pass as with the pass subject to minor revisions, although in this case the candidate has more at stake since the level of demand is initially higher, whatever the ultimate conditions of the settlement. This means that a skillful candidate negotiator could conceivably knock months off revision work by obtaining a "strict interpretation" (narrow) of the defense committee's demands. It is indeed possible, because of the "give" in the postdefense picture of what happened, for a candidate, for all practical purposes, to turn a pass subject to major revisions into one subject to minor changes, regardless of official labels to the contrary.

If after revision negotiations on a pass with major changes, it becomes clear that, say, another eight months to a year of serious sustained work is still required, many ABDs will no doubt have to deliberate continuing immediately, even going on at all. My own counsel would be to push on through your discouragement as long as you have reasonably tight assurances from the committee that if you make specified revisions they will pass you once and for all. Although

208

it is impossible at the present stage of American graduate education to rely fully on a contract theory of the dissertation in any strict legalistic sense, faculty will almost invariably honor a revision deal made with a candidate who has gone as far in the dissertation course as to have obtained a conditional pass in a full-scale defense.

Is there another formal oral defense after major revisions are made? I have no reliable data on this question, because there is no common policy discernible among the multitude of doctoral programs and committees. Some programs may require some kind of postrevision hearing, but whether it involves the formality of five examiners is doubtful. More common would be the candidate's being asked to meet informally with individual (or a couple of) members of the defense committee to have a "last round" on key revisions. From what I know of these postrevision "mini-defenses" (styled in some elite Ivy League programs as "chats"), I don't believe they are very formidable, or even really of a serious adversary nature at that late point.

A FAILED DISSERTATION.

What, finally, about the case we all dread but don't discuss very often—unconditional rejection of the thesis? It is true that one can pursue appeal and grievance procedures—sometimes full-scale lawsuits—to try to turn around the program's rejection of a thesis. But precedent and the assumption of competence and sound academic judgment on the part of graduate faculty is very much in the appellant's way. If your claim is one of personal discrimination (because of sex, race or serious personal animosity) against you, and thus against your thesis, by one or more thesis or defense committee members, and you can marshal *proof* of that discrimination (either through written documents or witnesses: and witnesses are very hard to come by, since professors, like MDs, will hardly ever testify against each other; and fellow graduate students withdraw at the last moment for fear that testimony will damage their own relations with faculty and jeopardize their dissertations), you have some moderate chance of winning a reversal or new hearing. If you seriously appeal a failed dissertation either on grounds of faculty's academic incompetence (you are arguing that at least five of the graduate faculty, after a judgment based on collective discussion, are wrong about your failure to perform the dissertation contract), or on grounds of personal discrimination, but without solid proof, you are guaranteeing yourself years more of hell, with little chance of ultimate vindication or victory—years which would much better be devoted to picking up the pieces and developing in a new direction.

That "direction"—except in the rarest of cases or circumstances—should *not* be another attempt at a doctoral dissertation, at all costs *never* in the same program, since the failed candidate and the faculty have definitely had it with each other. If another dissertation is mounted, it should come, in my judgment, only after much soul-searching reflection about the pain and life costs of a possible second rejection: years of one's career life have already been wasted, consolatory talk about "having learned something from the experience" being the thinnest and cruelest of sops. Intensive support psychotherapy seems to me much more unarguably indicated and valuable in helping one learn to live with a rejected thesis, than as help in writing one.

SUMMARY.

1. Dissertation subculture portrays the final defense in two contradictory fashions. One version sees it as a mere formality where the faculty judges "rubber-stamp" a foregone acceptance. The other views it as a serious, grueling, adversary procedure where the ABD must fight vigorously to pass a hostile committee. Most real defenses fall somewhere in the middle of these polar constructs, but the candidate is advised to prepare for the most difficult and unsympathetic reception, so that he can take in stride any defense climate which develops.

2. Preparation for the defense has to be conducted in three areas. First, the candidate must possess mastery of all substantive materials. Exercises with the devil's advocate file and "devil professor" role playing in one's dissertation group are useful in acquiring complete reign over materials.

Second, the dissertation must be strategically packaged for committee members. Important packaging elements include: a lucid and comprehensive abstract which appears at the front of the dissertation and, which may be the only part of the thesis read by latecomer defense committee faculty; professionally typed, impeccably edited and corrected copies of the thesis available to judges prior to the defense date.

For reasons which are not entirely clear, past candidates have made little concerted or systematic effort anticipatorily to obtain intelligence about what goes on in the defense, and so a folklore version, accented with fear, has been handed down from one ABD generation to the next. So, third, the ABD can reduce his trepidation about the defense by investigating its format, process and faculty decision options. Later sections of this chapter provide him with some of that information.

3. Defense committees have five decision options: a. to pass the dissertation unconditionally; b. to pass it requiring minor revisions; c. to pass it requiring major revisions; d. to pass the thesis but fail the candidate's unsatisfactory oral presentation and defense; e. to fail the thesis completely, with a judgment that no amount or direction of revisions will make it acceptable.

Passes subject to some kind of revisions are becoming modal. The candidate is urged to prepare himself mentally for construing even a pass requiring major revisions as basically an ultimate acceptance of his thesis. Failure in presentation of an otherwise acceptable thesis is almost always curable by a second formal or informal defense.

4. The conventional, official view of the student candidate set off against a united faculty defense group of five is challenged and replaced by a *realpolitik* model, where the defender is aligned with his long-term committee against—or at least in distinction to—the last eleventh-hour members of the oral defense. Such a realignment calls for an adjusted ABD defense plan, where the candidate plays basically to his thesis committee majority within the larger panel of judges.

5. A typical defense format, in terms of concrete elements such as seating arrangements, duration of the hearing, styles of faculty questioning (round-robin turn-taking versus cross-fire) is described. "Rehearsal" tactics, including visiting the examination room if possible, are indicated. The author anticipates common during-defense crises, such as "going blank," inability to answer particular questions, relentless attack by one judge who is turning the tide against the candidate, and offers some tactics for saving one's defense.

6. Procedures for converting passes with conditions to final passes are outlined. Strategies for negotiating or reducing demands for changes which faculty made during the defense—bargaining processes which are facilitated by the fact that a complete record or transcript of a dissertation "trial" is rarely kept—are discussed. Usually, another formal defense is not scheduled, but revisions are reviewed in informal

meetings with individual defense committee members, or with the adviser deputized to police changes.

7. The chances for overturning a truly failed thesis through appeals or grievance procedures are slim. A second dissertation effort is ordinarily counteradvised. At any cost, if undertaken, it should never be written for the same faculty and program as the first. The usefulness of support psychotherapy in the aftermath of dissertation failure seems less debatable than its effectiveness in helping a candidate successfully to finish.

NOTES

1. Even though the adviser and two other thesis committee members presumably read most of one's thesis, they probably retain, at best, 25 percent. But which quarter? Ah, that is the preparation question.

2. I *still* visit lecture rooms assigned for my courses some days prior to the first day of teaching to get a feel for size and ambience. I sometimes reshape my approach, depending on this reconnaissance.

3. Records of dissertation defenses are very hit or miss. I have never attended one that was taped, nor do we find dissertation stenographers transcribing the minutes. Individual faculty and the adviser/chair may take more or less systematic notes, but certainly talk of a full record is silly. This means that there is indeed room for negotiation about required changes, since a full, objective account of the whole proceedings is not available.

CHAPTER 9

Beyond the Dissertation: Surviving It and Professionally Exploiting It

DISSERTATION DAMAGE.

The ordeal of the dissertation course threatens postcompletion damage to the candidate in one or more of three different ways:

1. Loss of self-esteem, self-respect and self-confidence, the varied manifestations of which were discussed in detail in Chapter Seven, accompanied by counsel for avoiding or at least containing them.

2. Postdissertation paralysis, where the dissertation becomes the end of a career rather than the beginning. Here the candidate spends the next decade locked into a postmortem *angst und dram,* with no time, interest or energy to produce any new piece of work. The productive paralysis extends far beyond writing and researching: the burnt-out, lying-low professor's teaching is uninspired, his counseling of students unenthusiastic. If he becomes a graduate faculty member, he is likely to pass his indifference and negativism on to a new generation of ABDs, perpetuating the tradition of lack of support for dissertation writers.

Postdissertation atrophy is best countered in the manner of rehabilitation for all paralyses: exercise. The indicated exercise is pushing on with a new project after a very brief rest—long-term layoffs are counterindicated. Whether the new Ph.D. should strike off in a new direction or quite soon take up his dissertation for professional exploitation (discussed below) depends on how effectively the writer was able to employ the kinds of strategies for counteracting dissertation traumas, neuroses and disruptions outlined in this book.

3. Disrupted and sometimes irrevocably ruptured intimate relationships with spouses, lovers and close friends. Dissertation writing is, as Chapters Two and Seven spelled out, a "high-risk" occupation for divorces and breakups. The best way to avoid them is to attempt to bring your mate or lover into your project. There are styles for effecting this: informing him/her about it on a regular basis, including asking the partner to read and give feedback on sections and chapters as you write them; invitations to occasional meetings of your dissertation support group; having the partner actually work with you on some parts of the dissertation. My wife worked actively with me on a number of key areas of my research: she was responsible for my filing system being as thorough and effective as it was; she shared the enormous hand-tabulated correlation and table-partialing of the data; she provided invaluable angles of analysis when the data seemed to turn against me and my hypotheses. As it turned out, her involvement didn't save our marriage, but it did prevent its last two or three years from deteriorating into the kind of dissertation disaffection and role absenteeism detailed in Chapter Seven. Whatever the style of engaging the nonwriting partner, the idea is to limit as much as possible the other's feeling shut out from a large, unknown, even secret part of your life which is increasingly perceived as coming between you, or taking you away from him/her. How successful the ABD is in bringing the other into the dissertation enterprise depends on the idiosyncratic intellectual and emotional disposition of a particular partner.

In a certain number of cases, individuals will go their own ways after the dissertation. Others will stick with each other, hoping that time will bring matters back to the *ante status quo*. If the partner has continued to see the dissertation as alien and enemy, resisting attempts to bring him/her in, preferring a strategy of "just waiting until it's over" to cure estrangements the prognosis is poor for the two getting back together in the same old predissertation way. Postdissertation life is going to be a series of *new* extended career projects for the successful candidate (albeit probably not so tinged with desperation and anxiety as the dissertation) which the other may well experience as more of the same relationship diminishment.

An ABD who wishes to avoid the "I gave you the best years of my life" confrontation two years after the dissertation has to refrain from making promises he can't or won't want to keep. This entails disabusing one's partner of the idea that if he/she is just patient another year,

214

"it'll be all over," conveying instead that sustained work and a certain amount of role absenteeism will never be "over," from now on are an integral part of your intellectual, professional and emotional life. He/she may not accept this scenario for your future relationship and may decide to part company. The alternatives to honesty are subsequent years of squabbles, guilt-laying by one's partner which cripples every productive enterprise, mutually reinforced and spiraling resentment.

If a spouse or lover cannot accept your postdissertation pursuit of long-term serious writing and research—and this involvement is very important to you (which one would presume it to be for the great majority of persons who took on a task as demanding and unusual as the dissertation)—he or she may not be the "right" person for you in the years to come. The pain or resentment of living with a person who doesn't possess a kindred need to pursue intellectual projects, or at least respect and sympathy for such endeavors, must be experienced to be fully understood. At some point an individual, of course, has to make his own choice, weighing the pros and cons of continuing. It must be acknowledged that some persons of mighty intellect and drive toward publishing choose to stay with mates who are homebody types. Freud's wife kept, by all accounts, a comfortable bourgeois home but does not seem to have been a close intellectual confidante. Marx's wife appears to have offered more in the way of emotional than intellectual companionship. But both of these women were certainly sympathetic to their husbands' continuing projects, if not actively participant in them. A certain amount of complementariness between instrumental/intellectual and expressive/emotional roles in a marriage may be very functional, so long as both partners respect the other's values and worth.

SURVIVAL KIT: DISSERTATION MYTHS V. REALITIES.

Most severe ongoing and postdissertation disturbances develop because the ABD loses perspective about his problem/project and overreacts in desperation. Faulty perspective is often caused by the candidate believing in and living by dissertation myths reviewed in this volume. Postdissertation problems are the historical and biographical culmination of difficulties and distresses developed along the dissertation course; they do not spring from the brow of the defense committee's final inquisition. If such an accumulation, then, is to be prevented, or at least minimized, survival precautions have to be instituted from the start and practiced all along the journey of the thesis. One effective survival technique is neutralization of candidate- and dissertation-destructive myths. What follows is a brief restatement of the major recurring dissertation myths that the book has dissected, along with antidotal realities for neutralizing their detrimental effects on the student at the ABD and postdissertation stages:

1. *Myth:* "I've picked the wrong topic. It's not going to work."

Reality: If you've selected the topic with the care outlined in this volume, it is most unlikely that it will not prove viable. Almost all ABDs believe at one time another along the course that their particular topic was "wrong."

2. *Myth:* "I picked a dull topic."

Reality: Down the dissertation course, all theses go through stages of being perceived as dull or boring by their writers, no matter how exciting, "in" or relevant they appeared at proposal or research time. For their writers, regardless of evaluation by outsiders, all theses are equally dull and tedious in the framework of required research, statistical workup, analysis, writing, rewriting detail.

3. *Myth:* "X had an easier dissertation than mine."

Reality: There never was an easy dissertation. Although your problems and X's may vary both in substantive areas (he had a devil of a time with theory construction, you with statistics) and timing (twice he had to revise his proposal, you had to do two unanticipated pilots for your measuring instruments), the degree of difficulty roughly balances out in the end.

4. *Myth:* "Everybody's finished but me."

Reality: Half or more of the ABDs in your program who started the dissertation when you did haven't finished, either. Nor is there any "quota system," so that even if you do finish a year or two later than some of your cohorts, you'll receive your degree.

5. *Myth:* "Y over at Berkeley scooped me. There goes my thesis."

Reality: The journalistic analogy is invalid for doctoral dissertations. Ten people can, and would, write ten theoretically and methodologically independent dissertations on the same general topic in social sciences, education, humanities or literature.

6. *Myth:* "The faculty is out to get me."

Reality: If faculty have a dissertation supervision vice, it is almost always *indifference,* rather than persecution. It may be that in a given case one particular professor is hostile to a candidate, but to posit a conspiracy of several faculty plotting an ABD's downfall, given the

216

low priority of dissertation supervision for faculty career mobility, is to suffer from dissertation delusions of grandeur.

7. *Myth:* "I'm ruined. The data aren't panning out."

Reality: Outside of "fairy tale" introductory methodology books, the data never pan out with no hitches on first testing of hypotheses with original instruments. In the real world of dissertation writing, everybody has to use a range of *postfactum* adjustments, which are the general norm in social, life and physical sciences.

8. *Myth:* "I'm all alone with an unshareable problem."

Reality: On a purely statistical level, you have the company of over 50,000 other men and women starting out each year to write a dissertation. Although there is undoubtedly an unshareable, lonely core to dissertation writing, its proportion and importance relative to the entire thesis apple can be reduced by reaching out to significant others, particularly a dissertation support group, and receptive spouses, lovers and close friends.

9. *Myth:* "I'm selling my soul to the committee."

Reality: Souls are lost and saved in matters much larger than dissertation negotiations. The faculty-demanded accommodations and revisions that one makes with so much pain (soul-searching) during dissertation days will appear trivial upon five-years-hence reflection (if, indeed, one remembers them at all), especially if one has transacted two or three subsequent major projects.

10. *Myth:* "It won't come in any good, anyway. Ph.D.s are driving taxis."

Reality: You *knew* jobs were tight when you began last year, committed to finishing. So chances are that the recent not-worth-the effort argument reflects a rationale for quitting a tough project, rather than a reevaluation of economic circumstances and possibilities.

11. *Myth:* "When it ends, my career troubles are over."

Reality: Your dissertation is the first in a series of similar long-term projects you will be pursuing throughout your career. Many of the difficulties or "troubles" you have experienced with the thesis are built into academic professions which reward people principally on the basis of their continued production of dissertation-type scholarship and research. Added to the basically noncompetitive conditions of dissertation writing will be the "trouble" of contesting with colleagues for a limited number of tenureships and more senior professorships. The dissertation should be seen as anticipatory

217

socialization for the norms, demands and rewards of an academic career, rather than some kind of "one-shot" discontinuous effort by whose completion the new Ph.D. will have "arrived" once and for all.

It is also doubtful that troubles will be over with lovers and spouses on the issue of your continuing need for large swaths of time in your office for subsequent projects. In truth, you won't be able to "go home again," to the halcyon predissertation, preprofessional days of graduate student existence. And you won't *want* to. You may very well be able to work out a satisfactory new arrangement with family and loved ones, but time for yourself is going to have to be a nonnegotiable condition of the treaty.

12. *Myth:* "Once it's done, I'll never look at the damn thing again."

Reality: Although you may well lay off the dissertation for some undefined period immediately after completion, most candidates find themselves coming back to the thesis for a range of utilitarian purposes and emotional reflection. Dissertation exorcism or banishment attitudes reflect the dissertation-as-enemy theme, which makes it harder to finish; the enemy syndrome can also blind the finisher to his richest and most accessible source of professional capital angrily banished to the back of a filing cabinet.

GETTING PROFESSIONAL MILEAGE OUT OF YOUR DISSERTATION.

The most prominent national policy theme of late twentieth-century America is conservation and maximum exploitation of existing resources and capital. At an individual level, the largest resource or source of capital that the new Ph.D. is likely to possess is his recently completed dissertation.[1] The candidate has made an enormous investment in this project, a kind of "risk venture" that has now paid off. Although he cannot rest for a career on the laurels of this one success, it would be foolish not to exploit it for purposes and payoffs beyond receiving the doctorate. Even if you "hated" your dissertation and swear never to cast eyes upon it again, that mood will pass, and you will want to make use of your large resource in one or more of the following ways:

Publishing It As a Book,

not just in University Microfilms, Michigan. The potential for a dissertation being converted to a book varies enormously with field and subject. Although I played down the specific topic of a dissertation as being of primary importance in the decision to write a thesis, a candidate looking way ahead, with serious ambitions and expectations to convert his dissertation into a book, must consider the market for his topic. Of course, even such farsightedness in no way guarantees— or even increases the chances—that a publisher will want to publish an "in" topic dissertation three or four years later; the topic may have "peaked" by then, or the manuscript may be judged of insufficient quality.

Even if a publisher is interested in a dissertation-as-book, editors will insist that it be changed in numerous ways, the most important involving a "translation" from dissertationese to readable English. Then, too, even important, well-researched dissertations display a choppy and sometimes contradictory content and style which reflect the candidate's efforts to meet the demands of various thesis committee members.

People who are "sure" that somebody is going to contract for their dissertations sometimes keep double books—write one version of the thesis for the committee and their degree and another for Random House. My own sense is that this procedure, in the context of the already numerous demands of the dissertation, is too taxing for most ABDs and may well delay the dissertation itself by dividing one's energies. My inclination would be to set up a "conversion" file, where one would annotate areas that would require deletion, elaboration, change in style to qualify for a book; however, such a file should not become a major project in itself during the dissertation course.

It can happen that you *won't want* to publish your dissertation as a book, at least not for a good while, even if offers are made. Your materials may be perceived as damaging, offensive or occasionally even libelous to the group you researched, regardless of how scientifically ethical or objective you considered your procedures and conclusions. When the subjects of your history, political science or sociology dissertation don't come out smelling like roses, it might even be *dangerous* to publish as a book, as opposed to burying your findings in the University Microfilm archives. Contrary to conventional wisdom, one can publish *and* perish!

In my own case, several high-placed chiropractors got wind that my dissertation was critical of their professional organization (it *never* evaluated the therapeutic efficacy of chiropractic itself). On a number of occasions, it was indirectly communicated to me that my own health (chiropractic and otherwise) would be best guaranteed by letting the dissertation lie unpublished. At one point, representatives of one of the chiropractic associations offered to buy my manuscript "for publication." I knew, of course, that what they really wanted was the legal copyright to the materials, so they could prevent it from being published. I refused their offer. Within six months after my dissertation defense, I received serious interest about the thesis from a New England university press but did not pursue this tentative offer, primarily out of fear of unpleasant consequences, including physical retaliation, from the chiropractic profession. Although I used the dissertation in many of the ways discussed below, I never converted it to a book.* As time went by and I became engaged in other areas of sociology, my enthusiasm for such a conversion waned. In my judgment, if one is going to turn dissertation into full-scale book, the iron should be struck while relatively hot, within, say, a year of completion. Otherwise, one is going to encounter large mental obstacles to gearing up and reinvolving on such a complete and detailed scale.

Writing Articles or Book Chapters from the Dissertation.

Although getting a book out of your dissertation is the exception, reworking two or three chapters into journal articles or chapters for edited volumes is common enough to be the rule. The two advantages of this use of the dissertation are: you don't have to reinvolve yourself with the enormous job of reworking the style, organization and substance of the entire thesis; and, for better or for worse, journalese and dissertationese in a given discipline are more or less cognate, eliminating the need for much translation.

The Dissertation As an Important Credential for Teaching or Research Appointments.

It is quite common for employers to ask new Ph.D.s to include their doctoral dissertations (initially the too-often neglected abstract will be required; if the candidate gets to the final rounds of decision, he may be asked to send along the full thesis) in application materials. On more than one occasion I have seen a candidate land an assistant professorship primarily on the grounds of the hiring committee's being impressed with a fine dissertation from a "good" program. Al-

---

*It is ironic that its only major appearance in print comes in this present book on dissertation writing over a decade later.

though the dissertation is frequently crucial in obtaining one's *first* full-time "line, tenure-track" position, it can sometimes be influential as well in later career decisions, such as tenure, promotion or offers from other universities. Almost like the mystique surrounding the Phi Beta Kappa key, there is a kind of continuing corona around the first-rate dissertation which can open many academic and foundation doors for its author.

As an Entrée into the Speciality Area of the Thesis.

The ABD takes a very deep dive indeed into one or more subfields of his discipline. Not only does he become one of the nation's foremost specialists in his selected area during the dissertation course, but he often has occasion to correspond with or meet personally the established leading lights of the speciality to get advice or references concerning fine theoretical and/or methodological problems he has encountered. In my own case, I became a close colleague with a number of prominent medical sociologists, one or two of whom offered to take me on their grants as a "post-doc." Several of my clients have pursued, at my suggestion, correspondence with recognized researchers in their dissertation areas. I have no doubt this will multiply research or teaching opportunities for them. Specialities within disciplines are subcultures within subcultures. If you hook into one of their networks by virtue of your dissertation, the grapevine will spread it about, and you will be sought after. It should be stressed that most often the new Ph.D. has to take the initial step, creating advertisements for himself by contacting the currently recognized authorities in the field.

The Dissertation/Doctorate As Essential for Eligibility for Tenure-Track Professorships.

Until even the early 1970s it was possible to land a tenured university teaching job without the doctorate. Higher education lore is rich in tales and humor about how this was achieved (for even then, the formal rules of most departments required the doctorate for appointment to the rank of assistant professor or above, and for tenure): fifty-year-old men vowing to their university presidents that they would reregister in Ph.D. programs tomorrow; cleverly concocted cases for professors possessing the "equivalent" of an earned doctorate through work and/or experience in the field; sworn affidavits about the ABD

221

defending his dissertation the week after tenure is conferred (a defense which never materializes); even downright lying about possessing a doctorate, when the candidate dropped out of graduate school at a pre-ABD stage. Although it still happens that somebody occasionally squeezes through, enforcement of and adherence to the doctorate-required rule has tightened up to the point of near-universal application. This may be the university-sphere manifestation of post-Watergate aboveboard administrative policies. Even if one managed to be the exception here, his tenure would be limited to the specific university where he squeezed by, in effect sentencing him to career "life" in a particular department.

As a Model for Further Large Scholarly Projects in One's Career.

In the first chapter of this volume I argued that the majority of ABDs are at a loss to research and write the dissertation, because nothing in their theretofore graduate or undergraduate education has prepared them for such a vast and original enterprise. Willy-nilly, the dissertation serves as the great apprenticeship in a given field of intellectual craftsmanship. But the apprenticeship is not the classic one of serving under a master tradesman or senior guild member, since, as we have seen, the graduate faculty is generally unevenly or nondirectively related to one's project. The apprenticeship is a *self*-apprenticeship, where, cut off from pre-ABD graduate faculty support and guidance systems, the candidate has to use his ingenuity and improvisation to solve his dissertation problems.[2] In ways I cannot even count my dissertation has served as a model for me in writing a number of books and long articles. My contemporary style of organization of sections, presentation of materials forcefully to support arguments, analysis of data, construction of tables, figures, diagrams and much much more, all are rooted—not without modification over the years, of course—in that trial of fire and two years' time. I believe most Ph.D.s would similarly link their later work to foundations in their dissertations.[3] The groundwork function of the dissertation for a productive career in one's discipline cannot be overstated.

As a Source for Lectures for Years to Come.

In Chapter Seven I recounted how I used my dissertation as a main subject and departure point for several courses I was teaching during that time. Those lectures had a special vitality because I was living them as I taught them. But the lecture uses of one's dissertation out-live the existentialism of its writing days. A good dissertation is at root not about the culture of law students, or the validity of the Rorschach Test versus the TAT, or a reexamination of party alignments under the Weimar Republic; one starts, of course, with a specific topic, but during the course of the next two years one has to confront all the "big" problems of sociology, psychology, political science or history, with which the field has been engaged, most often for generations. So whatever the specific putative topic, in writing a dissertation one really writes, simultaneously learns, *por la libre,* his own version of the field. In a very real way your dissertation is your own interpretation, reading of, "textbook" on your discipline.

Because of the ABD intensity of your involvement and research, as well as the lonely and self-reliant conditions you must write it under, it may very well turn out to be the deepest and most comprehensive examination of all moments of the field you will ever conduct. Thus, there is a wealth of objectified knowledge capital contained in the dissertation about the ongoing—often "timeless"—core problems and issues of a discipline. Since it is probably your best, certainly your broadest, shot, there is every reason to use and reuse it for lecture materials far beyond the formal parameters of its subject. I have come to believe that the rap against professors constantly harking back to their twenty-year-old notes is often unwarranted. If the basis of those notes is their dissertations, supplemented by more recent literature touching on the same fundamental issues, students are probably getting a valid version of a particular course, buttressed by historical connections and continuities, and drawn from the stage in the teacher's career where he most thoroughly investigated matters.

The Dissertation As Support and Validation of Self.

The preceding seven uses of the dissertation dealt with quite specific career objectives. Now we come to three final functions of the dissertation, this and the next one which go to the emotional plane, and number ten which relates to the sociocultural one.

When I first drafted a list of dissertation myths and realities, I included the "myth," "You'll want to be proud of your dissertation when you look back at it over the years." But although this cannot be a major reason for writing it (indeed, I would contend that overattention to this aim during the research and writing period could lead to delay in pursuit of the *magnum opus* or perfect dissertation—which led me initially to classify it as one of the myths), it is nonetheless very true that long-term pride in the dissertation has important functions.

All of us, no matter what our prior accomplishments, positions or titles, suffer periods of self-doubt about our capacities and strengths. In such times, the dissertation is there as a permanent proof and reminder that one carried through to completion a very large, brave and demanding intellectual and emotional task. I vividly recall crises of self-doubt about my ability or fortitude to produce further major efforts in sociology or fiction, where I turned to the sheer and imposing largeness of my dissertation proper and its files for self-confirmation and validation: "My Lord, look what a work you produced!" Soon thereafter, I would open a new file and start banging away with a new ribbon and a new long-distance project.

The Dissertation As Changing One's Life.

I also believe there is much truth in the maxim that "finishing the dissertation will change your life." This is not to be confused with the aforementioned *myth,* "When it ends, my career troubles are over," but getting the degree does give one a new, prouder, self-esteeming image. It is of course true, as one of my colleagues put it, that if you check yourself in the mirror on the day following your defense you won't see a new person. There are related humorous (humorous at one level, sad at a deeper one) stories about persons who have undergone cosmetic surgery and then been disillusioned and disappointed that their social lives were not drastically ameliorated. But the analogy between getting one's dissertation and getting a "face lift" does not hold in terms of expectable consequences, precisely because the former was achieved and the latter passively received. Obtaining one's degree grants a passport to new circles of friends and colleagues, fundamentally changing the future direction of one's crucial life experiences.

Carrying On the Intellectual Tradition.

In most fields, one has to write the dissertation to be a full-fledged professor. Acquisition of the doctorate, then, allows a person to pursue full-time the life of the mind and train others in such an endeavor. In modern society, with increasingly antiintellectual values being exhibited by our young people, some of us have to "mind the cultural store," serve as role models for the intellectual craftsmanship, discipline and dialectic embodied in dissertations, if a tradition of thinking and scholarship is going to survive. It is in contributing to this vital survival task that dissertation writing and subsequent professing in the university is still a noble undertaking both for self and society, ultimately worth the hassle, pain and loneliness the ABD has to live through to get there.

SUMMARY.

1. The ordeal of the dissertation course threatens postcompletion damage to the candidate in one or more of three different ways: 1. continued loss of self-esteem and confidence; 2. postdissertation paralysis or atrophy, with the doctorate holder unable to produce subsequent work; 3. disrupted or irrevocably ruptured intimate relationships with spouses, lovers or close friends. These last disruptions are analyzed in a framework oriented to the Ph.D.'s future and calculated to reduce the guilt about changed feelings which are so often self- or other-imposed.

2. Postdissertation damage is the historical culmination of difficulties and distresses developed along the dissertation course. If such an accumulation is to be minimized, survival precautions must be instituted early on and practiced all along the journey of the thesis. One effective technique is neutralization of those candidate- and dissertation-destructive myths exposed throughout this book. Here twelve of the major myths are recapsulized, accompanied by their antidotal dissertation realities.

3. Consistent with our national 1980s resource conservation and exploitation emphasis, the completed dissertation is evaluated as the new full-fledged professional's greatest single resource or "capital investment" for his unfolding career. From that perspective, the chapter offers a list of major uses to which the dissertation can and will be put: 1. publishing it as a book; 2. writing articles or book chapters derived from it, if conversion to an entire published volume proves, as it most often will, unfeasible; 3. as an important credential for teaching or research appointments, at both the first and later stages of one's career; 4. as an entrée into the speciality area of the thesis; 5. as essential for tenure-track professorships; 6. as a model for one's subsequent scholarly projects; 7. as a long-term source for lectures.

The preceding uses of the dissertation were specifically related to career opportunities, objectives and problematics. Two more serve emotional functions, and a last relates to socio-cultural contribution. These are: 8. the dissertation as support and validation of self in subsequent years; 9. the dissertation as changing one's life, in the sense of conferring a travel visa into new collegial and friendship networks and circles; 10. licensing one to carry on the intellectual tradition. At a time in our society where intellectual values and pursuits are increasingly under the gun, some men and women have to "mind the cultural store," serve as role models for the intellectual craftsmanship and diligence embodied in dissertations, if a coherent tradition of thinking is to be perpetuated.

Notes

1. Conversely, an alarming amount of lost capital and wasted energy, both for our graduate educational system and the particular casualties affected, is represented in the high rates of nonfinishing for the dissertation doctorate. Although beyond the aims of this volume, plans for restructuring doctoral programs greatly to increase completion percentages are a pressing educational need.

2. In contemporary Cuba, a term one hears frequently is *por la libre,* which refers to myriad ingenious and imaginative ways which the Cubans devised to replace worn-out parts for industry, agricultural machinery, homes and autos denied to them during embargos. The ABD, exposed to a kind of faculty "embargo," often operates perforce *por la libre.*

3. Compare Darwin's assertion that the five years he spent as a young man on the *Beagle,* cruising the South American coastline were far and away the most important formative years in his life, determining all that was to come later in his theoretical modeling and research styles. Nora Barlow, ed., *The Autobiography of Charles Darwin* (New York: Harcourt, Brace, 1959), p. 76.

Index

227

231